HAROLD LLOYD

Harold and Mildred Lloyd, Port of New York, 1933.

TOM DARDIS

HAROLD LLOYD

THE MAN ON THE CLOCK

THE VIKING PRESS   NEW YORK

LIBRARY OF CONGRESS CATALOGING IN PUBLICATION DATA
Dardis, Tom.
    Harold Lloyd.
    Bibliography: p.
    Includes index.
    1. Lloyd, Harold, 1894–1971.   2. Moving-picture
actors and actresses—United States—Biography.
3. Comedians—United States—Biography.   I. Title.
PN2287.L5D37   1983   791.43′028′0924   [B]   82-42736
ISBN 0-670-45227-0

PHOTO CREDITS

Paul Guglielmo, page 294

Kas Heppner, reprinted by permission of Paul Schumach,
    Metropolitan Photo Service, page 297

Louis Hochman, page 272

Peggy Lloyd, pages 3, 40, 51, 72 (bottom), 103, 287

Gene Lester, pages 276, 277

John Meredith, page 292

National Film Archive/Stills Department, pages 46, 55, 56,
    57, 60, 64, 65, 94–95 (center), 94 (bottom), 226 (bot-
    tom), 226–27 (top), 256, 299 (bottom)

George Pratt/George Eastman House, page 293

Marc Wanamaker, page 29

All other photographs courtesy the Harold Lloyd Estate.

Set in the United States of America
Printed in CRT Primer
Designed by Kathryn Parise

For Ellen

ACKNOWLEDGMENTS

Gloria, Peggy, and Suzanne Lloyd have contributed much to this book. So have these friends of Harold's: Hal Roach, Peter Robeck, Dr. John Davis, Tom Sheppard, Harold Goodwin, Harvey Parry, Richard Correll, Linda Hoppe, Ben Pearson, Kitty Lippiatt, Colleen Moore, Joan Franklin, Mary, Richard, Jr., and Robert Simonton, Gaylord Carter, and John Meredith.

The following have generously shared their knowledge of Lloyd's work with me: Anthony Slide, Alan Hoffman, Maryann Chach, Elizar Talamantez, Jean Pierre Coursedon, Robert Parrish, Tom Fuchs, George C. Pratt, and Louise Brooks.

For permission to see and make use of materials I thank the following individuals and organizations: Peggy Lloyd, Richard Correll, Charles Silver of the Film Study Center of the Museum of Modern Art, Tino Balio of the Wisconsin Center for Film and Theater Research, Anne Schlosser of the Charles K. Feldman Library of the American Film Institute, the Theater Division of the Research Collections of the New York Public Library at Lincoln Center, the Oral History Project of Columbia University, the Margaret Herrick Library of the Academy of Motion Picture Arts and Sciences, the Library of the British Film Institute, and the National Film Archive. Joan Franklin permitted me to make use of the taped interviews with Lloyd, A. Edward

Sutherland, Elliott Nugent, Gloria Swanson, and Reginald Denny. Tom Sheppard of Sheppard, Mullin, Richter & Hampton in Los Angeles has allowed me access to the files of the Harold Lloyd Corporation. All figures for production costs and earnings of the HL Corporation are drawn from its files. Susan Prichard has generously supplied me with copies of articles concerning Lloyd. Ned Comstock of the Special Collections Library of the University of California at Los Angeles has been of special service in assembling the data concerning the Rolin-Roach Corporation.

Ellen Ervin, Patricia Lambert, and Benjamin Hellinger have made many valuable suggestions in the preparation of the manuscript. William K. Everson and Kevin Brownlow have given freely of their unique knowledge of silent film. My thanks to Cork Smith for his patience and care.

CONTENTS

CONTENTS

BEGINNINGS

Saturday afternoon, Hollywood, August 25, 1979. My screen-writer friend Tom Fuchs calls to ask if I'd like to see the last hours of Harold Lloyd's tremendous estate in Beverly Hills. The wreckers are hard at work, and this may be my last opportunity to see what's left of the splendors of Greenacres. As we drive out to Benedict Canyon, Tom and I talk about Lloyd and his mansion.

"Tearing down an old place like that makes me think of the last days of Kane's Xanadu," I say as Tom parks the car. "But *Kane*'s a film," he responds. "It'll be around forever, while Lloyd's place didn't last ten years after his death."

Lloyd's sixteen acres have been subdivided into more than a dozen plots. A new approach road to the main house is under construction; so, too, are the new sewer lines demanded by the Beverly Hills authorities. Giant fissures in the once-perfect lawn impede our slow progress up the hill; they're deep and it's necessary to leap over some of them. The Olympic-size swimming pool and its huge surrounding pavilion have been smashed to bits by the bulldozers; the great formal gardens lie in ruins. Devastation is everywhere; only the main house at the top is untouched. We circle around it slowly, seeing no one.

There is a furious tapping at what seems to be a kitchen window; a dark old woman glares out at us. We retreat immediately and move on to examine Gloria Lloyd's famous playhouse nearby, untouched in the midst of the havoc.

Under a cloudless sky, in the brilliant sunlight of the late August afternoon, Harold Lloyd's mansion is sad in the quiet desolation surrounding it. The main house has been bought by an Iranian who proposes to live there in the near future. Everything else on Lloyd's estate has been systematically destroyed. The gushing fountains have been overturned; the silence is complete. The famous golf course is now the storage site for the tons of machinery that will complete the destruction. It is as if the buyers of the property have been eager not to leave the slightest vestige of its past.

We start back down the hill toward the car, depressed by our Saturday afternoon expedition into Hollywood history. Tom notices someone waiting to greet us at the beginning of the property line on Benedict Canyon. It is a very tall Beverly Hills policeman standing in front of his radio car, with his hands on his hips. He is not smiling; the woman at the window must have called the police. Just as we reach the bottom, a second police car arrives at eighty miles an hour, its siren screaming. Two more policemen advance. Three tense men with guns on their hips now confront us. The first question is the critical one: "Where is your car?" Tom points to it and proceeds to give the first officer his registration. Once they have ascertained that this is really Tom's car, we are aware of a slight slackening of tension, although it's not over yet. It takes five minutes of questioning to determine why we have violated the no-tres-passing laws of Beverly Hills; police protection is excellent here. But eventually we establish we have done no harm and intended none. Now the officers politely explain how we may find our way back to Rodeo Drive.

We start talking again in the car. "You know, if we'd been on foot, we'd be in jail now. Are you sure you still want to write about Harold Lloyd?" he asks.

"Yes."

INTRODUCTION

Considerably more than half of the silent films produced in America before 1928 no longer exist. Entire studio outputs have vanished without a trace. Once-famous production firms with exotic names like Tiffany Productions, Truart, Mastodon, and Ritz-Carlton are now recalled only by their lavish ads in the film trade journals; most of their films have disappeared. In the early 1930s, millions of feet of film were systematically destroyed by their makers, who believed that there would be no further interest in silent pictures. The loss is tragic. Today, we can't be sure just what we've lost.

There are those who don't decry with much passion the losses in the area of silent drama; they mistakenly assume that a great deal of it can no longer be taken seriously. The popular view is that the characters wear impossible clothing; they roll their eyes far too much. Many of the films depend on an acceptance of antiquated social conduct, but this is equally true of the films of the thirties and forties. Silent dramas contain many of the outdated elements of American fiction of the same period—the behavior found in the novels of Joseph Hergesheimer, Booth Tarkington, and Harold Bell Wright. But the best silent dramas have outlived their sources. A particular tragedy is the nearly total loss of the films of such men as Maurice

Tourneur and Edward Sloman, and particularly Ernst Lubitsch's *The Patriot,* which won an Oscar in 1928, the first year of the Academy Awards. What we do have left makes us even more curious about the films lost.

The losses in comedy films are severe, but with profound differences. The questions about what has perished are equally valid. How good, for instance, were the feature-length comedies that Mabel Normand made in the early and mid twenties? Her films *The Thin Princess* and *Suzanna* are both gone. What about Roscoe Arbuckle's features made just before he was banned from the screen: *Gasoline Gus, Crazy to Marry,* and *Fast Freight?* Again, we don't know, and it's now pretty clear we never will.

By and large, however, the great films of the silent comedians have been well preserved. Almost the entire creative output of Chaplin, Lloyd, and Keaton is available. But it wasn't the determined efforts of their makers alone that preserved them for us. These pictures were *so* good, of such an amazingly high quality, that collectors obtained them, often illegally, and treasured them from the very beginning.

The best film comedy has never dated; it speaks to us as clearly as ever after sixty or seventy years. It has been said that some films age gracefully while some do not. Keaton's *The General* and von Stroheim's *Greed,* for instance, are even more meaningful to us than they were to the audiences of the twenties. It has taken time for our sensibilities to catch up with them.

Harold Lloyd's critical reputation as one of the great film pioneers of the silent era has not survived nearly as well as those of his two great rivals, Charlie Chaplin and Buster Keaton. Despite all the attacks on Chaplin's alleged sentimentality, both the critical and popular taste for his pictures has never weakened; his unique magic has withstood everything. Keaton, after years of neglect, has been gloriously rediscovered in the past two decades, and there are now many who hold him supreme among the great silent comedians. But Lloyd's reputation is still suffering, because his best pictures, which were simply un-available for many years, are finally being shown in forms that he would have detested, forms that prevent an accurate ap-praisal of their real worth.

Ironically, Lloyd himself was responsible for the withholding of his pictures. He preferred to keep them out of circulation be-cause he feared, and with good reason, that the films would be shown at the wrong speed or ruthlessly cut up into bits and pieces for insertion into TV time slots. Lloyd's decision to pro-tect his work cost him the serious attention of two generations of filmgoers. At least two of his finest films are virtually un-known to modern viewers: *The Kid Brother* and *Speedy.*

Almost as deadly to his reputation has been the determined effort of well-meaning admirers to characterize him as "The King of Daredevil Comedy," a false and misleading label that caught on and stuck because of our persistent memory of him clinging to the hands of a huge clock high above the street in his 1923 film *Safety Last.* The label has fostered a largely dis-torted idea of Lloyd's pictures—climbing stunts occur in only three of his eighteen feature films. Furthermore, Lloyd did *not* climb the sides of those buildings in the way we've been led to believe. Lloyd himself was partially responsible for perpetuating the myth that had him regularly risking his life to make his films. Although he didn't create it, he did little to prevent its being accepted as the truth.

The persistence of the daredevil myth has been damaging to Lloyd. If he was simply a glorified stunt man who climbed buildings at dangerous heights, how can he be taken seriously as a film artist? Yet isn't creating the *illusion* of extreme physi-cal danger ultimately more interesting than the banality of climbing tall buildings?

Lloyd himself presents special problems. To modern tastes,

fully prepared to accept the bizarre, frequently obsessive behavior of Keaton or Chaplin, Lloyd's offscreen personality is simply boring. He had no legendary history of scandalous behavior or alcoholism, no insane mother, no mental breakdowns; he was involved in no courtroom battles over sexual misconduct, no left-wing political activity. Lloyd, the affable millionaire owner of a palatial sixteen-acre estate in Beverly Hills, has always seemed a bit quaint among the Hollywood pioneers; he lacked excitement. His quirkiness, however, was of a different order. Only the fact that he was elected Imperial Potentate of the Ancient Arabic Order of the Nobles of the Mystic Shrine seems a bit odd for a Hollywood film-maker. In actuality, Lloyd's behavior was as obsessive and, in its way, as interesting as either of his rivals'. His career, like his behavior, also bears resemblance to those of Keaton and Chaplin.

Like them, his great achievements all lay in the silent era. Like them, he was seriously crippled by the arrival of sound and never really succeeded in reaching again the heights of his work in silent film. But of the three, only Lloyd has not received full critical and public appreciation of his genius. Although his best work is obviously worthy of comparison with the best work of Chaplin and Keaton, Lloyd's part in establishing silent film comedy as a major art still has not been fully understood or completely affirmed. When this has been done, perhaps we will have the opportunity to see his work in the way he made it, and to evaluate him as James Agee did in 1949 when he asserted that, in creating laughter, "few people have equalled him, and nobody has ever beaten him."

HAROLD LLOYD

CHAPTER 1

TOM SAWYER'S YOUNGER BROTHER

1

My folks were just folks. We weren't different from
other folks in Nebraska, except I think we moved
oftener. I think we moved oftener than any other
family in the state. . . .

—Lloyd

The birthplace was ordinary enough: Burchard, Nebraska, as
unremarkable as any of the other small towns to which the
boy's father dragged his family in his long quest for the success
that always eluded him. Some of the towns weren't as small as
Burchard (population 300, "so small you could pass through it
without realizing it")—Omaha and Denver were a lot larger—
but most were decidedly obscure: Humboldt, Pawnee City, and
Beatrice, all in Nebraska. There were seven moves between
cities and several more within them, all in Harold's first fifteen
years. He tried to treat the moving around as something that
was of little consequence, but one can hear a plaintive note in
his observation that "they seemed to be always moving on and
going to different places." The Lloyds' economic difficulties
often forced them to move from one neighborhood to another,

and the frequent moves meant that he changed schools nearly a dozen times.

Harold Clayton Lloyd was born on April 20, 1893, to a father who had not found his true métier by the age of forty and who appeared likely to remain without one. James Darsie Lloyd, or "Foxy" as he liked to be called, ventured into a number of occupations: he was a door-to-door Singer Sewing Machine salesman, manager of shoe and hardware stores that quickly failed, owner of a photographic gallery that attracted few cash customers, and restaurateur who closed his doors for good shortly after the grand opening. Each failure precipitated a move to still another town. There may have been something in Foxy's manner—a trace of the provincial con man—that worked against him so rigorously. In between his failed ventures, Foxy eked out a living as a shoe clerk—his "fall back" trade.

Foxy's wife, Elizabeth Fraser, remains a shadowy figure in her son's brief but revealing comments. In his 1924 *Photoplay* "autobiography," Lloyd indicated some of the difficulty he had in dealing with his mother by giving her birthplace and piously adding, "You know what every fellow thinks of his mother." He went on to admit frankly, "I don't remember that I thought much about her when I was a kid. I was pretty busy." He was indeed busy, even frantically busy, but his rejection of her here is unmistakable. In later years he freely admitted his disdain for the imperious, jealous woman, who in no way admired a husband who could not support her. Despite his father's all too obvious short-comings, however, Harold's emotional dependence on Foxy was clear-cut.

Lloyd always emphasized the ordinary, bland background he had sprung from. His simple account of success won through a combination of hard work and ingenuity was of immense appeal to his audience in the 1920s. Every last word of his story was true, and Lloyd never tired of telling it. There is little difference in either fact or tone between Lloyd's ghostwritten autobiogra-

Elizabeth, Gaylord, HL, and Foxy.

phy of 1928, *An American Comedy,* and the interviews he gave as late as 1970.

He was always a stickler for details, feeling that if he could relate them correctly and in the right order there could be no reason to misunderstand him. Even the slightest item in a story had to be just right: in describing Beatrice, one of the tiny Nebraska towns he had grown up in, he would interrupt himself to note, "We called it Be*a*trice there."

It is more than likely that Lloyd's continual stressing of his Horatio Alger–like success arose from a perfectly natural wish to convince his audience that the *real* Harold Lloyd had much in common with the furiously energetic young man of his films, the fighter who triumphed against the strongest odds. But Lloyd's early life cannot have been as idyllic as he liked to remember it. He was always anxious to convince people that he had emerged from a relatively stable middle-class background, a fact belied by the constant moves. The Lloyds were actually very unstable, economically as well as maritally, and didn't really belong to the middle class that Harold wished so much to

Gaylord and HL with their grandmother.

be a part of. It seems probable that he felt deep shame over his father's inability to make a decent living for his family, but since he was genuinely fond of his father, this shame couldn't easily be expressed. These early years of poverty can be seen as shaping Harold's later tight-fisted ideas about money and financial security.

Richard Schickel observed that Harold Lloyd's youth seems to have been "all Norman Rockwell stuff," because the anecdotes Lloyd told and retold were about a quintessential fun-loving, All-American Boy—a modern Tom Sawyer transplanted to the West. It was a childhood unlike the sensational ones of his two great contemporaries Chaplin and Keaton, both of whom endured extreme poverty and brutality. Lloyd's early life, as he liked to recall it, strongly resembled the life depicted in the pages of Booth Tarkington's novels about Penrod, a genteel reincarnation of Tom Sawyer: "I was just a plain, freckled, ornery, American kid." To complete the Norman Rockwell picture, Harold had a dog in Pawnee that he had acquired as a stray pup. Whenever he wished to summon the dog, he would call, "Here, Bill, yah, Bill! Yah, Bill!" In time this sound was heard by many as "Yabble," and it became Lloyd's nickname for the years he lived in Pawnee.

Lloyd had one brother, Gaylord, who was five years older. Many of Harold's stories center on his adventures with Gaylord, including one in which Gaylord saves Harold from certain drowning by dragging him from the old swimming hole just as he is about to go under for the traditional third time. A more interesting story concerned a skating excursion with Gaylord and his young friends in the dead of winter. At five, Harold was too young to skate, but he persuaded his mother to allow him to tag along with the older boys. Gaylord was carefully instructed to build a big roaring fire on the river bank to keep Harold warm. The fire was built as ordered,

> and I settled down, warm and comfortable. But after a while the fire went out. It grew colder and colder. I tried to build it up and couldn't. I cried and cried, but the boys had disappeared around the bend and couldn't hear me. I can still remember my terror, as dark came on. When the boys came back, I was nearly frozen. I remember I couldn't feel my feet as I walked home, nor anything under them. The sensation intrigued me, but I was pretty cold and scared.
>
> When we got home, my mother nearly collapsed. My feet were frozen black. She didn't know what to do first, take care of me or deal with Gaylord. Finally, she and Father split the difference and Mother began applying snow and other remedies to my little feet, while Dad took Gaylord into the proverbial woodshed. After much agonizing prickling, during which I howled valiantly, my feet were saved. In fact I think I could walk before Gaylord could sit down. . . .

Most of these stories about Lloyd's childhood feature him in a far more active role. Some concern his powerful, lifelong interest in magic and sleight of hand. He loved one particularly crafty trick called "the illusion." All his young friends were wild to know its secret, and Lloyd here does awaken the shade of Tom Sawyer:

> But finally my aunt wanted her back yard cleaned and the stable white-washed. It just seemed to me I couldn't get through it, so I told the boys if they'd help me clean up that back yard, I'd show them how I did the illusion. And though it nearly broke my heart, I did.

He mastered all the mechanical tricks for sale at the local novelty stores, especially those that required some sort of apparatus. In later life, he claimed that he could still perform these tricks "at any lull in the conversation." Lloyd did not like silences, and magic was one way to make sure there were none. He was a lifelong member of the Society of Magicians, and when he died, bits and pieces of these old tricks were found tucked away in his bedroom, along with their instruction manuals.

His passion for magic fed the fires of that intense curiosity about the way things worked that remained with him always. Besides making money at odd jobs, perfecting his sleight-of-hand repertoire, and doing all the other things that kept him busy, Harold began asking questions: Why does this work this way and not that way? What causes this to happen? Is there a better way to do this? Although never a particularly good student at school, he was an avid reader and developed a broad knowledge about a variety of subjects. Like Buster Keaton, Lloyd thought he might easily have become an engineer if he hadn't entered the world of the theater.

Foxy Lloyd's perpetual economic problems probably had a lot to do with Harold's early and abiding interest in making money. There was a wide variety of the usual odd jobs for boys: selling newspapers on street corners, stoking neighbors' furnaces and cutting their lawns. But with popcorn he really became an entrepreneur. He observed candy salesmen selling it on the local trains, and

> I got the idea of selling popcorn on my own. I bought the corn, bought a stack of sacks at wholesale from a local paper house, made a cut-rate deal with the grocer for butter, and promised my mother a percentage on sales if she would pop the corn. . . . I had the sales sense to keep the merchandise and myself spic and span, and netted from twelve to fifteen dollars a week, with which I bought all my clothes and started several savings-bank accounts which never lasted until the first interest date. Another move ended the job.

Although he doggedly refused to stress his parents' poverty in his story, its effect on him is clearly seen. At twelve or so, he decided to live by the maxims his film character later embodied. He was determined to pull himself up in any way he could. ("If you're short, grow. This is America.") In addition to his popcorn business, he managed to build a moribund newspaper route into a thriving one which soon required two additional boys to handle the deliveries. At twelve he possessed a sense of business that never left him, a talent for getting as much out of an enterprise as possible.

He was quite frank about his school performance: "I wasn't exactly dumb, though I never could write compositions or anything like that." It isn't surprising that he didn't do very well at school; a catalogue of his odd jobs in these early years is astonishing. He was a telegraph messenger in Durango, Colorado, at the time of the famous Johnson–Jeffries fight on July 4, 1910, a cash boy in a downtown department store in Omaha, and an apprentice in a blueprint shop. This *was* America and Lloyd was growing all the time.

Not all the stories were rosy. A note of fear sometimes changes the tone of Harold's idyllic boyhood story. He was

briefly a member in good standing of a gang called the Tenth
Avenues. The gang undertook an apparently successful raid on
their enemies' turf, when the tide of battle suddenly turned
against them. They were forced to make a quick retreat, each
falling back on his own resources, among them Harold: "I did
not stay to see the outcome, but fled for home for all I was
worth. When I got there no one was at home and I was so
scared that I locked the doors and pulled down every blind, although I had put the battle far behind me. . . ." He had no
compunction about telling stories like this, stories that drama-
tized his dread of the uncertain and unexpected, fears to be
kept at bay by superstitious rituals.

2

I was possessed from my earliest youth with a definite, violent desire to act that in no wise conformed
with the rest of my character.

—Lloyd

There was no doubt of it: his consuming passion and lasting delight was always the theater. He was encouraged from the beginning in this love by his mother, who had always wanted to be
an actress—so much so that she had wanted to leave home and
go on the stage, a daringly unconventional notion in the
America of the 1880s. Elizabeth Fraser had come out all the
way from Toulon, Illinois, to the Nebraska plains to visit her relatives, but instead she met and married Darsie Lloyd. She never
returned East, but she did not abandon her love for the theater:

She . . . kept in touch with everything theatrical she could.
She read all the plays she could get her hands on and even

took a New York paper for a while for the reviews it gave. She would drive for miles through a snowstorm to see a ham troop in some barn opera house, and she read Shakespeare for amusement. . . .

She also read Shakespeare to young Harold, who later recalled falling asleep in her lap, listening drowsily to a speech of Juliet's. At four or five, he began to put on his own solitary shows at home. He would collect old Halloween masks, cover them with sundry caps and hats and place the results in position all over the living room. With his captive players in full attendance, Harold would begin to act out the plays he had made up himself:

I would sit tailor fashion on the couch with the hats ranged in front of me. I invented and spoke their lines and moved them about. Of the plays, I remember only that they were as full of violence as Shakespeare's own.

He was only about eight or nine when he first appeared on a real stage. This was in a performance of *Macbeth,* given in Beatrice: "They needed a youngster for the scene where Macduff's sons are murdered, where the sons are with their mother and the assassins appear to murder them. . . ." Harold's debut had been arranged by both his mother and Gaylord, who had been appearing in bit parts for a year or so. Harold's initial venture began well enough:

So the prescribed time came, and I went out and was grabbed by the assailants. Of course, I was told to yell, "Help, help!" so I went screaming back across the stage which was fine. I worked beautifully there. But the moment that I got off and was supposed to continue yelling, I became embarrassed, with all the stagehands around, so that somebody had to take up voice and yell "Help" for me and finish it out. . . .

This was mortifying, but not at all discouraging: the intoxi-
cating excitement produced by the theater was like no other.
With the extraordinarily busy life he was leading in those early
years—school, the odd jobs, the enterprises—Harold's interest
in the theater might have been short-lived if it had not been for
a chance meeting with the man who permanently fired his passion. He was John Lane Connor, the producer and leading actor
of the Burwood Stock Company, a group of players, based in
Omaha, who traveled on what was known then as the "kero-
sene circuit." Lloyd's chance meeting with Connor on a street
in downtown Omaha was to be as fateful for him as Buster Keaton's initial meeting with Roscoe Arbuckle on Broadway in
1917.

Lloyd's curiosity led to this encounter. At twelve, Harold had
taken a sudden interest in the mysteries of astronomy, aided by
the appearance of an "astrologer fortune-teller," who had
rented a downtown store to attract the curious. The fortune-
teller immediately filled his windows with gaudily colored
charts of the solar system. Along with a small but faithful
crowd, Harold had repeatedly gone back to study these mysterious charts, finding them irresistible. One evening he heard the
sound of a fire engine, which came screaming along the street
past the store. The crowd dispersed at once to run after the fire-
fighters, leaving one boy still studying the charts: "What was a
fire more or less compared to Saturn's rings?" Assuming he'd
been left alone, Harold suddenly looked up to find himself being
sharply scrutinized by "a smartly attired young man, who
seemed to be the handsomest person I had ever seen."

Connor was impressed by the boy's indifference to the attractions of the fire down the street and the two began to talk.
Within minutes Connor had revealed his repertory background
in the theater with the Burwood Company, as well as his associ-
ations with the great Otis Skinner and other stage notables of
the day. More important, he indicated that he urgently needed

a place to stay in Omaha, particularly one with decent food. Tremendously taken with Connor's exotic stories, Harold offered Connor a room in the Lloyd home. Boarders were not a novelty with the Lloyd family; Foxy's financial troubles often made them a necessity. If Connor would agree, here would be a connection with a real actor from the living world of the stage. "All in one breath, I asked this immaculate and handsome young juvenile if he'd like to come and live at our house. He came the next morning, moved in that afternoon, and in the process acquired a young slave to do his bidding." Harold had met his mentor.

3

Inevitably, I became expert ... when Connor boarded at our house I knew already more about make-up than he, an experienced actor, did. . . . While yet in grade school few effects were beyond me.

—Lloyd

Harold's "effects" were entirely in the art of theatrical makeup, and it was in this area that he surpassed his teacher. He quickly read every book he could lay his hands on about the subject and began to make exhaustive notes about all the possible techniques. As Connor began to use him in supporting roles in the plays he was producing with the Burwood Company, Harold became acquainted with those members of the cast who knew the most about the art. The whole practice of physical deception became an obsession with him. He rapidly learned how to flatten his nose for ethnic parts by stuffing rubber tubes in his nostrils; he learned the properties of collodion and putty. He was soon infatuated with everything concerning stagecraft, especially lighting and directing.

His first appearances as an actor were carefully documented by his father, very much as Myra Keaton documented Buster's. Foxy Lloyd started keeping the first of a series of scrapbooks, which still exist; he gave them to Harold at the time of his son's first success in films in 1915. The inside front cover bears this inscription:

December 15   *Compliments of "Daddie."*
1915   *with best wishes.*

The very first item in the book is a review of a play called *Mistress Nell,* performed some time in 1907 at the Burwood Theater in Omaha. Harold's presence was duly noted: "As the call

HL on the right as a sixteen-year-old amateur boxer.

John Lane Conner when HL
first met him.

boy, Dick, in the theater greenroom scene of the first act, Master Lloyd, who appeared in 'Lovers' Lane,' is refreshing and appears perfectly at home despite his youth."

This was actually not his first appearance with the Burwood Company, as earlier that year he had played the part of Abraham, the dying young brother of Tess, in a dramatization of *Tess of the D'Urbervilles.* His big moment in the popular melodrama occurred when Tess leaves her humble abode in the company of the loathsome landlord who lusts after her favors. From his pallet on the floor, the very-far-gone Abraham staggers to his feet, crying, "Tess, Tess!" The effort is too much, and he collapses in a dead faint as the curtain falls. This was the kind of entertainment the audiences of the day adored, and Harold's playing of this juicy part brought him the strong admiration of at least one critic: "Harold Lloyd . . . demonstrated that he has a dramatic instinct which will doubtless carry him on to success in the histrionic art."

The prophecy might easily have failed: his voice changed that year and made him quite unsuitable for the parts Connor had been giving him. The voice change brought his stage career to a temporary but sharp halt, although he kept in touch with the company by selling its programs, lighting the plays, and doing anything else he could to stay within the magic circle.

Although he exerted a tremendous influence on Harold's early life, John Lane Connor remains a vague and shadowy figure in all Lloyd's accounts of him. At no time does he step forth as anything but a handsome young man with a gift for acting. Hal Roach, Lloyd's first producer, claims that Connor was extremely effeminate and probably homosexual. If this was true, it might make it easier to explain why Lloyd did little to dramatize the man who most clearly directed him toward a life in the theater. Lloyd found homosexuality troublesome, especially when it occurred later in his own family. Hal Roach may be correct in his view that Lloyd was simply being discreet in his depiction of this closest friend of his adolescence.

By 1909 Foxy Lloyd had taken his family to Denver, and was forced to leave them there in order to take a temporary job in Omaha. Harold's affection for his father can be seen amid all the local news he furnished him in this unedited letter of October 1909:

Two other boys and my self gave a show last Saturday, and had a 45¢ house, we are going to give another one Saturday after next, and we expect to make about 45¢ next time. I am getting homesick to see you papa, I'll bet its pretty lonesome there in Omaha for you isn't it. I would like to have a good old pitch game with you to night, I believe I could beat you 4 games out of five. . . . I am getting along fine in my studys, all except English. My Latin teacher told me I was a very strong Latin pupil. There are certainly strick here. If they catch you wisphering they will sent you up to visit the

Principal. I have only been there three times. After the first time they catch you they put your name on record, the old Professor forgot that I had been there 2 before, and as I didn't remind him of it, I have got my name on record once, there is one kid there that I know, as got his name on record about 5 times. There is a peach of a girl at school, I am pretty much stuck on her, I think she likes me pretty well too, as she talks to me all the time in school. Well papa as I have told you all the news I can think of now I will have to say good bye, With lots of love,

> *From your toady boy,* *
> *Harold*

English was indeed Harold's worst subject in school, and he always disclaimed any ability at formal composition. These letters of 1909, in his sixteenth year, reassert the Tom Sawyer image:

. . . that was an awful long time to wait for a letter from my Daddie. Well I got another report card from school I beat my old mark, I had three B's, One C, and one A. Last time I got two C's and three B's. . . . You know that old deck of card that I could tell what they were by their backs, I got a bran new deck just like them now. . . . I was to the Majestic theather last night, the Majestic is like the Orpheum, and there was some people skating on real ice. After the show I went back of the scenes and saw how they make it they had a machine that makes ice, they were making some when I got there. . . . Did you have a very good thanksgiving dinner, I wish you could have been here to help us eat ours, we had a great big fat turkey and maby you think he wasn't good. I would like to see you awfully swell papa and if you want me to come up and visit you Christmas vacation I will. I am working now I tend to a furnace next door, I have to get up at six o'clock in the mornings. I wouldn't mind beating you

---

* An affectionate term from a story that Foxy had read to him.

a couple games of pitch now. Well papa as I guess I have
told you all the news, I will close for this time, with lots of
love and kisses from,

> *Your Toady boy,*
> *Harold*

4

Heads for New York, tails for the Coast.
—Lloyd

Elizabeth and Foxy Lloyd were divorced in 1910. They had
been quarreling for years over Foxy's inability to settle down for
good in some job that would insure a steady income. A tall, regal
woman, a *grande dame* of the plains, Elizabeth Lloyd set a
sharp contrast to her defensive husband, who was always on
the verge of the chance that would enrich him. Harold later
claimed that his parents had waited to separate until the boys
had grown up. He reported the break quite matter-of-factly:
"While we boys were mighty sorry, it wasn't a tragedy to us.
They had waited until we were grown, and had our lives ahead
of us and were ready to get out into the world."

It is more than likely that Harold's picture of his mother is at
least partly false—it is made suspect by his insistence on her
"high falutin' " characteristics. She may well have been a
grande dame, but it is doubtful that she was perceived this way
by her husband and children.

Harold and Gaylord began to live with first one and then the
other parent, but it was Foxy who assumed the dominant role in
their lives after the divorce. Things had become a little better
for him in Omaha; it was there that he acquired his nickname,
largely on the strength of devising a scheme whereby his employers, the Singer Sewing Machine Company, could easily

track down stolen machines or those which had not been fully paid for on the installment plan. Foxy assiduously checked all the manufacturer's serial numbers on the machines he encountered in his wide travels and reported the culprits to Singer, whose Omaha sales manager hailed Lloyd as "Oh, you foxy Lloyd!" The name stuck.

Foxy's real success with Singer came about through his method of selling their machines from door to door. He became one of their best salesmen, driving a small buggy, which held two of the heavy machines. One day in 1912 his buggy was struck by a heavy brewery truck driven by a drunken driver. The result was a brief stay in the hospital and a lawsuit against the brewery. Foxy's lawyer was able to prove the driver was drunk, and obtained a compensation judgment of $6,000, which he divided equally with his client. Three thousand dollars was a small fortune at the time.

Foxy took the unexpected $3,000 as a sure sign that it was again time to move on, but the question was, where? Nashville, New York, and San Diego were the three places most often discussed. There wasn't the slightest doubt where Harold wanted to go. Connor had moved his operations to San Diego, "and said he could get me a position there if I came."

Foxy was sporting about the decision: he decided to let the spin of a coin make up their minds, either for Nashville/New York, Foxy's choices, or for Harold's San Diego. The tossing day came and the coin was a nickel, which "went up, hit the ceiling, dropped and rolled under a bed. It was a pre-buffalo nickel and it stopped wreath side up."

Harold had won: "It came up tails, so he headed out there for California, to Mr. Connor, who immediately got me a position to play in the stock company." All three Lloyds promptly packed their bags for the trip to California. But Foxy's luck hadn't really changed. The $3,000 windfall was merely that, and his business life in San Diego became still another version of what

The San Diego School of Expression in 1912.
HL second row on the right.

had happened to him in all those little towns back in Nebraska. He quickly invested his money in a combination poolroom and luncheonette in the middle of downtown San Diego. Knowing little about either the ways of pool players or the restaurant business, Foxy managed to run the enterprise into a gradual decline from which there was no recovery. Within eighteen months of his arrival in California, Foxy was back working in a retail shoe store.

Harold enrolled as a senior at the local high school; he had promised his mother he'd graduate, a promise he almost managed to keep. He played many of the leads in the school plays. More important, he became Connor's general assistant in his stock company, as well as an instructor in another Connor enterprise, the San Diego School of Expression. At the School of Expression Harold gave instruction in fencing, dancing, and elocution. A picture taken there in 1912 shows a group of the expression seekers, along with Harold, who is wearing one of the standard ironlike starched collars of the day; he has the serious, dedicated, almost staid look of a young business trainee.

He was incredibly busy that year. His high school operated
on a split schedule and was

> so crowded that they had to start classes at seven-thirty. So I'd
> work through the first three periods, dash merrily to rehearsal
> at ten, be back at noon, finish at two, give lessons at the dra-
> matic school until five, help Dad in the restaurant until time
> to go to the theater at eight—and then, after the performance,
> I went home to bed. It was a great life. I loved it. . . .

It was now that his lifelong habit of constant activity began to
crystalize—KEEP BUSY!

Harold and Foxy attended a vaudeville act that featured a boy
called Harold who hated his name, especially when his uncle
addressed him with it. Every time he did, the boy would whine:
"Don't call me Harold; call me Speedy!" Foxy liked the name
well enough to bestow it on Harold and was still calling him that
thirty years later. "Speedy" became Harold's nickname to
nearly everyone; it became the title of his last silent picture.

The combination of the earlier stage experience and his
friendship with Connor virtually guaranteed Lloyd all the leading parts in the presentations of the Burwood Stock Company.
He quickly formed an inflated opinion of his talents. He loved to
relate the severe dressing-down he received from Connor, to
whom he had come for an expected dose of praise after appearing in *Going Some,* a play Connor had directed. Lloyd foolishly
approached Connor in a joyful mood:

> "Well, how'd you like the show?"
> "Not so bad."
> "And how'd you like me?" I asked, beaming.
> "You were terrible. . . . I have seen worse actors some-
> where, but I can't remember where."

Connor then told him plainly and precisely what was wrong
with his performance. Lloyd always stressed the fact that Con-

nor didn't rant or rave about how bad he'd been that night. It was a calm, closely reasoned recital of just where and how Harold had been guilty of bad timing, wrong emphases, and all the other basic errors of acting technique. It was a lesson he never forgot. He became equally sensitive to praise; he found it embarrassing, even if there wasn't the slightest doubt he'd earned it.

Connor's fire-sermon can be dated with precision, because Foxy's scrapbook contains an ad for *Going Some,* a "five act farce comedy." Harold appeared as J. Wellingford Speed, the head teller, on December 6 and 7 of 1912 in San Diego. In the months to come he took on a wide variety of roles: Tonga, the poisoned-dart thrower in an adaptation of Conan Doyle's *Sign of the Four,* the Reverend James Bartlett in *Cousin Kate,* the sheriff in *House of a Thousand Candles,* Caleb Plumber in Dickens's *Cricket on the Hearth,* and the unctuous clerk in *Dr. Jekyll and Mr. Hyde.* He played the male lead in *The Prince Chap* opposite a diminutive leading lady who played the part of an eight-year-old in the first act, a twelve-year-old in the second, and who was eighteen in the third act. This was nineteen-year-old Anita Loos, who played her part wearing a huge blond wig.

At nineteen Lloyd gave every sign of being firmly embarked on a successful career in the theater. There had been a brief transitional period when he was suddenly too old for juvenile roles and still too young for romantic ones; at this point he became aware of the films being made up the coast in Hollywood.

He had been going to the movies almost from the beginning—as far back as Porter's *Great Train Robbery* of 1903, but they never seemed as exciting as the stage: "They had no reality. I never associated them with so romantic a place as the theater and did not think of the actors as beings, but as puppets. . . ."

Through his work at Connor's school, Harold became one of these puppets in the early spring of 1913, when members of the

HL in 1912.

Edison Film Company came down to San Diego to shoot some scenes for a Western being filmed in Long Beach. They needed extras and the Connor School of Expression was an obvious place to get them. Harold was sent for the day's work, "to be kind of head of the group of about a dozen that were taken over. And they still didn't have enough, so they asked me if I wouldn't mind sitting in also. It was a costume thing—kind of a Spanish thing—so I put it on. . . ." What he put on was actually a loincloth, for his role was that of a Yaqui Indian serving food to his white masters. In the next week or so, he appeared fleetingly in another Edison production, a Dutch costume film, but this brought his screen appearances to an end. The work had not intrigued him, nor had he the faintest intuition that film-making was to become the center of his life.

Lloyd's initial coolness to films, similar to Chaplin's, was totally unlike the reaction of Keaton, who had been fascinated by film long before he ever had the chance to appear in one. It was sheer economic necessity that drove Lloyd back into moviemaking: "nothing else offered." He could have resisted more strongly if his luck in obtaining parts to play in San Diego that summer of 1913 had held out. But he was suddenly faced with the prospect of a long summer with no work in sight.

Connor's company had disbanded for the summer (so had the school), and there was now virtually no theatrical activity in San Diego. Harold was soon forced to give up the furnished room he had recently taken by himself, as Foxy had left town for Los Angeles on one of his new ventures. Harold exchanged the room for a tent on the roof of his apartment house: the owner had no objection to his former tenant's taking up squatter's rights on his property. But the cash available for eating quickly dwindled away to nothing (he lived on a diet of doughnuts and coffee for weeks). He then recalled the work he had done in the spring for Edison. That world of film-making was only 120 miles away in Los Angeles. So, too, were a number of the stock companies he had worked with in San Diego, companies that would be working right through the summer. He left San Diego, never to return, lacking just a few of the credits required for graduation from high school.

He took the cheapest room at the Belmont Hotel in downtown Los Angeles, a hotel whose clientele was largely composed of vaudevillians. He was almost immediately joined by Foxy, now working again in a shoe store, and by Gaylord, who had not prospered any more than his father. Harold found work instantly with a local stock company, but that petered out and he was soon in the same situation he'd been in back in San Diego—close to starvation. Perhaps the Edison Company might oblige with more extra work; they did, until the company returned to New York at the end of summer. With no hope of any stage work, Harold turned all his energies into getting work as an extra where it was most plentiful, the busiest studio in all of Hollywood—"Big U," or Universal, at the corner of Sunset Boulevard and Gower Street.

CHAPTER 2
KING OF THE BRODIES

1

Why don't you see if maybe you can't get some work
in these movies?

—Foxy Lloyd

In those days we had no lights, remember that. We
hadn't heard of lights. . . . They used what they
called diffusers. They were these big cloths over the
stage to screen out the sun. They were on wires, and
you pulled them across as you would venetian
blinds. . . . There were no indoor sets—oh, no.
Everything was outside. You were purely dependent
on the weather. . . .

—Lloyd

The Harold Lloyd who came to Hollywood in 1913 was a likable
young man of twenty, a man of huge energy and a tremendous
desire to succeed. He liked to please: nearly everyone who recalls his early days agrees on his intense need to be accepted.
Women found him exceptionally attractive. His taste in women
probably was influenced by his troubled feelings about his
mother, whose imperious behavior had left its mark. Lloyd dis-

trusted girls who posed problems by their forthrightness; he preferred them to embody the traditional gentleness and sweetness then popularly associated with women. The heroines of his films reflect this taste.

Good-looking, athletic, and fiercely ambitious, he appeared to possess all the requirements for success in these new and increasingly talked-about movies. But it is clear that he was deeply mistrustful of them: after all, almost everybody felt that films were only a passing fad. The stage was the real place to demonstrate your acting talents—not those crude mime shows in the dusty uproar of Universal Studios.

His acting abilities were not going to be any help in obtaining work at Universal. The studio used a simple "shape-up" system for hiring extras. This entailed a large room, or bull pen,

> where the aspirant would go and sit down, and the assistant directors would go into this room and look around to see what atmosphere they wanted. Not knowing your name, they'd point at you, and then you were to follow them, and you got the required work for the day.

None of this appealed to Harold, as he felt this was scarcely the way to recognize the kind of acting talent he knew he possessed. An alternative method of getting a director's attention would be simply to present himself for an interview. But how to get past the guard at the gate? It was manned by a crusty old fellow whose sole job was keeping hopefuls like Lloyd off the premises. After studying the situation for an hour or so, he noted that the guard admitted without challenge anyone who wore visible make-up. Taking the hint, he hastily applied some greasepaint to his face, turned up his hat, and strolled casually through the gate. He repeated this method of entry for the next two days, by which time the guard had accepted him as one of the regular extras.

Taking a stroll through the tightly packed acreage of a Hollywood studio in the pioneer days of 1913 was rather like viewing
the booths for the various attractions at a carnival or country
fair. As Lloyd has indicated, everything was shot outdoors, utilizing natural light to the utmost. Most sets were relatively
small, just large enough to appear convincing when photographed by the heavy, stationary cameras mounted on tripods.
The sets were very noisy places: the air was filled with the
sounds of hammering and sawing wood for sets under construction, and of directors barking out instructions to their
crews. Music could often be heard: many directors required
portable organs to create the right mood for the sequence being
filmed. Encircling everything were the light diffusers; they
were adjusted regularly as the light changed during the day's
shooting.

Hollywood, 1914. J. Warren Kerrigan listens to a mustached HL.

Westerns, historicals, and "straight" dramas were the staples at Universal. Harold's first regular work there was for a popular director of Westerns on the lot, J. Farrell Macdonald, whose biggest star was J. Warren Kerrigan, an actor famous for his cowboy roles who was being paid the fantastic sum of $300 a week. The pay for extras at Universal was three dollars a day, which Harold was soon earning on a regular basis. Within a few weeks he was making five.

Another of Macdonald's regular extras was a solidly built, cherubic twenty-one-year-old from Elmira, New York. Hal Roach, who was to become a vital force in Lloyd's career, had started at Universal just a few weeks before Harold. By his own admission then and now, Roach was a terrible actor; he couldn't do the simplest thing without immense effort. But Macdonald liked Roach and was patient with his inadequacies. Lloyd later recalled Roach rehearsing a scene with Macdonald again and again with no visible improvement. Macdonald's patience finally wore out and he told Roach, "You just haven't got the idea." He abruptly turned to Harold, who had been observing his new friend's difficulties, and said, "Let this other fellow try it." Harold got the thing right on the first try.

Several weeks later, while both men were waiting around on a bench in the hot sun, costumed as Hottentots—grass skirts and greasepaint—Roach made a prophecy that would be fulfilled in a remarkably short time: "Some day I'm going to make a picture myself. I'm going to make a comedy. People like to laugh and there's always room for real comedy . . . and when I do, Harold, you'll be in it."

2

I saw an ad in the paper. "Wanted, men in Western costume. Pay: a dollar, carfare, and lunch. Be in front of the post office."

—Hal Roach

The ad Roach saw appeared in a Los Angeles paper at the end of 1912. He tried his luck down at the post office and was chosen on the spot for his first job, as a film extra at Universal. Roach proved to be a godsend to his new employers because of his expertise in all gambling matters:

There was a big argument among the film people about how to run a roulette table. From my experience in Alaska, I knew how to run one.
I breezed up to the director:
"What do you want to know? I know all about roulette."
"We want the leading man to win at the start and then to lose all he's got."
I told him how to do it.

Then the new resident authority on gambling remembered to ask one important question:

"How much are you going to pay me for that?"
"You get five dollars a day."
You say five dollars today, it means nothing. Bear in mind that when I was a kid, a laborer got ten cents an hour, a dollar a day for ten hours, This was 1913. . . .

Hal Roach had come by his gambling expertise the hard way. After leaving home at seventeen, he had gone to Alaska to seek his fortune. He prospected unsuccessfully for gold and then became a mule-skinner for a while. He worked at odd jobs in a number of saloons, where he learned to gamble. He resumed mule-skinning in California, at nineteen becoming superintendent of a hauling company in the oil fields for sixty dollars a month. He was awaiting his next assignment when he read Universal's ad.

Still a solid, chunky man with a ruddy complexion, Hal Roach grins broadly at the fun Harold Lloyd and he enjoyed in their early days of film-making. While having lunch with Roach in 1980, I had the feeling that the man across the table, once Mack Sennett's only serious rival as a producer of film comedy, hadn't changed very much in the nearly seventy years since Lloyd and he had first met. Roach is a man of total self-confidence, with a stunning belief in his own abilities. He produced the early Laurel and Hardy films, as well as those of Charley Chase, and the endless series of *Our Gang* comedies, which spanned three decades and involved eight sets of children. He tries hard to convince you that he also invented the screen *persona* of Harold Lloyd.

Lloyd and Roach were enjoying their five-dollar-a-day life back there in 1913, when Universal suddenly decided to pay that rate only to those who at least had small acting parts. The ordinary extras were promptly demoted to three dollars a day. Roach and Lloyd retaliated by going on strike against Universal. They soon exhausted their funds and went their separate ways in search of work. Harold sought the advice of his old friend Connor in San Diego, who recommended him to Allan Dwan, a novice director at Universal. The letter to Dwan went unanswered, and Harold began to subsist on a diet of doughnuts and not much else.

Finally, he landed work as an extra from a man called Gottschalk, who was making a series of cheap sequels to *The Wizard of Oz*. When Harold arrived for his first day's shooting, he found

The old Bradbury
Mansion in Los Angeles.

that Roach had beaten him there by a day. It was while they
were both attired as Hottentots that hot day in the park that
Roach began to talk seriously about making comedy films.

In the summer of 1914 Roach inherited $3,000; it was
enough for him to acquire briefly a business partner named
Dan Linthicum. Roach combined the first two letters of his
name with the first three of his partner's, giving the firm the
name Rolin, which it retained for several years. The few films
they produced were so bad (Roach can't even recall what they
were about) that not one was ever sold in the chief marketing
place for films, New York. Linthicum and Roach parted company, and Roach was forced back into seeking work as an extra
for Gottschalk.

Roach's luck took a sudden, unexpected turn for the better,
however, when a local film company hired the well-known New
York actor Edwin August to play the lead and direct a picture
called *The Hoosier School Master*. The nervous backers of the
film discovered that their director was always too busy to listen
to them. Aware of the situation, Roach talked his way into becoming the assistant director or main line of communication

between the parties. The backers also hired a Los Angeles attorney to keep his eye on the money being spent. When not
spying on the director, the attorney passed most of his time
talking with Roach. He told him about a wealthy young man
who operated an automobile agency in downtown Los Angeles
but was eager to make films. This was Dwight Whiting, a young
Englishman and the man Roach had been waiting for. Roach
had no difficulty in convincing him that he had mastered the art
of film-making, and Whiting became his second partner. Whiting took care of the business side of Rolin; his chief task was attempting to sell the firm's product to Pathé in New York.

The reactivated firm rented office space in the old Bradbury
Mansion, on Court Street over the former Hill Street Tunnel in
downtown Los Angeles. The rambling Victorian edifice, known
to some as the "old Zodiac Studio," was being used by a number of the smaller film companies around town. Complete with
turrets, bay windows, a grand staircase, and sixteen-foot ceil-
ings, the mansion looked positively baronial in the hundreds of
films shot there. Chaplin made some of his early films at the
mansion in 1915. Roach constructed *his* shooting stage in the
back yard and then turned his attention to producing the comedies he had promised to make with his new friend, Harold
Lloyd.

3

Well, the nicest place in Los Angeles, where the sun always shines, is out where we live—a place called Edendale.

—William Hornbeck's mother

We have no scenario. We get an idea, then follow the natural sequence of events.

—Mack Sennett

While Lloyd and Roach had been eking out their uncertain day-to-day living as extras, slapstick comedy was just coming into its first days of triumph over at Mack Sennett's Keystone Studio in Edendale. Actually, in these early days of 1913 and 1914, most of their output was, as Chaplin described it, "a crude mélange of rough and tumble."

Mack Sennett earned his familiar title of "King of Comedy" in two ways: as a discoverer of new talent and as a major film pioneer who introduced radically new material into the American film. His discoveries included Chaplin, Charley Chase, Roscoe Arbuckle, Ben Turpin, Gloria Swanson, and Frank Capra. Sennett was the first to bring slapstick to America from France, where it originated. He was quite open in expressing his deep indebtedness to the French pioneers:

Now, I have been posing for many years as the inventor of slapstick motion-picture comedy and it is about time I confessed the truth. It was those Frenchmen who invented slapstick and I imitated them. I never went as far as they did, because give a Frenchman a chance to be funny and he goes to the limit—you know what I mean. But I stole my first ideas from the Pathés. . . .

What he "stole" from them was the art of comic improvisation, seen to perfection in the antics of his celebrated Keystone Kops. James Agee has suggested it better than anyone else:

> . . . he gave inanimate objects a mischievous life of their own, broke every law of nature the tricked camera would serve him for and made the screen dance like a witches' Sabbath. . . . The thing one is surest of all to remember is how toward the end of nearly every Sennett comedy, a chase (usually called "the rally") built up such a majestic trajectory of pure anarchic motion that bathing girls, cops, comics, dogs, cats, babies, automobiles, locomotives, innocent bystanders, sometimes what seemed like a whole city, an entire civilization, were hauled along head over heels in the wake of that energy like dry leaves following an express train.

All the early Sennett films played havoc with the world of everyday life: time became dizzyingly accelerated and place succeeded place with astonishing ease and speed. Sennett's films played endlessly with new combinations of thrills and laughter, creating the foundations of an entirely new form of art. In time, it would be called filmic surrealism; its influence can be seen in talents as diverse as Buñuel's, Jean Cocteau's, and the Marx Brothers'. The early Sennett comedies were crude, but the directorial taste of actors Roscoe Arbuckle and Mabel Normand prevailed and the general level of Sennett films quickly improved. But it was the genius of Charles Chaplin that changed everything about film comedy and transformed the hurly-burly antics of the Keystone Kops into a world of grace and beauty. Only with luck and perseverance did Sennett manage to hire Chaplin. The star comedians of Sennett were Ford Sterling, Roscoe ("Fatty") Arbuckle, and a delightful young lady named Mabel Normand, who was then Sennett's fiancée. She was the main reason that Chaplin ever bothered seeing any of the Keystone films.

While Chaplin was on tour with the Karno Company in 1913, Sennett and Mabel Normand observed his work in Los Angeles. Both were impressed with Chaplin and attempted to contact him the next day, but neither could recall his name. Only the name of the Karno Company and its general manager, Alf Reeves, had stuck. They sent him this wire:

IS THERE A MAN NAMED CHAFFIN IN YOUR COMPANY OR SOME-
THING LIKE THAT STOP IF SO WILL HE COMMUNICATE WITH KESSEL
AND BAUMANN 24 LONGACRE BUILDING BROADWAY.

When Chaplin discovered that Sennett wanted to hire him to appear in films, he was reluctant to give up his promising career in vaudeville for the uncertainties of the movies. Sennett received this answer to his wire:

FELLOW'S NAME CHARLIE CHAPLIN STOP HAS FORTY WEEKS' SOLID
BOOKING STOP WON'T TAKE CHANCES WITH MOVIES.

Only by nearly quadrupling his stage salary of $40 a week to $150 did Sennett finally get Chaplin to agree to sign a contract in the late summer of 1913.

Initially, Chaplin had difficulties working with Mabel Normand and some of the other company members, but his triumph was assured the day he first donned his tramp's costume. The pants were baggy, the shoes were immense, the bowler hat too small, and the whole ensemble was topped off by a preposterous cane. He later liked to identify the costume as one of "shabby gentility," a phrase he took from Dickens.

Chaplin tried out the costume in a picture with Mabel Normand. He quickly improvised some business on the set of what was supposed to be a hotel lobby:

I entered and stumbled over the foot of a lady. I turned and raised my hat apologetically, then turned and stumbled over a

cuspidor, then turned and raised my hat to the cuspidor. Behind the camera they began to laugh. . . . When it was over I
knew I had made good.

This was the beginning of the laugh heard round the world;
Chaplin's tramp character had a magical effect. That success
began the series of pay hikes that had him earning ten thousand dollars a week at the beginning of 1916. By that time slapstick film comedy had achieved the status of a brand-new art
form, as well as an extraordinarily lucrative business. Lloyd,
Roach, and Dwight Whiting had picked just the right time to
start making their comedies.

4

I was born at a time when they were so glad to have
anybody stand in front of a camera, it didn't matter
who if only they had two legs, and could stand
up. . . .
                                        —Gloria Swanson

All right, how do we start? Well, we're going to have
a couple meet in the park. . . .
                                        —Eddie Sutherland

Roach began making two-reel dramatic films starring Roy
Stewart, a former Western heavy. He alternated these with
one-reel comedies starring Lloyd. The burly Stewart would play
the villain in the comedies, while a young actress named Jane
Novak furnished the romantic interest in both types of film.
Lloyd's first film comedy, which has not survived, depicted him

as a chauffeur-chaperon for two mischievous little boys having fun at the beach. All of the initial Rolin productions were apparently so terrible that not a single one was sold to a distributor. They were made cheaply enough—$200 or $300 a film, experiments that failed. "I suspected for a while that he'd robbed a bank or something . . . that first picture cost two hundred dollars and it was exclusively exteriors," Harold recalled later. It finally dawned on Roach that if he were to have any hope of selling his films Harold had to come up with some kind of identifiable comic character. He startled Harold by telling him, "Hell! You're a comedian! I'll pay you five dollars. Now think up a character for yourself and we will be set." For the first time, Harold began to consider himself not as an actor but as a comedian—whatever that was. The result was his first screen character, a Chaplin derivation that the Rolin company called "Willie Work."

Willie Work had a lurking question mark built into his name—would Willie "work" or wouldn't he? Willie was a feeble imitation of Chaplin's tramp character, with Harold wearing a cat's-whiskers mustache, a beaten-up old top hat, and a long, heavily padded coat. Roach directed Harold in several of these Work comedies before they finally sold one to Pathé in New York, *Just Nuts,* one of the few Lloyd films from this period that have survived. It wasn't much: heavy-handed pranks in the park, lots of brick-throwing, the usual pratfalls, culminating in a barroom brawl. But on the basis of *Just Nuts* Pathé offered Roach a distribution contract if he could guarantee the services of Stewart, Novak, and Lloyd. Roach joyfully agreed, and several more of the Work films were made. As Harold recalled:

We just would go out in a park. We built a set or two, but really, we'd go out in a park like Echo Park or Hollenbeck Park, with no script, no idea, just characters, and we'd make up our comedy as we went along. . . . For instance, say we'd have the girl sitting there, and the comedian comes along, and he flirts with the girl or gets acquainted with her. Then her sweetheart would come along, and then altercations would start. You'd work up your own ideas, your own business and everything—work it right out while you were doing it, with people around. Maybe sometimes you'd have a hundred people standing around watching you. . . .

All went well until Harold discovered that Roach was paying Stewart ten dollars per day, five more than he was getting. He protested that it was unfair; Roach agreed, but claimed that Stewart wouldn't work for less. Harold then decided to quit and managed to land a job almost immediately at Mack Sennett's Keystone Studio. Roach hired a substitute for Harold who proved hopeless, and Rolin's production came to an end. Roach was able to obtain a director's job at Essanay, the firm to which Chaplin had gone after leaving Sennett. In the next few months, Lloyd and Roach separately attended the two best schools in the world for learning about film comedy.

Harold's stint at Keystone lasted only a few months, but it was invaluable. There he mastered the fine art of taking falls— not just ordinary falls, but the spectacular ones that were standard for Arbuckle, Ben Turpin, and Chester Conklin. These falls were known as "bumps," or "Brodies," after Steve Brodie, who had survived a plunge from the Brooklyn Bridge. The artist taking the fall was called a "bumper."

At first, Keystone didn't know what to do with him—after all, he *did* have acting credentials—but Harold was used frequently once he had demonstrated his sensational ability to take the falls expected of a purely physical comedian. He appeared in a supporting role as one of Fatty Arbuckle's suitors in *Miss Fatty's Seaside Lovers*—Arbuckle frequently appeared in drag in his films. But the Brodies kept Harold on the payroll. He liked the excitement of working with Sennett:

There were companies working all over the place. You see, nobody interfered with anyone else, because it was silent, and you could have one company just 25 feet from the other one. There might be four or five different comedies working there, with different ones in each, cameras grinding all over the place. Sometimes they would get someone with a violin, for atmosphere, but that was a little high-toned for a comedy lot. . . . we didn't aspire to that. . . .

Ford Sterling, Sennett's leading comedian until he was displaced by Chaplin and Arbuckle, felt that despite Harold's genuine abilities at roughhouse comedy his talents were being misused: "Harold, you've got a different quality from the rest of them," he would say. Sterling's place in the Sennett hierarchy was still high enough for him to use Lloyd as the juvenile in his pictures, and Harold began to appear in all the Sterling films. Between his Brodies and the Sterling pictures, Harold was well on his way to success at Keystone.

Back in New York, Pathé decided they wanted Roach to reunite his three principals, but there were difficulties:

It seemed that Stewart was tied up with someone else and they couldn't get him, and they couldn't find Jane Novak. I was the only one of the trio that he could get. So they said, "All right, you get Lloyd, the comic, and we'll give you this contract."

Fully aware that there would be no Rolin without Lloyd, Roach offered Harold fifty dollars a week, double what he'd been making just a few months previously. "That was more money than there was in the world or ever has been since." But Sterling strongly advised Harold not to accept the offer:

"Oh my God, what do you want to go with a little one-horse independent company like that for? You've got a big company

HL as Lonesome Luke.

here with Keystone, and you've got places to go. . . . Don't go with Roach!"

All of this was extremely flattering, but Harold had made up his mind, telling Sterling, "No . . . I'm going to go there. I'm going to be the comedian. Besides, if I go there, I'll be the big fish in the little pond. . . . "

Roach's first question to Harold on the day of his return to Rolin was: "How about a new character?" Lloyd had anticipated him, and "Lonesome Luke" was created within the next few days. It was Foxy Lloyd who devised the costume, which consisted almost entirely of variations on Chaplin's tramp attire. This time, everything was reversed: the trousers were tight and far too short, the vest equally short, the whole costume the exact opposite of Chaplin's outfit. The ensemble was topped off with a mustache that consisted of two dots of grease paint. Luke did the things that Chaplin's tramp did—almost exactly the same things. It was total imitation, and in later years Lloyd

A 1917 trade ad for Lonesome Luke.

An aquatic
Bebe Daniels.

was embarrassed to talk about the scores of Lonesome Luke films he had made.

Roach acquired a new actor to appear with Harold as the chief male foil in the Luke pictures. This was "Snub Pollard," who had come to the United States as a member of an Australian vaudeville troop, Pollard's Lilliputians. When the group broke up, most of its members took the name Pollard as their own, and Harold Fraser became Snub Pollard. Like the British-born director Eddie Sutherland, Pollard "decided to stay on in Hollywood because this looked like the new gold rush to me." Pollard was aware that his talents as a roustabout comedian were very much in demand there in 1915. He sported a walrus mustache based on that worn by the German Kaiser. One day he absentmindedly applied it to his upper lip upside down; the result was thought to be comically intriguing, and he kept it as his trademark for the rest of his career. Pollard continued to work with Lloyd until 1919, when Roach began to star him in a series of his own.

After the fourth or fifth Luke film, fifteen-year-old Virginia Daniels, accompanied by her mother, visited the Court Street offices of Rolin for an interview with Roach and Lloyd. Virginia, or Bebe Daniels as she became known, had appeared on stage since the age of four. She had begun her film career when she was only seven and by 1915 was able to regard Harold Lloyd as a relative newcomer to the field. Known throughout the twenties as the "good little bad girl," Bebe Daniels is perhaps best remembered today for her portrayal of Dorothy Brock, the tough singing star in the 1933 Warner Brothers musical *42nd Street,* but this role does no justice to her considerable gifts as a comedienne.

HL, Estelle Harrison, and Snub Pollard in an unidentified film.

Bebe possessed an extraordinarily expressive face, her huge eyes well suited to register the full impact of the wild antics of Harold and Snub Pollard. She was quite dark; the studios later liked to boast of her "Castilian beauty." In the twenties, Paramount claimed her as "a descendant of relatives of the Spanish Empress, Josephine. . . . royal blood flows in the veins of this young actress." The truth was plainer: Bebe's Jewish mother was from South America; her father, from Scotland.

At a starting salary of ten dollars a week, Bebe quickly became quite athletic and was soon up to being thrown off trolley cars, suspended from cliffs, and hurled from one actor to another. She was a talented dancer, as was Harold. The couple became regular contestants in the countless dance competitions held all over the Los Angeles area. She was vivacious and absolutely irresistible.

Harold fell in love with Bebe Daniels not very long after the day of her interview at Rolin. She seems to have been the first woman he became emotionally involved with. Harold was twenty-two in 1915, and his petite young leading lady was barely fifteen. Her youth as a film star is not at all surprising when it is recalled that the direct sunlight utilized by the early film-makers was cruel to women's faces, making them appear far older than they were. Directors demanded young faces: the Gish sisters were also in their mid-teens when they began their career with D. W. Griffith, as were the Talmadge sisters, Norma and Constance.

Despite her youth, Bebe was tremendously ambitious and independent in her thinking. She and Harold would often quarrel, but their genuine liking for each other would quickly overcome any bad feelings. Bebe's forthrightness, her strong will, and especially her ambition—as strong as his own—were qualities that might easily have turned Harold away from her, but her vitality and beauty overshadowed all of them. They soon became inseparable.

5

There was no such thing as a producer. The actor
and the director sat around and talked about a
scene, and everyone put in his two cents.

—Gloria Swanson

Both Lloyd and Roach recalled that all of their early films were
made without a script of any kind. Roach remembers it this
way: "Monday morning I would bring the group in and say,
'*You* make up as a cop, *you* make up as a garbageman, *you*
make up as a pedestrian.' We'd go out in the park, and we'd
start to do something. . . . I don't think we ever had anything on
paper until we started making two-reelers with lights."

This was definitely not true of the early years at Rolin, as
there was a brief but significant time there when the Lloyd
films *did* use scripts. Roach's young partner, Dwight Whiting,
started soliciting them from a young lady named Dolly Twist of
Santa Ana, a friend of his family, as early as June 1915. Miss
Twist wrote to Whiting on June 15, telling him, "I certainly
would like to try my hand at a comedy about Lonesome Luke
and will start as soon as I receive the scenario." She was refer-
ring to a copy of an earlier Lonesome Luke script which Whiting had promised to send her as a guide to what they wanted. In
the course of the next few weeks, Whiting bought the scripts
for *His Wash Laundry* and *He Is Some Photographer* for the
agreed-upon price of twenty dollars per script. In August, Whiting wrote Dolly about her golf story:

We are changing it all around, and when you see it on the
screen, I do not believe you will recognize it at all. We are cutting out the dream stuff, as it has been worked to death

lately. . . . You have perhaps noticed in seeing some of the Keystone stuff, that there are two separate threads of comedy all through the story. That is—there are separate and distinct pictures run together, of different people, who simply come together at the end with a big splash. You have probably noticed how hard it is to end up a scenario, also how weak all those we sent you were, and how weak your own was. . . .

Whiting went on to explain that it was often necessary to splice a completely different plot line into the Luke films, just in case some of the material proved to be dull or flat. This kind of picture-making permitted a lot of leeway in the editing process. He concluded by telling her, "Of course, it is essential for the whole thing to wind up together in a rough house finish, so that there is a logical end to the picture. . . . I do not know if you quite got the idea from what I have said, as it is a pretty hard thing to explain. . . . '"

Whiting also told Dolly that all her scripts required the approval of Pathé in New York before they could be purchased by Rolin. By October of that year, the situation had changed and he was able to write that they had started on their fifteenth picture, "which is being put on without any scenario at all. Mr. Roach made arrangements with Pathé whereby we are permitted to put on comedies without submitting scenarios and without using them, as this is the way we get the best results." He also told her, "we are . . . still in the market for good slapstick ideas."

Dolly Twist was disappointed to discover a shrinking market for her scenarios, but could see "how it would easily be as good, or better without them." But she was perplexed as to how to present her new ideas for slapstick situations. "Can you tell me how to write them? As a kind of synopsis or should I try to put in the funny stuff?"

Dolly's career as a script writer for Harold's films was brief, only a few months, but her correspondence with Dwight Whiting shows how the shooting techniques of these one- and two-reelers gradually evolved. Their letters do much to explain why so many of the Arbuckle and Keaton films of a slightly later period (for example, *Good Night, Nurse!* of 1918) have two entirely different plot lines in the same picture.

Money was always tight at Rolin; there was very little cash, and things often got desperate. Dwight Whiting was responsible in these early days for obtaining distribution contracts for the firm's products from Pathé in New York. It was not an easy job. On March 19, 1915, Whiting wired Roach in Los Angeles, explaining his difficulties with Pathé:

$1.10 PER NEGATIVE FOOT CAN GET NO CONTRACT. . . .

The following day Whiting spelled out more bad news:

THEY WILL TAKE 2 OF THEM AT MOST. . . . IT IS NO USE TRYING TO PUT OUT BUM STUFF AND UNLESS WE CAN DO THE WORK IT IS HOPELESS PATHÉ WILL TAKE GOOD COMEDY ONLY AND THAT MEANS EXCELLENT THEY LIKE LLOYD'S WORK.

Roach took all this in his usual tough-guy style, replying to Whiting on the twenty-first:

DON'T LET THOSE NEW YORK WISE GUYS SLIP ANYTHING OVER ON YOU.

By the twenty-fourth, things had become so bad financially in Los Angeles that Roach sent this to Whiting:

ALL OUT OF FUNDS CAN YOU MAKE ANY ARRANGEMENT FOR US HERE?

Whiting's reply the following day was stark:

Inscribed photos from Bebe
Daniels's collection.

HAVE NO FUNDS TO ADVANCE HUSTLE SOME CASH TO LAST UNTIL
NEGS ARRIVE AND ARE ACCEPTED BY PATHÉ.

With the firm on the brink of going under, Whiting had some
strong advice for his partner:

TAKE YOUR TIME AND DO IT RIGHT OUR BEST IS NONE TOO GOOD
BUT WILL GET BY. . . . IN PAST WE HAVE HURRIED TOO MUCH AND
WE MUST PROFIT BY OUR MISTAKES IF YOU FEEL STUFF IS NOT
GOOD DO IT OVER.

It wasn't until the following day that Whiting had any good
news for Roach and Lloyd, but it wasn't all good:

WILL SELL COMEDY [number] ONE PATHÉ SAY DIRECTION VERY
POOR IN ALL PHOTOGRAHY FAIR SAY ALL IMITATIONS . . . AND NOT
GOOD IMITATIONS BETTER LAY OFF WE SEE WHERE WE GET OFF IF
WE KEEP LOSING NO USE CONTINUING WE WILL KNOW SHORTLY
DON'T LOSE HEART OLD SCOUT.

The people at Pathé were correct: the Lonesome Luke comedies
were poor, blatant imitations of Chaplin's work. Pathé's critique
worked: in the next few months Lloyd and Roach pushed hard
to improve the quality of the films. By October 14, 1915, Whiting had much better news from New York:

SUCCESS PATHÉ ACCEPTS ALL PICTURES.

The Lonesome Lukes were formula pictures, with Luke consistently cast as a young ne'er-do-well who gets into scrapes
with trolley-car conductors, cops, pretty girls, and almost anyone else Roach and Lloyd could devise. Harold's few months'

Picnic at Santa Monica. Dee Lampton at extreme left;
HL and Bebe Daniels at right.

experience at Sennett proved invaluable in making these pictures, and he rapidly acquired a reputation for rough, physical
comedy. A trade paper took notice: "Harold Lloyd must be
made of India rubber. The way he suffers himself to be kicked
all over the map, hit on the head with a mallet and fall down a
dizzy flight of stairs is marvelous."

Not very many of the fifty or sixty one-and two-reel Lukes
have survived; four is the current estimate. Most of them went
up in smoke in a 1943 nitrate explosion in a film vault on
Lloyd's estate. The few that are extant demonstrate clearly that
they were ground out as fast as possible to fulfill Pathé's release
schedule.

In later years, Lloyd was doggedly evasive about Chaplin's influence:

> But I never did, really, even in the slightest sense, try to imi-
> tate Charlie. . . . The only thing I did was a comedy character
> with big shoes and probably some comedy mannerisms I used
> may have been borrowed, inadvisedly, from Charlie. But I was
> never happy with that whole situation. . . . I had the feeling,
> and rightly so, that I would never get any farther with Lone-
> some Luke than I had, because underneath it all, he was a
> comedy character that couldn't possibly rise to the heights
> that Chaplin had. And while you didn't try directly to imitate
> Chaplin, Luke was a character that belonged in that category.

He might have gone on making these Lonesome Luke films
for at least another year or so—they were doing sufficiently well
for Pathé to want at least three a month—had he not overheard
a small boy talking to a friend in a theater one night, just as a
Luke picture was about to begin. What he heard was, "Oh,
here's that fellow who tries to do like Chaplin." In the boy's
words were coalesced all the contempt that Lloyd had begun to
feel for his Luke character: "I went back and told Roach I
wasn't going on forever being a third-rate imitator of anybody,
even a genius like Chaplin."

When Roach informed Pathé that his star comedian wished to abandon a character that was making money for all of them, they took the news badly. Roach was not happy about it either, and Harold might not have succeeded in dropping Luke if Roach had not just then become involved with a new comedian called Toto, a pantomimist of the first order from the New York stage. When Roach saw that nothing was going to change Harold's mind, he said, "All right. . . . I'm going to turn it over to you. You pick whoever you want to direct you. I'll take over Toto." Lloyd was left to develop and perfect his new character, the "glasses" character, the one that was to make him world famous.

CHAPTER 3
A PAIR OF HORN-RIMS

1

> I liked the glass character, because it allowed you to
> be a human being. It allowed you to be the boy next
> door or anyone. . . .
>
> —Lloyd

Lloyd always gave himself credit for inventing his "glasses" character. He had recalled seeing a film about a shy, quiet, bespectacled churchman who, when provoked strongly enough, is magically transformed into a fighter who defeats his enemies and wins the girl: a premature Clark Kent. It wasn't the parson's calling that fascinated Harold, it was rather the idea of "a character that belied his character, you thought he was a Milquetoast, then in certain situations he turned out to be just the opposite." Significantly, Lloyd also discovered that he could be anything he wanted to be with these glasses; he had permanently freed himself from the exaggerated costumes and elaborate makeup of the other film comedians. Harold's development of his glasses character was a process of rediscovering himself: *he became an actor again*—what he had always wanted to be— not just another slapstick comedian in the shadow of Chaplin.

Hit Him Again, 1918.

There were other advantages: the new character could maintain a love interest. The presence of romance led to a more sophisticated treatment of character. In time this began to enhance the reality in his films. It would be more accurate to describe the process as the realistic fleshing-out of some common, deep-seated fantasies about the nature of ambition, perseverance, and success. Lloyd's enormous audience all over the world in the 1920s found him the living embodiment of these fantasies. It wasn't simply humor that his audience encountered: they could discover the joy of seeing a meek, mild-mannered man just like themselves transformed into a dynamo of furious, unflagging energy and wild success.

Harold purchased his first pair of horn-rimmed glasses at an optical shop on Spring Street in downtown Los Angeles for seventy-five cents. He removed the lenses immediately, as they were likely to catch the reflection of the klieg lights now being used more and more frequently in film-making. He had gone through thirty pairs before finding the right ones, which he wore for the next eighteen months, patching and repairing them as necessary—action films were as tough on glasses as they were on actors. When the glasses finally gave out, he tried to have them replaced by an optical supply house in New York. The firm sent Harold twenty pairs without charge: his glasses character had become so well known by the end of 1918 that sales of horn-rims were booming all over the world.

The first of Harold's glasses pictures was *Over the Fence,* which he directed himself. He made it as a one-reeler, precipitating a minor crisis with Pathé, which could see no good reason to retreat from the two-reel Luke films. Harold's argument for starting with one-reelers was persuasive:

> I'm getting started in a new character, and you want people to get used to the character. . . . Besides, if you make a poor or

Unidentified film.

mediocre or even a bad picture in a two-reeler, it will tend to sour the people on you, because they won't see another for a month. But if we make one-reelers, we'll get one out every week. So if a couple of them are not so good, and the third one is, it will cover up the other two.

This one-reel formula worked, and Harold's new character, the boy next door, *the winner,* began to catch on quickly. One of his fans expressed the pleasure she and many others felt:

Will you permit a movie fan to congratulate you about discarding your Lonesome Luke make-up, and becoming just plain Harold? Harold is different. . . . Your comedies have improved 100% and it was a long time before I could believe that the sober-faced "Harold" with big rimmed glasses and Eton Tie, and the silly Luke were one and the same.

The Eton tie she mentions here was a mistake, and Harold quickly dropped it for more conventional neck garb.

In both subject matter and quality, the early glasses pictures do not differ significantly from the last of the Lonesome Lukes. The situations and their treatment are often quite similar. Only very slowly did the quality of Harold's films in 1918 improve; he was feeling his way with this new character. It was not until the beginning of 1919 that he began to make the films by which he is remembered today. They were all directed nominally by Roach, but the signs of Harold's collaboration are easy to see. Lloyd's apprenticeship was a long one, and his rate of progress was remarkably slow compared with Chaplin's and Keaton's, although one could argue that both Chaplin and Keaton actually had much longer apprenticeships if their childhood theatrical experience is taken into account. Harold was just as consistently cautious about what he did in films as he was in his personal life, a trait that never left him. He hated making mistakes and preferred to deliberate as long as possible before going

Probably *All Aboard,* 1917.

ahead with a project, but this was impossible when making a film a week. It can be truthfully said that none of the other major silent comedians made so many relatively poor films.

There was very little money available to make them: all profits were immediately ploughed back into the corporation. The financing of Rolin was simple: Pathé in New York would advance all production costs, at this time about $1,500, and retain 30 percent of the net proceeds from whatever sums the films might earn in rentals. This 70/30 split between film-maker and distributor was common to the industry at the time; banks wouldn't dream of lending money to film producers, and there simply wasn't enough private capital available to satisfy even their modest demands. In 1918 the Rolin films (also known to the film trade as Phun Films, a horrendous appelation devised by Roach) were earning at best between $2,000 and $3,000; there was very little left over after paying the staff's salaries. Cash was always extremely tight, and it was this situation that came close to forcing Harold to leave Roach and Whiting and go off on his own.

While it is true that Harold and Roach preferred to remain outwardly friendly in later years, it is clear that they didn't really get along as well as they claimed. There were frequent quarrels in these early days, some of them admittedly foolish, but significant to Harold, who increasingly thought he knew more about film-making than Hal Roach. In his 1928 autobiography *An American Comedy*, Harold went out of his way to preface his criticism of Roach with a crude sort of testimonial, calling him "a born leader, an excellent businessman and an original comedy director." All three were true enough, but Harold may have felt that he had to spell it all out before stating that Roach found the two-reel length tedious, that he would often ask after a week or so of shooting, " 'How much footage

Snub Pollard, Bebe Daniels, and HL in *Bees in His Bonnet,* 1918.

have we now?' '' When he got the answer, he would call out, '' 'Well, boys, let's finish her up,' and shoot the remainder as if he had a train to catch.'' Harold was a good deal franker when he talked with Kevin Brownlow in the sixties: "Hal . . . wasn't actually a very good director. He had fortitude, he had drive, and he had worlds of confidence. But in the early days, on the Lonesome Luke pictures, he would work until he got up to the last five or ten minutes, then he would say, 'All right, this creaks.' And he'd quit. He'd just wind it up.''

Roach claims that Harold had little or nothing to do with the genesis of his glasses character. As Roach tells it, there was an actor named Earl Monahan on the Rolin lot who specialized in playing drunks. Monahan arrived on the set one day wearing a pair of lensless horn-rims. Roach and some others in the company thought this idea would be "just right" for Harold, and the

She Loves Me Not, 1918.

The Dutiful Dub, 1919.

character was born that very day. Harold's recollection of this tale was rather different, but in his usual good-natured way he let the matter ride, preferring not to make an open break with the man who had given him his first start in the business. But it must have rankled, as their differences kept escalating.

Roach's policy of putting the profits back into the business didn't help his relationship with Harold. The success of the Lloyd films made Roach double Harold's salary of $50 a week to $100, beginning in August 1916. In February 1917 his weekly rate rose again, this time to $125. In March of that year, Roach increased it to $150, where it remained stuck for the next year.* By that time the glasses pictures were gaining hugely in box-office appeal each week. Roach and Whiting had promised Harold another 100-percent jump in pay by the spring of 1918. When the time arrived, both Whiting and Roach announced that they were not taking in as much from Pathé as they had expected and that Harold would have to wait for his raise. He was invited to inspect the firm's books if he doubted their picture of Rolin's cash position. There was no need: he was perfectly aware they were telling him the truth, but he felt that it was *their* company, *their* investment, and *their* profits. Since he didn't participate in any of these, why should he be denied what they owed him? His reaction to Roach's going back on his word was exactly the same as it had been earlier, when Roach had refused to pay him that ten dollars: he quit, gave up his hotel room, and moved back in again with Foxy Lloyd.

---

* Harold was not required to serve in the armed services during the first World War—the authorities decided that his appearances in pictures like *Kicking the Germ Out of Germany* and *A Sammy in Siberia* were of far greater importance to the war effort.

2

Harold Lloyd has, in less than a year and a half, become one of the great screen comedians in the country.

—*Moving Picture World,*
April 17, 1917

When he suddenly quit working for Roach and Whiting in March 1918, Harold was not particularly worried. He had saved several thousand dollars, and his glasses character was becoming familiar enough to guarantee him work wherever he wanted to go in Hollywood. But when he looked for work, he found that the other studios believed his contract with Rolin was still in full force. Whiting had passed the word around that it was, and his competitors refused to hire Lloyd.

The decision to quit Roach had not been motivated entirely by money. Harold violently objected to Roach's insistence that he be present at the studio every single working day, regardless of whether he was appearing before the camera. Roach's notion was that Harold's presence was a morale-builder for the rest of the company. One day Harold did not appear; shortly before noon his phone rang. It was Roach, demanding to know if he was ill. Harold's reply made Roach smash the phone down as hard as he could. When Harold arrived at the Bradbury Mansion that afternoon, Whiting informed him that Roach insisted that the presence of both Lloyd and Roach was too much for the Rolin Company: one of them had to go. Whiting made it clear that he considered himself Roach's partner and refused to get embroiled in the quarrel. Harold went home to begin thinking for the first time about leaving. A reconciliation was achieved that time by bringing the two principals, unbeknownst to each

Young Mr. Jazz, 1919.

Pistols for Breakfast, 1919.

other, to a room down at the Alexandria Hotel. After a short period of mutual glaring, Roach and Lloyd shook hands and
Harold returned to work the following day. But disputes like
this were symptomatic of some deeper quarrel, and it is clear
not only that Harold disliked working for Hal Roach but that he
hated working for *anyone*. When the split came up over the
money, Harold must have been aware that more than dollars
was involved: it was independence that he craved, although he
may have known that he wasn't ready for it yet.

For a man who thrived on work, the inactivity was terrible.
Harold did some hard thinking in the next week, realizing that
under the circumstances neither he nor Roach could yield to
the other with any grace. A third party was needed to repair the
situation, and this was obviously Pathé. Lloyd quickly packed a
bag and left on the noon train for New York. It was the first time
he had been east of Chicago and he had lots to think about on
the long, five-day trip across the country. He was more than half
convinced that his trip would accomplish nothing.

After registering at the Bristol Hotel on West 48th Street,
Harold bought theater tickets, one for a matinee that day for Al
Jolson in *Sinbad* and the other for a show starring Fred Stone.
After leaving the Jolson show shortly before five, he decided to
call the Pathé office and make an appointment for the following
day with Paul Brunet, the firm's general manager. He was told
that Brunet had left for the day, but when Harold informed the
operator that "Mr. Harold Lloyd" was calling, she interrupted
him excitedly, repeating, "Mr. *Harold* Lloyd?" She then told
him that Brunet was expecting him the following morning at
nine o'clock; someone at Rolin (probably Whiting) had called
Brunet about the hasty trip to New York.

His meeting with Paul Brunet was a complete success.
Harold told him all about the promised raise and Roach's failure
to live up to it. Brunet knew all about it; he also knew perfectly
well that Rolin's films without Harold Lloyd were not worth

distributing. Brunet had been having his own troubles with Roach, as Roach did not like Pathé's critical opinions about his work as a director. The previous year Roach had wired Whiting concerning Brunet's attitude: "I REFUSE TO MAKE PICTURES FOR PATHÉ TO BE EDITED IN NEW YORK. . . . PATHÉ CANNOT EDIT COMEDY. . . . BRING HOME THE BACON." Brunet had no illusions about his abilities as a film editor; he had gone along with Roach's refusal to accept editing in New York. He had also been gradually increasing the cash advances on the films, believing that Lloyd had a tremendous future. Starting at $1,500 in early 1916, the advances had reached $2,300 by the fall of 1917. Brunet knew even better than Roach that the market value for Harold's films was climbing day by day. He could see no difficulty about raising Harold's salary to $300 a week, even if Pathé had to guarantee it whenever Roach and Whiting couldn't pay that much. To celebrate his visit, Brunet gave Harold a dinner attended by various local exhibitors in the New York area, as well as an all-expenses-paid tour of the city.

As Harold made his way back to California the following week, he was aware that he'd won more than just the money: he'd gained the respect and admiration of one of the executives of a major film distributor. He also knew that there would be a time when he would be able to make his films the way *he* wanted them made. He realized that he was the drawing card they wanted in New York—and the rest of the world.

3

In those days . . . it was one big family—a lot of crazy people, but a lot of them very smart and very, very lovely.

—Reginald Denny

Harold Lloyd was a mechanical man. . . . I don't mean bad mechanics. I mean great mechanics. If he stepped on a pig it wasn't a pig, it was a rock. . . . his pictures were funny because he worked like a slave. He really directed himself mostly, I'd say.

—Eddie Sutherland

Harold returned to work in the last week of March 1918 to resume making some of the thirty-four Lloyd one-reelers that Rolin released that year. In *Kicking the Germ Out of Germany*, Harold dreams that he gets to Berlin to rescue a beautiful Red Cross nurse from the clutches of the Kaiser. In *Somewhere in Turkey*, Harold is a professor whose rival for the girl he loves is the Sultan. In *Hit Him Again*, Harold must fight Boiler-Nose Bill in order to win the girl he adores. The girl was always Bebe Daniels, whose genuine talents for comedy roles became clearer each week. She started working at Rolin at ten dollars a week in 1915 and by 1918 had worked her way up to one hundred, a lot of money then for a girl who had not yet reached her eighteenth birthday.

Bebe and Harold remained constant companions. They continued to enter the dance contests at all the famous night spots of the day: the Ship Café, the Sunset Inn at Santa Monica, Watt's Tavern, and Nat Goodwin's at Venice. They regularly won prize cups in competition with other young film stars:

Bees in His Bonnet, 1918.

Gloria Swanson and her first husband, Wallace Beery; Wallace Reid, the ill-fated narcotics addict, and his wife Dorothy. Harold later believed that some of the cups he won with Bebe may have been awarded because of their fame as film stars rather than for their dancing.

Bebe's intense vitality came through strongly on the screen. In 1927, when Luis Buñuel was attempting to indicate why he preferred certain types of "non-literary" film, he singled out her acting to demonstrate what he meant. As Bebe's talents began to emerge, so too did her image of herself as a performer. She began to participate actively in the discussion of her roles, often arguing with Roach and Harold. At one point she became sufficiently angry with them to refuse to appear for work. In March 1916, Whiting wrote to Roach in New York, "Today is payday and everyone got full checks with the exception of Bebe Daniels, who hasn't got anything seeing as she will stick for nothing." In the spring of 1917, Roach and Whiting were convinced that Bebe was about to leave them for a rival firm. Dancing one night with Harold at one of the local cafés, she had been observed by both Cecil B. De Mille and Jessie Lasky of Famous Players-Lasky, who asked her over to their table. When Whiting heard that his rivals had then proceeded to make an offer to his second most important star, he wrote an indignant letter to Frank Garbutt, the general manager of Famous Players:

> Mr. Lasky and Mr. De Mille noticed our star, Miss Bebe Daniels, on the dance floor, and after calling her over to their

Bebe Daniels in the early twenties.

table, offered her a position on the Lasky forces. Miss Daniels replied that she was satisfied to remain where she was as she was under contract and receiving her salary regularly whereupon they told her that they would be glad to have her join their forces at any time she could arrange to do so, and that they would pay her a figure of around twice what she is now receiving. . . .

Whiting's use of military terminology served to emphasize the fury of Roach and himself over the proposition. His letter went on to cite the provisions of the Hollywood Producers' Association, which stipulated that raiding was strictly forbidden. Garbutt's answer of the following day loudly proclaimed the innocence of his firm's principals:

> Mr. De Mille advises me that he and Mr. Lasky saw Miss Daniels dancing at the Café, as stated, and thinking she was an attractive girl, and not knowing who she was or that she was employed, asked her to call at the Studio. Later, when Mr. Lasky found that she was employed and under contract, he told her frankly he could not pursue the matter further, and the question of salary, Mr. De Mille says, was never mentioned at all. . . . there has been a misunderstanding. . . . neither Mr. Lasky nor Mr. De Mille would talk to anyone whom they know was under contract. . . .

With Harold the man in her life, as well as a steady series of raises, Bebe was kept relatively happy. But De Mille never gave up his hope of having her work for him and kept tempting her with ever higher offers. She refused all of them and continued to work out her contract with Rolin, while she and Harold remained as close as ever. There is some indication that she was anxious to marry him, but he felt he was far too young to shoulder the responsibilities that went with marriage. It seems probable that, despite his tremendous fondness for her, Bebe posed a kind of threat to him: here was a young woman of only eighteen with fully developed career plans all her own. This was scarcely what Harold wanted. There was also his timidity in making major decisions. His ambivalence toward Bebe Daniels can be seen as characteristic of this reluctance to make up his mind about things—a need to postpone decisions until he had examined the problem in all its aspects, a process that Bebe must have found difficult. In the meantime, the relationship was a good one for both of them; their genuine feeling for each other never wavered.

Their work together was always a kind of spontaneous, unpredictable fun. Each week found the Rolin Company in some new and hitherto unexplored part of the greater Los Angeles area, in quest of a locale for the stories they invented as they rode around a country that was a paradise in those pre-smog, pre-freeway days. Lunchtime was always a picnic and an especially fine one if the company was near the beaches at Santa Monica, Balboa, or Redondo.

Film-making in those early joyous days was often a communal experience in which almost anybody might get involved. Agnes De Mille, the famous choreographer and niece of Cecil B. De Mille, recalls this aspect of Hollywood in its infancy:

> [When a picture was finished] they'd paste it together and run it and they asked everybody—all the families, all the children, even neighbors, sometimes—"Come in, come in and see our picture." Then they'd ask everybody what they thought. . . .

It was about now that Harold began to indulge his passion for exotic automobiles, a passion that intensified as his income rose to keep pace with it. One of his first cars was a Chandler phaeton, which he had painted a brilliant blue, in flagrant imitation of a car owned by Wallace Beery. The phaeton became an important part of Harold's professional life; cameraman Hal Mohr* recalled:

> . . . he and Bebe used to sit in the back seat going on location while Gil [Pratt] would drive them. . . . We had a little yellow bus that was like a miniature of the present-day school buses . . . and this little bus contained the Rolin Stock Company (exclusive of those in Harold's Chandler), Snub Pollard and others, and that little bus would follow this blue Chandler around town. As we'd drive, we'd discuss. We had some kind of format, an idea as to how the picture would be made, but actually the comedies were made by the inspiration of the moment. We'd get an idea: we'd see a park or we'd see a bench or we'd see a drugstore, or a saloon with a post in the center of the door and it was a springboard for a gag.

4

. . . RECEIVED NO ANSWER FROM BEBE
—Telegram
Hal Roach to Dwight Whiting
April 12, 1919

If Harold and Foxy thought they were breaking away from Elizabeth Lloyd for good when they left for California in 1912, they were mistaken. The divorce was real enough, but Elizabeth became determined to join her youngest son soon after the first sure signs that he had become successful. Mother and son ex-

---

* Hal Mohr, one of the major Hollywood cameramen in the twenties and thirties, was a co-director (with Gil Pratt) of one of Lloyd's two-reelers.

Vehicle used by Roach Company for transporting
cast to shooting locales.

changed letters with some regularity, but Harold was apparently nowhere near as faithful a correspondent with her as he was with Foxy. Her letters attest to her displeasure at his long silences. After leaving Denver, Elizabeth had settled down for a time on a ranch in Wyoming, and on New Year's Day of 1919 she wrote Harold a letter that indicates what the other members of the Lloyd family had long been contending with:

> *Hagie Wyo*
> *Jan 1 1919*
>
> *My dear Son:*
> *This is the beginning of a new year and I'm going to start right by writing to you although it will be my last unless you do your part for Harold it isn't right for you to neglect me. Not a word or line for 5 mon past, if you haven't time send a telegram or something. Harold dear don't think your little box I sent you is your real Xmas present for I wrote to Uncle Roy to see if he could get me a Navaho blanket & just heard from him so will get him to get it & send it from there I hope dear you are well & happy. This is a lonely day for I'm alone here at the ranch except for hired man. Geo has to*

*be in Torrington & our own man went to Cheyenne for New
Years & one of the neighbors does the chores. . . . You don't
mean to be neglectful dear but you are, so try to improve in
1919. Just think I'll be fifty years old the 10th Your mother
will soon be down & out. Now my dear, dear Son, I call
Gods blessing on you for each & every day to give you
health & happiness love & everything good—I know He will
for you have been wonderfully blest in past years so may all
things be yours for 1919—and I hope to see my boy,
Gaylord & Mayo* are still in Denver so I am alone—*

*Good night dearest with love,
Mother*

I would love to have ½ doz more small pictures of me—

Harold's response to letters like this was to buy his mother a
modest house in Los Angeles, the first of a series of ever more
imposing ones as his fortunes rose.

Elizabeth's self-pity, her constant whining, as well as her
"grande dame-ism," may have had a good deal to do with
Harold's deepest feelings about women. She would seem to be
at least partially responsible for Harold's attitude, which would
now be classified as sexist. Women were supposed to be soft
and vulnerable; those who weren't, caused trouble. Bebe Daniels was hard to categorize.

By the spring of 1919, the Lloyd films were doing so well for
Pathé that they thought it was time for Harold to begin making
more expensive two-reelers. Such films could not be made
without a considerable increase in production advances, but
Paul Brunet indicated to Roach that Pathé would be willing to
pay a lot more if Harold's presence in the films could be assured: " [If] you can see your way clear to put him under contract for a period of three years. . . . Then we can pay more."

---

* Gaylord's wife.

After talking this over with Harold, Roach wired Brunet: "HAROLD SAYS YES. . . . STATES HIS WILLINGNESS TO SIGN FOR AN ADDITIONAL 2 YEARS AT 500 A WEEK AND A PARTICIPATION IN THE PROFITS."

The first of the vastly enhanced Lloyd contracts between Rolin and Pathé, sometimes referred to as the "A" contract, specified nine two-reelers, each of 1900 feet and "acceptable" to Pathé. A clause was inserted in this April 12, 1919, contract giving Pathé the right to judge the films according to four categories: "Good, nearly good, fair, and poor." Sixteen thousand dollars was to be advanced on each film, $3,500 on commencement and $3,500 per week for three weeks, with a final payment of $2,000 on delivery. Rolin was to keep 65 percent of the gross U.S. receipts; the two parties would split the foreign market on a fifty-fifty basis.

Harold's participation changed dramatically: he received another raise of $100 a week, bringing him up to $400. He later claimed that it was at this time that Roach began paying him $1,000 a week, but that figure was still two years away. His pride may have dictated changing the facts here, since compared with the earnings of his two major rivals in the industry, Roscoe Arbuckle and Chaplin, Harold's new salary of $400 was really quite small. Arbuckle was then receiving $1,500 a week from Joseph M. Schenck and his Comique Corporation in addition to $3,000 per week from Paramount. Chaplin's salary had risen to $10,000 a week as early as 1916, and by 1919 he was paying himself out of the huge proceeds of his self-financed films. The film comedian that Harold was currently on a par with financially was Buster Keaton, whose salary was raised to a level approximating Harold's in 1919.

In later years Lloyd was generally reliable whenever he quoted figures about the financing or earnings of his early films. But by the time he was telling Wesley Stout his life story in 1928, many of these financial records had been out of his

His Royal Slyness, 1920.

Mildred Davis in 1919.

hands for at least ten years. Most of the figures he gave Stout in 1928 have been accepted as correct, but an examination of Hal Roach's ledgers, as well as the Pathé files, indicates that Lloyd's memory was not as accurate as has been believed.

With the much larger budgets available, the Lloyd films were now made more carefully. The first two under the new arrangement were *Bumping into Broadway* and *Captain Kidd's Kids*. As usual, Bebe was the leading lady, but these were her last pictures with Harold. She had finally decided to take up Cecil B. De Mille's offer of 1917, which he now boosted to $1,000 a week. Her decision to leave the company was probably based as much on her hopes for a major film career of her own as on her personal feelings about Harold. One clear way to show him she did play an important part in his life would be to leave him *and* Rolin. Perhaps she wanted Harold to call her bluff. But he didn't, and Bebe eventually married the actor Ben Lyon, with whom she had an extraordinarily successful professional and personal relationship. She never regretted her move: within a year or so she had become a first-rate comedienne in films like *Why Change Your Wife?* and *The Speed Girl* (1920). By the time she appeared in *Miss Brewster's Millions* (1926), *She's a Sheik* (1926) and *Feel My Pulse* (1928), she had become a major Hollywood star all on her own.

If Harold was depressed or disturbed by Bebe's departure, he kept it to himself. Unlike Buster Keaton, who had severe difficulty in articulating anything about his feelings, Harold was always adept at telling people about *good* news; if the news was bad it was best not to say a word.

Harold and Roach decided that they must find a new girl as unlike Bebe as possible. A blonde was part of the answer, and they found her in Mildred Davis, a seventeen-year-old whom Roach had seen in a comedy film starring Bryant Washburn. She was quite attractive in a childlike way, and when Harold saw the film he was all for hiring her on the spot: "The more I realized how inexperienced and young she must be, the more anxious I was to get her. . . . On the screen, she reminded me of a big French doll."

Roach was far more cautious; he wired Paul Brunet in New York: "I AM TRYING TO GET MILDRED DAVIS TO PLAY LEAD WITH LLOYD STOP KINDLY ASK THE OPINION OF PEOPLE THERE REGARDING THIS GIRL." Brunet's reply was immediate: "MILDRED DAVIS VERY SATISFACTORY WE SUGGEST YOU GET HER."

Obtaining Mildred's services proved to be a problem; no one in Hollywood seemed to know where she had gone. Roach finally discovered that she had left California "for good," in order to return to her home in Tacoma, Washington, and complete her high school education. Once Roach and Lloyd had located her, she and her mother returned to Hollywood on the basis of the promises contained in Roach's telegram. Both Mildred and her mother were convinced that Mildred should appear to be as mature as possible; when Harold and Roach met her at the studio they found it hard to reconcile this beautifully dressed young woman with the unsophisticated girl they had seen in the film clip. After they made her discard all her plumes and feathers, Mildred proved to be what they had hoped: Harold's new and demure leading lady for the third two-reeler, *From Hand to Mouth*.

By the summer of 1919 Harold had much to be pleased about. He was now the third most popular screen comedian in the country and gaining fast on both Arbuckle and Chaplin. The rental fees on his films were increasing day by day. The sound of money was loud in the air, and it surely looked as if he was going to get his share of it. He had a brand-new leading lady who, while lacking Bebe's sexual vitality and charm, did not pose the problems that Bebe did. But on a quiet Sunday afternoon in August, Harold's dreams were shattered by the sound of an explosion.

CHAPTER 4

"THE YOUNG MOLIÈRE OF THE SCREEN"

1

What the hell, Bill, what the hell . . . Suppose you
hadn't lowered your hand?

—Lloyd

With the impending release of the first of their new two-reelers,
Roach was anxious to obtain a new selection of publicity photographs of Harold. The Rolin Company couldn't afford the luxury of a staff photographer, so the services of the Witzel Studio
in downtown Los Angeles were scheduled for Sunday afternoon, August 14, 1919. Roach's property man, Frank Terry,
thought a pose of Harold lighting a cigarette from the fuse of a
property bomb would be in order and selected one from inventory for Harold to take to Witzel's studio. It was a papier-mâché
bomb, painted black, with a long, delayed-action fuse, the kind
of property bomb that the Rolin Company often used in their
comic films. Harold recalled what happened when Terry
handed him the bomb:

> I put a cigarette in my mouth, struck a sassy attitude and held
> the bomb in my right hand, the fuse to the cigarette. The

smoke blew across my face, so clouding the expression that the photographer, whose head was buried under the black cloth, delayed squeezing the bulb. As he continued to wait and the fuse grew shorter and shorter, I raised the bomb nearer and nearer to my face, until, the fuse all but gone, I dropped the hand and was saying that we must insert a new fuse, when the thing exploded.

If Lloyd had not lowered his hand at that precise moment, the chances are that he would have been killed instantly. The force of the blast was principally upward; it tore a gaping hole in the sixteen-foot ceiling above him, broke all the windows in the room, and smashed the upper plate of Frank Terry's false teeth. Harold was in a state of shock; his face was a mass of blood and he could see nothing. His right hand was steadily losing blood; part of it appeared to be missing. Frank Terry flagged down a passing car, and they were both rushed to a nearby hospital, where Harold was given ether to lessen his agonizing pain.

The explanation of what happened never really satisfied Lloyd or anyone else at Rolin. Two property bombs had been made for a social event of the firm up at Bear Lake. One of these was used to demolish an oak table as part of a stunt; the force of that explosion was so powerful that the second bomb was returned to the studio inventory and defused. How it was later given one of the long, delayed-action fuses remained a mystery, but when Harold awoke the next day in the hospital his main concern was whether or not he would ever see again. His doctors were cautious, as they were convinced that his right eye had been penetrated by some of the metal in the bomb. But their prognosis was wrong, and in a few weeks Harold regained normal vision in both eyes. His face was another matter. It was, as he said, "raw meat and the first efforts were concentrated on preventing gangrene. The antiseptic treatment accomplished its purpose, but, in turn, set up a maddening rash and an outbreak of boils. Then my painfully swollen lips cracked in four deep crevasses as they began to heal."

It was his hand that wasn't going to heal: the explosion had completely torn off the thumb and forefinger of his right hand. The impact of this loss must surely have been traumatic, since Harold went out of his way to conceal the fact for the rest of his life. There is not a word about it in his autobiography. It may be argued that for a physical comedian such as Lloyd, the loss of part of his hand might well have been a terrible burden; Harold's reaction seems to indicate that he found the loss so devastating that he pretended it had never happened. In the following months he obtained the first of a series of prosthetic devices that he used for all his work in front of the camera. Socially, he always wore gloves to conceal his deformity.

The hand was bad enough, but he couldn't avoid thinking how close he had come to death. He kept repeating one of his favorite phrases to himself, "What the hell, Bill, what the hell." It was a nervous phrase he always used when concentrating on something difficult or disturbing. Always a careful man, Harold cursed the arbitrary quality of the accident that seemed to have smashed his career just when it looked as if he was close to success.

His face swathed in bandages for weeks on end, Harold became convinced that he would never appear in another film. He began to think seriously about a new career as a director. Hundreds of "get-well' cards arrived from admirers all over the country, including one from Stan Laurel, temporarily tramping the boards in Alberta, Canada: " . . . trust it is not as serious as they say. . . . Mae joins me in kind regards to all & self." Mabel Normand and Fatty Arbuckle sent cards, as did almost every other major star in Hollywood. Bebe Daniels's was signed, "To Boy with love from Girl." In the following weeks Foxy Lloyd dutifully pasted every one of them in Harold's scrapbook.

A comic aftermath of the explosion arrived in the form of a

bill for damages from the photographic shop that Roach had chosen to take the ill-fated series of pictures. The bill from Witzel's (PORTRAITS THAT PLEASE) was accompanied by this letter, printed here without changing a comma:

> *September 29th*
> *1919*
>
> *Dear Sirs:—*
> *As per your request we are inclosing you, bill for actual repairs for the damage done on that fatefull Sunday that poor Harold meet with his accident.*
> *As you probebly know we were compelled to close the Studio shortly after the accident as all sittings were to nervous to sit for there appointments, and our operator was all in.*
>
> *With the best for you,*
> *We are very truly yours,*
> *Witzel Studio.*

The year 1919, the first year after the Great War, was a time of unparalleled growth in the film industry. Hollywood had become the chief film producer for the world. New and ever larger theaters were constructed at fever pitch; box-office receipts spiraled upward from week to week. The public came to see their favorite stars and the stars knew it. Contracts were being torn up and rewritten all over Hollywood. The new salaries granted these stars caused the expense of picture-making to escalate steeply. In 1916 a feature film had cost about $10,000 to $30,000; by the end of 1918 the costs had reached the $30,000-to-$75,000 range, with the figures for some major films soaring as high as $100,000 to $125,000 if the picture included ranking stars. Huge sums of money began pouring into Hollywood, and it was only a short time before profit-sharing became an eagerly discussed topic around town. It was known that Arbuckle, in addition to his combined salary of $4,500 per week from Paramount and Schenck, was receiving a quarter of the profits on

Recovering, 1919.

his films. Mary Pickford was earning over a million a year, including one half of the profits made on her pictures by Adolph Zukor's Paramount. Harold was aware of what was going on in the film world as he lay in his hospital bed, deeply troubled about his future. His view was dramatically changed on August 28 when he received a wire from Douglas Fairbanks, who had also been thinking about Harold's future:

WILL YOU WIRE ME IN STRICT CONFIDENCE . . . WHEN PRESENT CONTRACT THROUGH AND WHAT YOU ARE GETTING STOP CAN SWING A BIG DEAL FOR YOU IF YOU WILL TRUST ME REMEMBER I HELPED YOU RIGHT ROAD ONCE AND CAN DO IT AGAIN.

Whatever Fairbanks had done for Harold in the past is now lost in it. What he now had in mind, obviously, was taking him on as one of the partners in the group of stars that was to create United Artists in the fall of that year: Chaplin, Mary Pickford, D. W. Griffith, and Fairbanks himself.

For reasons that remain mysterious, Fairbanks and his asso-

ciates were convinced that Harold's accident made his contract
with Roach null and void. In a few weeks the opportunity to join
United Artists was made definite by what Harold later described as an offer of a five-year acting contract at a salary of
$100,000 per year. An offer like this seems unlikely, because
United Artists was created as a distribution organization by the
stars who owned it. By becoming their own distributors, the
stars could avoid the hefty cut taken by releasing organizations
such as Paramount and Associated-First National. Harold
didn't have the kind of money to become a partner in United
Artists and perhaps he changed the story about the nature of
the proposed deal out of simple pride. But there were good reasons for his rejecting *any* kind of offer from United Artists.
Even as a partner in the new firm he would be competing with
Chaplin for the attention of the exhibitors, a fate that overcame
Buster Keaton in 1926 when Joseph M. Schenck began to dis-
tribute his Keaton features through United Artists, of which he
had become president. With a Chaplin film, Schenck could always demand his own terms; with a Keaton, it was an "also
ran" situation. Shifting Keaton from MGM to United Artists
produced a marked decline in the revenues of Keaton's films
and signaled the decline of his career. Harold knew perfectly
well how good he was, but 1919 was still too early to take on
Chaplin, the man every comedian in Hollywood knew simply as
"The Master." Things might have been even worse if the partners had actually wanted to hire Harold simply as an actor. It
would have been demeaning: working for Roach was always a
problem, but in effect working for *Chaplin*? Whatever the nature of the offer, Harold wisely rejected it.

However, the dickering with Fairbanks and his partners was
an ideal way for Harold to induce Roach to give him a share of
the business. By October, Harold had signed a new contract
with Roach that increased his salary to $500 per week and, far
more important, gave him 50 percent of the profits. His new sal-

ary began immediately and was to be increased again to $750 on January 1, 1920. While scarcely in the Arbuckle or Chaplin league, Harold had made a big advance in his career, and he may well have had the accident to thank for it. He was absent from the screen for seven months, and the exhibitors were all too aware of it.

Another reason for Harold's being able to extract these terms was the terrifically expanding market for comedy films. In 1919 and 1920, when Chaplin, Keaton, and Lloyd were making their now-classic two-reel comedies, these films were, in fact, the main reason many people bought tickets. The titles of the two-reelers and their stars were frequently in letters at least as large as those of the feature films on the same bill. There were plenty of filmgoers who could only be persuaded to sit through seventy-five minutes of a Norma Talmadge tearjerker or a Gloria Swanson "high living in high places" film if they could be assured of seeing Buster Keaton in films like *One Week* and *Cops,* or Chaplin in *Payday* and *The Idle Class.* In time, the popularity of short comedy films would lead their makers to produce feature-length films in order to obtain their fair share of the moviegoer's dollar.

2

I made practically all of Harold's films, and basically he had not a funny bone in his body, but he was such a good actor that if you gave him a good script, he could play it to the best advantage for laughs.
—Hal Roach

Roach's remarks may apply to the Lloyd of the mid-thirties when, in fact, the script *was* nearly everything in film, but they most certainly do not apply to the 1919 Lloyd, when there were no scripts to worry about, and the sight gag was supreme.

Sheer vitality was the quality that characterized the nine two-reelers Harold made for Roach in 1919 and 1920. These films, along with the Keaton and Chaplin short films of the same period, reflect their makers' desire not to waste a moment; *every second counted* as it never has again in the history of film. A two-reeler ran for only about twenty to twenty-two minutes, but it was always packed with incident. There would be a plot line of sorts, nothing very elaborate, just enough to maintain a narrative thread on which could be mounted the improvised visual gags that made up the heart of the film.

Bumping into Broadway, the first two-reeler featuring Harold's glasses character, was released in November 1919, nearly three months after the accident. The film had been completed prior to May of that year and it co-starred Bebe in her next to last appearance in a Lloyd film. The picture begins early one morning in Bearcat Simpson's boarding house in a sleazy section of New York. Bebe is a young dancer who can't pay her rent; Harold is her next-door neighbor, a budding musical-comedy writer. We see him completing his morning toilette with the half inch of water left in his wash bowl: he moistens his face with a few strategically placed drops and vigorously dries himself with a huge towel, with which he then polishes his shoes. After the landlady slips a FINAL NOTICE TO PAY BILL under all the doorsills, Harold puts together enough to pay his by disgorging the entire contents of a baby safe concealed under his mattress.

He leaves his room and finds Bebe sobbing in the hallway. Touched by her tears, he gives her all his money to pay her rent. About to leave the building, he observes another tenant being savagely beaten by the landlord for nonpayment. Harold thinks of trying to get his money back from Bebe, but she thanks him so profusely that he gives up and returns to his room to plan his next move. The dreaded landlady enters, and what she sees is a Harold who begs for her mercy upon bended knees. Not so, for a closer look reveals that we are looking at a dummy created from Harold's hat and coat, cleverly draped over a chair. By the time the landlady has caught on, Harold has slipped out of the room and begun a dizzying series of moves to evade the clutches of her husband, the bestial landlord, Bearcat Simpson. Harold hides in a laundry basket about to be removed by two Chinese: the bottom drops out and he flees yet again. In these scenes Harold shows that he is clearly the equal of both Chaplin and Keaton in the realm of pure physical comedy, using his body as a comic instrument that continually surprises and delights. The pace is relentless, and several minutes pass before he makes his getaway.

On his way to the theater for a decision about his new play, Harold hops onto a passing car. He climbs into the back seat and finds himself sitting next to a pompous old gentleman reading a newspaper. Calmly, Harold takes the paper and begins reading it himself. When they arrive at the theater Harold honors the oldster with a mocking bow as he descends to the pavement. The stage door attendant won't let him into the building, so he hides inside a grandfather clock that is being delivered. Once inside the theater, he presents himself to the general manager, who proves to be the old man from whom Harold stole the newspaper. The manager throws Harold and his play out of his office.

About to leave the theater, Harold notices Bebe rehearsing on stage. Bebe's boss, the musical director, suffers an accidental fall through a hole in the stage floor; furious, he berates Bebe and fires her without cause. Harold comes to her defense and soundly thrashes the director. For his pains, he is thrown out of the theater. In despair, Harold sits by the curb and tears up his manuscript. He is nearly run over by a limousine that whisks up to the stage door. A rich young man steps out and enters the theater. He is attracted to the saddened Bebe and invites her out to a supper club. Bebe accepts the invitation, and an angry

Harold observes the couple entering the limousine. Without a pause, Harold climbs into a street cleaner's cart and ties it to the back of the limousine; the linked vehicles roar off down the street.

When Harold manages to get inside the "supper club," he discovers a large group of people arranged in a semicircle with their backs to him. After picking up some money lying on the floor, he attempts to hand it to one of the men, but is shoved away. He then tosses the bill into the middle of what proves to be a roulette table. A certain number wins the entire pot, and the number is Harold's. Stupefied, he begins filling his pockets with thousands of dollars as he is being vigorously congratulated by the other players. Just then, the police arrive to raid the place. Harold and Bebe, having made up their quarrel over her

Bumping into Broadway, 1919.

escort, manage to evade what seems to be the entire New York Police Department as they flee hundreds of police officers from room to room—a scene strangely similar to Keaton's *Cops,* filmed nearly three years later. The officers collect the supper-club gamblers and depart, leaving Harold and Bebe alone for their kiss at the very end.

This is a film of continual movement, punctuated only by Lloyd's efforts to show the ingenuity of his character. Compared with his great features of the twenties, *Bumping into Broadway* is relatively slight, but it clearly foreshadows many of the techniques he was to bring to perfection in the later films. The sight gag of Harold begging his landlady for mercy is a primitive version of a technique that became ever more elaborate in the feature films. Sheer chance is an element in all these early films, giving rise here to the success Harold achieves at a roulette game he didn't know existed. But only his firm will to get Bebe back from the hands of her new admirer has propelled him in the direction of the gambling club in the first place. From first to last, *success* is the keynote in this film: success in evading his brutal landlord, success in winning a fortune, and success in winning his girl. He owes most of it to his sheer energy and ingenuity; it was the interplay of these two elements that began, at the outset of the twenties, to fascinate filmgoers all over the world.

3

Slapstick will be taboo. The public taste has gone beyond the rough-and-tumble performances that used
to be classed as humorous. Instead, a more subtle,
clean-cut production, with at least some semblance
of a story, is the current demand in the comedy line.
                              —*Moving Picture World,*
                                  September 27, 1919

When the bomb exploded in August, Harold had completed
about half the shooting of his fifth two-reeler, *Haunted Spooks.*
Before going back to it in the late fall of 1919, he took his second trip to New York. One of the reasons for the trip was to celebrate his new contract with Hal Roach. Another was to meet
Charles Pathé, who was on one of his infrequent trips to
America. But the real reason was to be on hand for the first
screenings of *Bumping into Broadway,* which opened with
enormous success during Harold's visit. He never forgot the experience of seeing his name in lights on the marquees of the
two largest movie theaters in New York, the Strand and the
Rialto. In both cases, the theaters equated Harold's name with
the feature films they were currently showing, pictures starring
Dorothy Gish and Pauline Frederick. The sensation of seeing
his name in lights on a Broadway theater was overwhelming:
"My heartbeat jingled the coins in my pocket, my legs wavered
weakly and I stood staring, mouth open, until I woke to a fear
that I might be attracting attention. So, closing my mouth, I
strolled back and forth, but never took my eyes from that rainbow."

The film-going public throughout the country was just as en-
thusiastic about *Bumping* as the New York theater managers.

Word of mouth, then as now, was the largest single factor in a film's success. Pathé backed *Bumping* heavily, running two-page spreads for the film in the trade papers. One of the ads included excerpts from telegrams like this one from a theater owner in Salt Lake City: "BUMPING INTO BROADWAY ... POSITIVELY GREATEST KNOCKOUT OF THE YEAR. . . . STOOD THEM UP FOR OVER THREE HOURS. . . ." An Indiana manager's patrons thought Harold was "BETTER THAN CHAPLIN." A few weeks later, in sophisticated New York, the manager of the huge Strand Theater placed the words CLEVER HAROLD LLOYD on the marquee for the second two-reeler, *Captain Kidd's Kids.*

By the beginning of 1920 Lloyd's name on a theater marquee had taken on a special magic. Prior to the accident, he had completed *From Hand to Mouth* and *His Royal Slyness,* released by Pathé early in the year, one month apart. The financial results were impressive. Pathé had advanced Rolin a total of

The Strand Theater, New York City, November 1919.

$17,000 to make *Bumping into Broadway*; the film's cost was just over this, at $17,274. The gross rentals for its first three years were $150,356. After Pathé deducted its 35 percent plus their original $17,000, Rolin was left with a net profit of $63,-987, one half of which belonged to Harold. A personal profit of nearly $32,000 on a film that had cost only $17,000 to make was startling, but it was only a prelude to the success of the next half dozen two-reelers, for which the gross rentals kept rising.

While Harold's films at this time were nearly all first rate, their ever-increasing popularity is explicable on other grounds: Buster Keaton spent nearly a full year in the U.S. Army in 1918–19, causing a hiatus in his career of exactly twelve months. Chaplin released only two short films in 1919 and none at all in 1920. With a public avid for outstanding comic films, Harold's productions stood out sharply. Aside from Chaplin, his only serious competition at that time was "Fatty" Arbuckle, still far ahead of him in popularity.

A year later, at the beginning of 1921, Lloyd's short films were earning as much as $200,000 apiece. His own earnings increased dramatically because of the new terms he soon demanded and got from Roach. On June 4, 1920, Pathé and Rolin had signed a new contract for six films, one every eight weeks; the Pathé advance money was increased to $100,000 per film, guaranteeing superior production values. In this contract Roach finally had his way on what had been a sore point: there were to be no cuts by Pathé in the films, no editing of any kind, not even title card changes.

On the strength of his rising power at the box office, plus Pathé's higher advances, Roach gave Harold a new contract in November 1921. It raised his weekly salary to $1,000 and, more important, it increased his share of the profits to 80 percent. On the eleventh picture of the series, *Among Those Present*, Harold received $48,000 in profit sharing, out of total gross of $212,-079. Amounts of this size, plus his thousand a week, soon had

him earning about a quarter of a million dollars a year, or somewhere in the neighborhood of three or four million by 1980
standards. Except for his continuing interest in exotic cars,
Harold saved nearly all his money: he had plans for his future
that did not include working for Hal Roach.

As for Roach and his Rolin Company, there were many
changes made in the organization. The name Rolin was
changed in late 1921 to Hal Roach Productions, Inc. Roach and
his partner of five years, Dwight Whiting, had parted company.
(Roach later stated that the people at Pathé had pressured him
into getting rid of Whiting.) The most drastic change of all was
the departure of the company from the old Bradbury Mansion,
the birthplace of the firm. With half a dozen production companies busily at work, the old place had become impossible as a
functioning work site. Roach chose to build an entirely new
studio on Washington Avenue out in Culver City, not far from
the place that MGM would occupy in just a few years. Besides
Harold's pictures, the firm was turning out Snub Pollard comedies, Ruth Roland adventure serials, and, briefly, a series of
comedies starring Gaylord Lloyd, who had none of his younger
brother's charm or talent. In time he became Harold's aide-de-
camp while the Lloyd pictures were in production.

When the company moved into new quarters in Culver City,
Harold was shooting *An Eastern Westerner,* co-starring Mildred
Davis in her second film with Harold. Despite the company's
departure from the premises, Harold insisted on being driven to
the abandoned Bradbury Mansion each day in order to put on
his makeup there. Only then would he join the others for the
shooting at Culver City. Harold Lloyd was an extraordinarily
superstitious man all his life. He felt that to ensure the picture's
good luck it was necessary to put on his makeup in the place
where the shooting had started. When the film was completed,
Harold and his Japanese chauffeur went back to the mansion
for a final visit: "We went about bowing and saying farewell to

Get Out and Get Under, 1920.

Shooting *Get Out and Get Under* in 1920.
Hal Roach standing next to left camera.

each room, the stable and the yard. . . . On the sidewalk we made a final salaam and drove away. . . . "

His superstitions took many forms. He believed that he had to leave a building, any building, by the door through which he had entered; this was just as applicable to a sports stadium as to a private house. In the years of his great mansion, Greenacres, if his car of the day was parked in the front drive, his chauffeur knew that he would have to back it around the center fountain; only then could he drive away. Whenever Harold went somewhere by car, he had to return by precisely the same route. He was inflexible about these matters.

Harold's various chauffeurs over the years learned about some of his other superstitions. There were certain areas around Hollywood that were to be avoided at all costs. He regarded certain streets as "bad," streets such as Roxbury Drive, where his mother had died, and Bedford Drive, where Gaylord Lloyd had spent his final years. Harold never went out of his way to explain any of these quirks; the reasons seemed to be sufficiently clear to him and required no justification. His miraculous escape from death on the day of the explosion may have started the entire process.

After the ninth two-reeler, *Number Please*, Hal Roach ceased directing Harold's films for good. His replacement was Fred Newmeyer, a former southpaw baseball player from the minor leagues who had met Roach and Lloyd in their days at Universal. He started with them as a prop boy and worked up to directing Roach's all-girl *Vanity Fair Maid* in 1920. It is clear that Harold had wanted for some time to free himself from working directly with Roach; the firm's rapid expansion after 1920 made this possible without an open break. As for Newmeyer, Harold once summed up the nature of his working relationships with all his various directors; it echoes what Eddie Sutherland had observed, that Harold mostly directed himself. Lloyd usually described his films as being the work of a team. But when asked just what he meant by "we," he replied, "Oh, what the hell. Why say 'I.' It sounds better to say 'we.' "

Late in life, Harold told an audience at the American Film Institute that he had regularly given director's credits for his films to writers and idea men who had never directed pictures. "My thinking was this: that I was getting all the credit I needed by being the main comic, and the audience was giving me the full credit. Why did I have to have the credit for doing the direction? . . . So it was good for the boys; it helped them. . . . "

Harold's method of working with his directors strongly resembled that of Keaton with his. Both Keaton and Lloyd's silent films are largely their own productions. Although both stars depended heavily upon the work of professional gagmen (sometimes even the same men, Jean Havez and Clyde Bruckman), the decisions about *how* the pictures were to be made were the stars'. Bruckman's work for Keaton, for example, does not at all resemble the work he did for Lloyd.

One of the main reasons why the classic comedy shorts of this period are so miraculously good is that they were made by a trial-and-error method which relied on audience response. When a new film was completed, a finished print was taken out to a theater in a nearby town such as Pasadena or Glendale. The film would be shown to the theater's patrons without prior warning, to see just how they responded. This was the beginning of the "preview" system, credit for which has often been given incorrectly to Irving Thalberg. It is clear that Harold was doing it in 1918; by 1920 it was standard procedure for Keaton and all the others. If the audience reaction indicated there were slow sections or "difficult" scenes in the film, cuts would be made and sometimes new footage substituted. The goal was perfection, which was sometimes achieved only after two or even three of these previews.

4

Harold Lloyd is the young Molière of the screen.
—*Moving Picture World,*
March 5, 1921

Harold was rapidly catching up with Arbuckle and Chaplin all through 1921. To assist him, Pathé sought to impress the exhibitors with the message that Harold's two-reelers had more box-office potential than most of the feature films currently in circulation. They began to run four-page spreads in the trade magazines, printed in color on glossy paper, asking the exhibitors these questions: "Have you ever considered that the comedy may be a bigger asset to your program than the feature? Have you ever thought that quality should be the true test of a feature and not length?"

Paramount, with its Arbuckle-Keaton two-reelers, was delivering very much the same message. In an ad for *The Garage* in 1921, they told theater owners, "You can run it for a long time and bring it back again." Many owners took this to heart and began to promote these two-reelers just as prominently as their nominal feature films. A Pathé ad for Harold's *I Do* claimed, "Harold Lloyd is the only star featured without any long picture whatever; and this at the Capitol Theater, New York City." It was true—the Capitol bill consisted of Harold's film, a travelogue, and some live musical numbers. One newspaper ad for Harold's *Now or Never* was divided so that the Will Rogers fea-

(*Right*) Shooting *Look Out Below* in 1918. Roach at left; Pollard center; HL and Bebe Daniels on beam. The effect of great height was achieved by shooting straight down into the street below. Locale: Hill Street Tunnel.
(*Bottom left*) HL and unidentified stand-in.
(*Bottom right*) *Never Weaken*, 1921.

On the pier at Santa
Monica: HL, Mildred Davis,
unidentified woman,
Roy Brooks.

ture film *Boys Will Be Boys* received only 10 percent of the space.

The public's appetite for good comedy films, especially short ones, seemed insatiable. Every year or so, the distribution rights to the early Chaplin one-reel films of 1915 and 1916 would change hands, the price going up with each sale. As much time and energy went into making the short films as the current features. A strong competitive feeling was in the air in 1920 and 1921, which did much to raise the quality of these films. The market for comedy became so brisk that many lesser talents entered the field. Some were unjustly consigned to obscurity and have been nearly forgotten: Lloyd Hamilton, Charley Chase, and Larry Semon. Still others have vanished into oblivion: Jimmy Callahan, George R. Clarke, Jimmy Adams, and Sid Smith (The Hall Room Boys), Harry Sweet, and an energetic young lady named Alice Howell, whose films were correctly labeled "Every One a Howell."

It may well be asked, if comedy was prized so highly, why

didn't the great silent comedy stars begin making features much earlier? First of all it must be understood that while many feature-length comedy films *were* being made in 1919–22, they were nearly all "story" films, usually based on popular novels and plays or *Saturday Evening Post* serials. They would star performers like Constance Talmadge, Will Rogers, and Mabel Normand. The story was always the main thing. The art of Chaplin, Keaton, and Lloyd was based on the radically different notion that the *gag* was supreme; to them the story was completely secondary. It was for these reasons—disregard for literary sources and reliance on the sight gag, always closely allied to the even more "vulgar" slapstick*—that the two-reel mas-

HL's production crew in 1920: Roy Brooks in rear;
Sam Taylor on HL's right.

---

* The dialogue between Rufus's parents on the first page of James Agee's *A Death in the Family* expressed this fear of slapstick:

" 'Well, 'spose we go to the picture show.'

" 'Oh, Jay! . . . That horrid little man! . . . He's so *nasty!*' she said as she always did. 'So *vulgar!* With his nasty little cane; hooking up skirts and things, and that nasty little walk!' "

terpieces of these men were held suspect for so long. To conservatives, their proper place on a film bill was as an appetizer for the serious drama that would follow. But the wider public didn't agree; they adored the short comedies and clamored for more.

Douglas Fairbanks made feature-length comedies (including *His Majesty, The American* and *Knickerbocker Buckaroo*—both 1919), but they weren't presented to the public that way; they were marketed as thrill or adventure movies. When a splendid gag comedian like Roscoe Arbuckle began making feature films, he appeared in such pictures as *The Roundup* and *Gasoline Gus,* in which he was forced to abandon all the comic devices that had made him famous; he simply became an actor. So, too, with Keaton, who began his acting career at Metro in a "straight" part in *The Saphead,* just prior to his great series of shorts at that studio. Chaplin was indecisive about producing

Charles Pathé signing HL's contract in New York in 1921;
Roach, HL, and Brunet.

features. Although he made one of his greatest films, *The Kid*, as a feature in 1920, he chose not to make another until *The Gold Rush* of 1925.

Harold Lloyd was the very first comedian to begin producing the kind of feature that kept all the best qualities of the short gag pictures, along with a carefully prepared story element. He did this almost by accident, in the same year that he surpassed Chaplin in popularity. In a 1922 poll that asked the readers of *Photoplay* to name their favorite comedian, Lloyd received 4,650 votes to Chaplin's 3,060.

CHAPTER 5
CLIMBING TO FAME

1

Mildred is never still. . . . she makes me think of
nothing so much as a little canary.
—*Picture Play*, 1922

Myrtle Gebhart's *Picture Play* article about Mildred Davis, a
typical piece of fan-magazine puffery, described her as a wide-
eyed young thing of twenty-one, intensely devoted to ball
games, Mary Pickford, making her own clothes, and perhaps a
certain Mr. Harold Lloyd. He was mentioned frequently in the
story, but Miss Gebhart made it clear that she had no real idea
of what went on between them and could only breathlessly
guess about their plans to marry.

The comparison of Mildred Davis with a canary was probably
not meant to be unkind: Myrtle Gebhart was not the first to notice that Mildred was birdlike. She was also excitable and warm;
she radiated enthusiasm. She acquired the nickname "Glow-
worm," which conveyed something of her character. When
Harold had first seen her on the screen, he had thought of her
as "a big, French doll," and there *was* something curiously

Trip to the East, 1921.
Unidentified woman,
Mildred Davis, HL, Roach,
and Mrs. Roach.

doll-like about Mildred; it can be seen in virtually all the films she made with Harold. Bebe Daniels had been the perfect foil for Harold, especially her shocked or quizzical *What can you be thinking of?!!?!* expression. Mildred was quite different on screen: pretty, but in a tame sort of way. Mildred performed her acting chores adequately enough in Harold's first four feature films, but she did not stand out in any of them. There was little chance for her to do so, since her parts were simply decorative, somewhat like Buster Keaton's heroines—pretty, but just a bit dumb.

Harold had been taking her out with some frequency in the year or so after his injury. It was all very proper: when Mildred visited New York with Roach and Harold, she was accompanied by her mother. She wasn't the only woman in Harold's life: Hal Roach insists that there were many, most of them girls met on his various trips to New York. As Roach tells it, Harold would return to California flushed with the success of a new conquest. His triumphs were usually short-lived, however, since the girl would soon prove unfaithful or, even worse, the carrier of a venereal disease.

While it is obvious that most women found Harold tremendously attractive, he, on the other hand, seems to have always

Wedding day,
February 10, 1923.

been on his emotional guard with them, as if he simply couldn't afford to take any chances. In the words of his daughter Gloria, "women were either whores or vestal virgins, with nothing in between." With the exception of Bebe Daniels, he preferred quiet women; as his friend Harvey Parry says, "Harold always liked his girls to disappear into the wallpaper." He couldn't stand women who were in any way assertive; they had to be demurely sweet. By the beginning of 1923 Harold was convinced that Mildred possessed these qualities.

There was a strong practical reason to marry Mildred: she was about to leave the Roach organization because of a better offer—the Bebe Daniels situation all over again. Nearly forty years after his marriage, Harold was frank about his reasons: "I married Mid because I found she was about to leave me to do pictures for somebody else and I figured that was the only way to keep her around." This is not disingenuous; he always told it this way. Nine years after this interview, he told Anthony Slide,

"I thought I was going to lose her, and so I thought that was the best kind of contract I could make, and it seemed to prove a very happy one—went on for many years. She went into another type of production—we had three children, so she kind of accepted that situation, seemed to be happy with it."

Although the marriage probably began as one of convenience, in time it turned out to be more than that. It seems likely that the convenience Harold desired was having Mildred available in his personal life, but he apparently wasn't really sure he wanted to marry her. Hal Roach tells a story that supports this idea. He claims that Harold, on the night before the wedding, offered him $20,000 if he could think of an honorable way to back out. Roach couldn't, and the wedding took place on February 10, 1923. Not all of Roach's stories about Harold are

John Davis, Mildred, unidentified baby, HL.

necessarily true, but if this one is, it indicates just how he felt about embarking on this marriage.

Despite the intense interest of the press, the wedding at St. John's Episcopal Church in Los Angeles was thoroughly private. Roach's publicity director, Joe Reddy, had informed the newspapers of the event, but Harold was able to coax the reporters into staying away from the church until after the ceremony. Besides Mildred's mother, the small wedding party consisted only of Gaylord Lloyd as best man and Jane Thompson, a young friend of Mildred's, as maid of honor. Harold chose not to invite his parents. His ambiguous feelings about his mother hadn't changed much. He had purchased a house for her in an affluent suburb of Los Angeles, where she had plunged into the center of all the local civic affairs. Foxy Lloyd continued living with Harold at their house on Hoover Street. In many ways he functioned as a sort of watchdog over Harold's career. It is likely that neither parent was invited because one or the other would have suffered a slight if he or she alone had been ignored; inviting both had been simply impossible.

Harold and Mildred went on a short honeymoon to San Diego, returning to Los Angeles in ten days to a rented bungalow on the grounds of the Ambassador Hotel. Harold then took his bride to the house on Hoover Street, but living there proved impossible because of the presence of the ever voluble Foxy. Harold then rented a large house on Irving Boulevard in Los Angeles, which they later bought. This was the only house they lived in together before the construction of their Greenacres mansion. At the end of his allotted two weeks, Harold returned to work on his current film, *Why Worry?*, the fifth in less than two years. These were the films that had made him the most talked-about actor in the United States.

2

Among the principal clowns of the silent screen,
Harold Lloyd was the exception. He had to think it
all out. . . . Lloyd was an ordinary man, like the rest
of us: ungrotesque, uninspired. If he wanted to be a
successful film comedian he would have to . . . learn
the hard way. That was what took him so long.

—Walter Kerr

Think slow, act fast.

—Buster Keaton

Keaton is telling us more here than the mere fact that he
thought carefully before moving. He is also telling us that he
worked out the finer details of his pictures with a rigor of
thought that still astonishes. Even a casual viewing of *The General* or *Sherlock, Jr.* will convince skeptics that here is film-
making of an extraordinarily complex nature, in which all the
details have been worked out with a fine precision that perhaps
has never had its equal in American film.

Walter Kerr seems to hold it against Harold Lloyd that he had
to do a lot of thinking before achieving the films by which he is
best remembered. He sees Harold as a very slow and painful
learner. Kerr believes that both Chaplin and Keaton became accomplished film artists in a very short time, almost overnight,
without much need for "thinking" about the development of
their art, while Lloyd—as noted earlier—had to serve a much
longer apprenticeship. Kerr's ideas are based on choosing to ig-
nore the long apprenticeship that both Chaplin and Keaton
served in the theater from the time they could walk; it can be
argued that their entire lives had been spent preparing to ap-

pear in films. When the film medium opened up, they were
more than ready. This was not the case with Lloyd: his stage apprenticeship had been very short; he required a lot more time to
master film.

Kerr also asserts that Lloyd's creative skills were acquired:
"He got no gifts from the gods." Neither Keaton nor Chaplin
depended solely on inspiration or gifts from any gods above—
they were both tremendously hard workers, possessed of the
considerable analytic skills they had discovered in their early
years in the rough-and-tumble world of vaudeville. Lloyd's
background was completely different: pseudo-middle-class all

Production crew for *A Sailor-Made Man,* San Diego, 1921.
Behind cameras: unidentified man, Walter Lundin, unidentified man,
Robert ("Red") Golden. On Golden's left: Jean Havez and Sam Taylor.
Front row: Fred Newmeyer, Mildred Davis, and HL.

Production crew for *Grandma's Boy*, 1922.
Left to right: Golden, Newmeyer (kneeling), HL, Walter Lundin,
two unidentified men, Havez, and Taylor.

the way, he came from the world of "straight" or legitimate drama, the thing taught in genteel "schools of expression." Coming from this background, Harold had to think out his problems with much more effort than his two great rivals. The gift that all three artists did have was their extraordinary physical coordination and agility. They also had in common an enormous capacity for hard work, as well as a passion for precision. It is that painstaking care lavished on every detail of their films that has kept them so exciting.

As the twenties began, movie audiences were thirsting to see full-length films starring their favorite comedians. But there were serious problems in the switchover to features, problems as serious as those waiting at the end of the decade with the introduction of sound. Feature films would have to be far more carefully planned than the two-reelers. Scripts would not yet be the order of the day, but the story content would obviously have to be a lot stronger.

At the very end of 1921, Harold became the second silent comedian to make a feature, but he did so almost by accident. *A Sailor-Made Man,* although technically the first of Harold's feature films, barely qualifies. It is only four reels (slightly over forty minutes), and was released in that length because Lloyd felt that "We liked the footage in it, and when it came to editing it and cutting it down, we just kind of hated to cut the rest of it out, so they [Pathé] said: 'Well, we think it's too good to delete.' So we left it that way, and it stayed a four reeler and was more or less our first feature."

The "more or less" clearly indicates that Harold and his crew were aware that *A Sailor-Made Man* was really an expanded two-reeler. The result is a film that moves rather jerkily from one sequence to another; the individual parts don't fit together as well as they might. The story concerns an unbearable rich young idler who, after some clever demonstrations of his sassiness, joins the navy in order to win the hand of a girl (Mildred) whose wealthy father strongly disapproves of his character. Once in the navy, Harold's character becomes far more sympathetic: we now see him using his brains for completely practical ends. His ship lands him in the Middle Eastern land of Khaipura-Bhandanna, where, predictably, the girl is being held by a lustful sheik who abducted her from her yacht. Harold pole-vaults his way over the wall into the closely guarded seraglio and accomplishes a miraculous rescue involving some wonderful sight gags. He uses a pipe from the sheik's hookah as an underwater breathing device while evading his murderous henchmen in the harem pool. It is fast-moving and quite entertaining, but there is none of the solid characterization found in Harold's succeeding films. It is really a brilliant cartoon. In its extended four-reel form, it bears comparison with Keaton's first feature, *The Three Ages* (1923), a film that also breaks down into what Keaton himself admitted were actually three two-reelers spliced together.

The critics loved *A Sailor-Made Man* as much as the public did. It grossed $485,000 in its early years, but this amount was small compared to that earned by Harold's first true feature, *Grandma's Boy,* of 1922. This was the first of what Harold liked to think of as his "character pictures," in which the story line is held together by our concern for the hero. The idea for the picture was Harold's own, "A very good idea too, in my estimation, one of the best we ever had. . . . " Once again, the film started out to be a short one, as this was still the basic contractual arrangement with Pathé. "Just because one had gone long didn't mean it would be standard procedure. . . . We started it as a two-reeler, but it had a strength to it that we just couldn't keep in two reels. It kept going and going and finally we said, 'Well, let's just play it out,' and it developed into a five-reeler, which was really our first true feature picture."

Harold subscribed to the notion that if you want something badly enough, you'll get it; his own burgeoning career was proof of that. So, too, with faith; if you believe in something strongly enough, it's bound to be true. In *Grandma's Boy,* it was "an idea of a boy who was a coward, who was given a talisman by his grandmother in which he implicitly believed, as she'd never lied to him. . . . " Harold is the Boy, and he has recently been thrown down a well by his Rival for the Girl (Mildred). His history of cowardice dates back to his grade school days: "The boldest thing he ever did was to sing out loud in church." A sudden chance for a change in his character arises when a local prowler starts terrorizing the community. Harold is duped into being deputized to catch the culprit by his hated Rival, but all of his old fears leave him powerless. It is then that Grandma tells the despairing Harold a tale, in flashback, that features Grandfather's adventures in the Civil War.

He, too, had been a coward, but, armed with a magic amulet he had bought from an old gypsy woman, Grandpa (also played by Harold) performs heroic service by capturing four enemy generals. Now, in his hour of need, Grandma gives Harold the magic amulet. With his talisman in hand, Harold follows the example of Grandpa, captures the murderous prowler after a brutal fight, and brings him back to town in a baby buggy. Then it is time to settle his affairs with the cursed Rival, with whom he has a long and convincing fight. Harold briefly loses the amulet, and with it his new-found courage, but on regaining the amulet manages to throw the Rival down that same well seen in the opening sequences. At this point, Granny reveals all: she has made up the entire story about the amulet; "it was just the handle to her umbrella, and it was surely his own faith that had won." Harold's new-found courage is strong enough to convince the Girl that she must marry him *at once.*

Upon its completion, the picture was previewed in Glendale before a stony-faced audience: there were not very many laughs in the film, because the stress was on *telling* the story. Harold later recalled that Roach, still technically his boss, told him, " 'Harold, you're a comic, you've got to get laughs. Let's go back.' So we went back and worked for months—at least a month—and just put comedy-business gags all over the place. . . . The second time we previewed it, it blossomed. It was fine and it's been fine ever since." Getting it to be fine was no easy task: the total shooting time for *Grandma's Boy* was extremely long for those days, from October 22, 1921, until March 14, 1922, nearly five months.

It was worth it, since besides the basic values of its vaguely mythical quest theme, the comic scenes that were added enhance the picture tremendously. There is a sequence in which Harold comes to court his Girl in his Grandpa's best suit (circa 1862) and immediately discovers that her black butler is wearing an identical outfit. Grandpa's shoes had been shined bril-

Grandma's Boy, 1922.

liantly with goose-grease, and the Girl's kittens rush up to lick them greedily. The Girl begins to notice a strange odor rising from Harold: it is the old mothballs that fill the pockets of Grandpa's garments. The mothballs wind up in the Girl's box of candy: Harold and the Rival begin to eat them with feigned pleasure. James Agee noted that Harold possessed "an expertly expressive body and even more expressive teeth, and out of his thesaurus of smiles he could at a moment's notice blend prissiness, breeziness and asininity, and still remain tremendously likable." In the sequence where he must eat the mothballs with relish, Harold used every smile in that thesaurus.

There can be no doubt that Agee was right about the public's enormous liking for Lloyd, which went far beyond merely liking his pictures for their entertainment value. They really *liked* Lloyd. Here was someone they could identify with, Herr Jedermann (Everyman), as he was sometimes referred to in German reviews. Chaplin and Keaton may have been just as funny, but their worlds were often distant from everyday American life in the 1920s. In a profound sense, Harold's films were frequently at dead center in their depiction of some shared deep concerns about courage, social mobility, growing pains, and even love.

Grandma's Boy is a landmark in American film comedy; it is the first Lloyd film in which he was able to incorporate gag and story material in an admirable, even magical combination. It is basically the same combination that Keaton hit upon the following year in *Our Hospitality* and that Chaplin had already used in *The Kid*. Chaplin was a great admirer of *Grandma's Boy*: "It is one of the best constructed screenplays I have ever seen on the screen. . . . the boy has a fine understanding of light and shape, and that picture has given me a real artistic thrill and stimulated me to go ahead."

Grandma's Boy did extraordinarily well everywhere it played, which was very nearly every movie house in the United States, even in towns with populations of only two or three hundred. It finally grossed just under a million dollars, a sum for those days, comparable to the grosses of today's *Jaws* and *Star Wars*. At his 75 percent rate, Harold's share of the profits came to $232,000. Beginning with his next picture, *Doctor Jack,* Harold's share rose to 80 percent, as part of the new contract signed with Roach and Pathé in October 1921. Roach's 20 percent could be viewed as the rental fee for his studio facilities—a high price for them. Harold had also insisted that the new contract stipulate that the words "Hal Roach Studios" be omitted from the credits of the three films to be made under its terms. It is clear that Harold wanted to indicate that, good or bad, these were *his* films.

The first, *Doctor Jack,* was shot in just four months, but was released only ten weeks after *Grandma's Boy.* This was not a film that "grew and grew"; it was planned as a feature from the start. Harold liked to divide his films into two categories: character films and gag films. Technically, *Doctor Jack* belongs to the first of these classifications. Jack Jackson, or Doctor Jack as he is known to everybody in town, has a fatal character flaw for some modern viewers: he is just *too* nice to be believable. Young Doctor Jack begins as a fully developed "nice" character and stays that way. *Doctor Jack* is a very funny picture that relies for its success almost entirely on the gags that Harold and his writers were able to insert. Most people who have seen it recall the wonderful opening sequence in which Doctor Jack receives an early morning phone call informing him that he must come at once, for "Mary is dying!" Jack leaves his house with the speed of light; in a flash he is at the wheel of a 1922 racing car. He tears down the road, but is as quickly slowed down by the local cop, who proceeds to hand the doctor the rest of his breakfast (as is his custom). The car breaks down; Doctor Jack switches to a child's scooter, falls off, switches this time to a broken bicycle. Upon his arrival, Mary is found at the bottom of a well. Doctor Jack speedily rescues Mary, who proves to be the favor-

Shooting *Doctor Jack*, 1922.
Walter Lundin, unidentified man, HL, unidentified man.

ite rag doll of a charming little girl. Without missing a beat,
Harold gives the doll artificial respiration, and smiles fill the entire screen.

There is a plot of sorts: Mildred plays the unfortunately
named "Sick-Little-Well-Girl," who is kept in seclusion and
semidarkness by her quack doctor, Ludvic von Saulsbourg.
Doctor Jack knows instantly that nothing is wrong with Mildred
that light and exercise, and maybe a little excitement, can't
cure. She gets the excitement thrice over when Doctor Jack
disguises himself as an escaped lunatic roaming through the
house after dark.

Of all Harold's feature films, *Doctor Jack* is the one that
comes closest to deserving the verdict that his work was mechanical. It *is* a mechanical picture, "the embodiment of
American cheek and indefatigable energy," as Gilbert Seldes
wrote in 1924. But, as Eddie Sutherland wittily observed,

Doctor Jack, 1922.

Lloyd's mechanics are always good, even *great,* mechanics. Some of them are at work in the scene where Mildred has her first encounter with her new consulting physician, Doctor Jack. Her black maid has been reading her fortune in a deck of cards; the maid draws one, telling Mildred, "That's the old Jack of Spades—he's ridin' straight into your life!" The fortune-telling is interrupted, and the card remains face-up on the floor. Another maid pushes an amorous butler away from her in the adjoining corridor; he in turn bumps into the eagerly approaching Doctor Jack, who collapses backward onto a serving cart, which goes careening across the room to where Mildred is taking her rest in an armchair. Her Fate has arrived with the force of a blow; his sudden appearance is breathtaking. Unable for the moment to face his bright regard, her gaze falls to the floor, where she sees his picture on the card in place of the Jack of Spades; it *was* in the cards. The whole sequence is lightninglike and probably occurs in less time than it takes to read this.

Although nearly all the critics of the day agreed that *Doctor Jack* was considerably less of an achievement than *Grandma's Boy,* predictably it did even better at the box office, grossing $1,275,423. Harold's share was $512,123. His star was rising, and it was his next picture for which the world remembers him best: *Safety Last.*

3

They are tearing the arms off the chairs and laugh-
ing so loudly the organist can't hear himself play.
—Theater manager,
Portland, Oregon

Comedy comes from inside. It comes from your
face. It comes from your body.
—Lloyd

Harold Lloyd's long, torturous climb up the side of an office
building in downtown Los Angeles is among the permanent
images in screen history. Its rivals for sheer memorability include the Odessa Steps sequence in Eisenstein's *Potemkin*,
Chaplin's lonely dance of the rolls in *The Gold Rush*, and Keaton's flight from all the police of the world in *Cops*. In the
climbing section of *Safety Last*, the most persistent single
image is of Harold literally holding on to his life by clinging to
the hands of a gigantic clock at the top of the building. When
the face of that clock collapses outward, the effect on audiences
is galvanic, as it has been for the better part of this century. The
shock is produced by a mixture of laughter and fear that has
never been equalled in any thrill film.

Safety Last, the most famous of Harold's self-styled "gag
comedies," was the result of enormously hard work. As Harold
liked to say, "You studied comedy, it just didn't happen, believe
me." One day in July 1922, Harold noticed a group of people
staring up at the Brockman Building on 7th Street in Los Angeles:

I discovered that someone was going to scale the side of the
building. . . . Being curious, I waited around. . . . By the time

he had climbed up two stories and was starting the third one, I began to feel so sorry for him, and thought, "Oh, he can't possibly make it." . . . Being a little chicken . . . I walked up the block, intending that I wasn't going to watch him kill himself. But my curiosity got the better of me, so that when I was about a block away, I went around the corner, so that I was out of sight from where they were, but I could peek around the corner every so often to see where he'd gone. . . .

I watched him scale this whole building, by just occasionally peeking at him, until he finally reached the top. He got up there, and he had a bicycle and he rode the bicycle around the edge of the building. Then he got on the flag-pole, and he stood on his head. Well, it made such a terrific impression on me, and stirred my emotions to such a degree that I thought, "My, if it can possibly do that to an audience—if I capture that on the screen—I think I've got something that's never been done before."

Harold returned to the building and introduced himself to the climber, a young steelworker named Bill Strothers, who accepted his invitation to come out to the Roach studio for a meeting with Hal. Roach placed him under contract to appear in Harold's new project. Impatient for the film to begin shooting, Strothers requested permission to make another climb on a downtown building, a simple climb of only three stories. That resulted in a broken leg and a pronounced limp, which earned Strothers his name in the picture: "Limpy Bill." As Harold and his crew began to develop the idea of an extended climb for the film, they quickly realized that no suspense could be generated if Harold was the human fly; this would be Strothers's role. The extremely rough idea they came up with was for Bill to be a professional climber who can't, for some reason to be worked out, execute his scheduled climbing, and for Harold to take his place. With little more than this to go on, the shooting of the climb began on Sunday morning, September 17, 1922, on the roof of the International Bank Building at Temple and Spring streets in Los Angeles. Hal Roach's company work diary indicates these facts:

> Weather Bright—Very hot—some heat haze
> Companies working
>
> Lloyd—L 17 Climb at International Bank Building
> all cameramen worked

These terse entries don't tell us anything about how the climb was accomplished, something people have been arguing about from the day of the film's opening. There are good reasons for the confusion.

In most instances, Harold preferred to tell the truth about how he made his films, but in the case of *Safety Last* a number of problems arose about what to tell and what not to. Since it became the best known of all his thrill pictures, identifying him permanently as "The King of Daredevil Comedy," a certain amount of latitude was used in telling people how it was done. In the early days, at the time the picture was first released, Harold was somewhat franker than in later years. He did not object to telling Adela Rogers St. Johns for *Photoplay* in 1923 that he had used a double in all the long shots. More important, she reported that he told her that

> they [Harold and his crew] found three other buildings, of different heights, all shorter than the main building. On the tops of these, they built sets exactly [re] producing and paralleling the real building. Thus, the set where Harold was working corresponded exactly in height and position to the story where he was supposed to be on the real building. But these sets were built several feet in from the edge of the roof, thus making it possible for him to work only two or three or four stories above the roof, instead of the eight or twelve above the street. . . . They were built in just far enough so that the fall could be broken and so that a platform could be erected for

the camera. Yet they were close to the edge so that by shooting with the camera at a proper angle the drop to the street looked straight down.

When questioned in the fifties and sixties, Harold usually suppressed all information about the sets they built on the roofs of the four buildings used for the film, preferring instead to talk about "safety platforms" covered with mattresses that presumably jutted out over the street, some ten or fifteen feet below where he was working. The implication was that, despite the presence of these platforms, Harold was in grave danger. He relished repeating one story, in which "we dropped a dummy onto one of the platforms and it bounced off into the street. I must have been crazy to do it." Not really, for although there is no question that there were mattresses used to protect him from a fall, that fall would have been directly onto a roof not very far below.

It is clear that Harold was often a bit embarrassed while telling interviewers how *Safety Last* was shot. At the beginning of his friendship with Joan and Bob Franklin,* in 1958, he rattled off the familiar details about those dangerous little platforms: "It did look like sort of a postage stamp, when you looked at it from on down. It meant that if anything happened, you had to jump to this platform, and you had to fall flat, because if you bounced, that would be the end." At this point, Bob Franklin asked Harold if he had ever fallen. His reply may indicate that he had become uneasy about the way the questioning was going:

Not fall, actually, but I was to a point once where I knew . . . I think I could have held on. As I recall, it was only once that I

---

* A young Boston couple who became fascinated with the silent era in the late 1950s and interviewed many of the survivors of the era.

did. . . . This one time, I was working up there, I believe around the clock, and I thought there was a good chance that I might lose my balance, so I just let go and dropped flat. It was better.

With no transition whatever, Harold abruptly interrupted his platform story to tell the Franklins, "We built our own sets up there," following this with a full, truthful account of the built-up sets:

You see, what we did was this. We started on a one-story building, built sets on there, about two and a half floors, ourselves. Then we went to a three-story building, made sets and built them up on there. Then a five-story building, finally to the last, the highest we could find in Los Angeles. . . . It took quite a long time to make this sequence. I guess we were a month and a half, two months on it, because we could only work a certain length of time in the daytime. You had to work from 11 o'clock till about 1. Then the shadows came in, and of course the shadows would have been very noticeable, but as long as it was bright in there, they didn't see. . . .

For a basically truthful man, the deceptive aspects of shooting *Safety Last* must have been a trial. Once caught up in it, Harold was in somewhat the same position as William Faulkner, who liked to talk about his fictitious crash flights for the Royal Canadian Air Force, or Arshile Gorky, who liked to recall his days working with Kandinsky. If Harold respected the interviewer, he might give a pretty accurate picture of what happened. He seems to have been reluctant, however, to clear the matter up for good: if he did, wouldn't it damage his role as The King of Daredevil Comedy?

■　　　■　　　■

Safety Last, 1923.

Once the climb had been shot, Harold and his writers (Sam Taylor,* Tim Whelan, and Roach) began to work out the justification. What they came up with was the archetypal story of the Boy who leaves his small hometown for the Big City to win success for the sake of the Beloved One. The story begins with what is perhaps the most famous of Harold's sight gags: we see the young couple saying a tearful farewell through iron bars; to the left of Harold stands a member of the clergy, and a noose hangs ready in the distance. But the camera slowly pulls back to reveal that we are not in the death house: Harold is simply saying good-bye to Mildred at the railway station, the clergyman is her father, and the noose is a rope for mail pickups.

---

* Lloyd regarded Sam Taylor and Clyde Bruckman as his two most talented workers. Taylor's later work included the Beatrice Lillie film *Exit Smiling,* as well as the Pickford-Fairbanks *Taming of the Shrew.* Long after his retirement from films, he wrote a brilliant detective thriller, *The Man With My Face* (1954).

When Mildred arrives unexpectedly in the city to visit Harold at the store, disaster is close. Although he has written her that he works there as an executive, he is merely a harassed sales-clerk. Searching for a quick route to executive status, he comes up with a promotional idea involving a human fly climbing the side of the building to produce a large crowd and stimulate business. For the climb, Harold hires his roommate, "Limpy Bill" Strothers. Strothers has unfortunately made an enemy:

> When the time comes for Strothers to climb, his enemy the cop is found to be patrolling the beat in front of the store. He gives chase to Strothers. The store manager impatiently de-mands to know where my human fly is. The crowd is waiting, and in order to save the situation I reluctantly start to climb for Strothers, who tells me that he will take my place at the second story.

But the cop won't give up the chase inside the building, and Harold is forced to go on climbing, floor after floor. At this point the climb obviously becomes the decisive event in the Boy's life: he *must* climb if he wants that raise, that promotion, that girl. In the midst of this comedy sequence, Lloyd strayed into areas of intense emotion: audiences have never ceased being power-fully moved by Harold's lonely struggle.

The climb becomes a series of increasingly difficult chal-lenges as he mounts higher and higher. We are reminded of the primordial tests of strength in mythology. A flock of pigeons adopt his shoulder as a place to rest and eat—someone has thrown peanuts out a window. A tennis net is thrown out of an-other window; he becomes entangled in its web. A painter's trestle is suddenly thrust out through a window, nearly throw-ing him into the yawning chasm. He attempts to change places with Bill on one floor by entering a window, but Bill has exactly the same idea concerning the window. When Bill advances out on the ledge to meet Harold, he succeeds in knocking him off the window ledge. Harold luckily grabs hold of the top of the huge clock that he passed on the way up. When his hands begin to slip, he catches hold of the minute hand, which immediately begins to descend. Then occurs the most memorable of all the Lloyd images: the entire clock face bursts outward with Harold clinging for life to the minute hand.

Limpy Bill throws his friend a rope that he ties to an office desk. Another brush with death: the knot becomes undone and the rescue rope is attached to nothing. Only the combined efforts of Bill and his pursuer, the cop, save Harold from disaster. They manage to grasp the end of the rope just as the last bit of it is slipping away. "Saved" by the rope, Harold gets to the ledge and resumes his climb. He attempts entry on the next window ledge but is so badly frightened by an angry bulldog that he crawls out onto a flagpole, which promptly breaks off, throwing him back down into the innards of the demolished clock below. Undaunted, he again gains the side of the building and resumes his epical climb. Perhaps the most brilliantly absurd moment in the sequence occurs when he reaches a ledge near the top; a mouse runs up his leg, and Harold begins an involuntary twitching that the spectators on the ground interpret as an embryonic Charleston: they applaud his performance vigorously.

James Agee memorably defined the silent comedian's art of topping a gag in his discussion of *Safety Last*:

> As Lloyd approaches the end of his horrible hegira up the side of the building in *Safety Last,* it becomes clear to the audience, but not to him, that if he raises his head another couple of inches he is going to get murderously conked by one of the four arms of a revolving wind gauge. He delays the evil moment almost interminably, with one distraction and another, and every delay is a suspense-tightening laugh; he also gets his foot nicely entangled in a rope, so that when he does get hit, the payoff of one gag sends him careening head downward through the abyss into another. Lloyd was outstanding

even among the master craftsmen at setting up a gag clearly, culminating and getting out of it deftly, and linking it smoothly to the next.

With *Safety Last,* Harold Lloyd became stereotyped as the undisputed master of daredevil comedy, although such films were a fraction of his output. This was an honor which he never welcomed. He was much happier with the roles he played in what he called his "character pictures." But there was little he could do about it: *Safety Last* was one of his finest pictures and is still the one that many filmgoers recall best.

The film broke box-office records all over the country. One theater manager summed up his feeling: "*Safety Last* is a once in a lifetime picture that makes you sore because your house is not three times as big." Harold went on tour with the picture across the country, with some interesting results in the Middle West:

They met me about an hour out of Chicago, with a long list of things that I was to do, which were the usual things: greet the mayor, get the key to the city, etc. But among them, they had "Christen the Wrigley Tower," the clock, because our picture had a clock in it. . . . They said, "Well, they figured that you'd break a bottle of champagne over it, like christening a ship. It would be the first time it's ever [been] done." I thought, "Well, we can get along without that." I drew a line through that. He said, "I'm afraid it's not as simple as that." He said, "The crowd's already waiting there for you. It's set about half an hour after you get in, and there must be at least 10,000 people there by now." So I was in what you might call a trap. . . . At that time, I think it was the highest building in Chicago—up, up, up. And we get up there. Of course, they had figured that I might not do it, so they had hired a steeple-jack up there. They figured that when I went in, he would put on my hat and coat and glasses, and he would do it. Well, they were crazy in what they were going to do. They had like a boatswain's seat, a board with two holes in it and a rope goes

Safety Last, 1923.

through and underneath—no windlass, just lowering it down over the edge of the building. Well, of course, he was a smart cookie and he looked at it. He knew what the wind velocity was going around that building, and he said, "Gentlemen, I need the money but I don't want to commit suicide," and he walked out on them. When I got there, there was no one to take my place. So they said, "What are you going to do?" It's quite a question. Someone said, "Well, if Harold does that he'll cancel all of his insurance. He's got quite a bit. In pictures, he really tries to protect himself." . . . So I got the idea what I'd do. I knew damn well I wasn't going to be lowered down there and break the bottle over that clock. So I got a megaphone . . . and I went downstairs. . . . I got up on a taxi cab, I got the crowd's attention and I told them exactly what had happened. I told them I didn't want to commit suicide and had no intention. Of course, it became a big joke. We got tremendous play in all the Chicago papers, more than if we had gone through with the stunt.

Human flies soon became the rage. One of these, named Harry Young, fell to his death while climbing the facade of the Hotel Martinique in New York; Pathé had paid him fifty dollars for the climb.

The word about *Safety Last* spread to Washington: Warren Gamaliel Harding's doctor advised the ailing president to see it. He viewed it at the White House and his verdict was the common one: "Loved it!" Publicity like this was invaluable at the box office. As part of an ever-upward curve in grosses, the picture took in $1,588,545, with Harold's share amounting to $643,842.

4

A lot of the stuff was ad lib when we were on the
sets. . . . Harold would have the last word. . . .
—Fred Newmeyer

At the heart of the entire operation of making a Lloyd film was
the work done in the gag room, a sort of think tank where the
most significant elements of his pictures were created. The
structural principle underlying all of Harold's best work, as well
as that of Keaton and Chaplin, is the absolute supremacy of the
gag. There were no confining scripts; the closest thing to a
script they ever used was a two- or three-page outline. Fred
Newmeyer, one of Harold's two main directors, recalled how he
and Sam Taylor worked in conjunction with the gag writers:

> Usually they would sit and work in the office all day long, and
> while they were preparing a sequence we would be shooting
> one. We would be shooting this sequence while they were
> preparing the next one; and then we would hold a conference
> after we were through shooting that sequence, and then go
> out and make the next one.

Newmeyer described how the ideas were developed:

> Here is the way you do; one man will get an idea, and if it is
> good, then somebody else will elaborate on it, and he will say
> something, and pretty soon maybe it is thrown out altogether,
> and another germ comes; so finally all these boys agree, and
> believe it is O.K. and then they O.K. it, and then finally call
> Harold in at the finish of that. Practically at all times he would
> say, "don't like it," or "I like it," and maybe we will elaborate
> on it; and if he O.K.'s it, then we go out and shoot it. But the
> germs are all formed right in that gag room with those boys.

Improvisation was common once the shooting began:

> We would probably put down notes, you know, of this gag or
> that gag, and then shoot right from them. We never had a
> scene number. We always had on our slates "O.K." or "N.G.,"
> but no scene numbers at all. It was what we called "shooting
> from the cuff."

The foregoing gives some idea of how a film like *Why Worry?*
came about. Oddly anticipating Owen Davis's play *The Nervous
Wreck* of 1924, which concerns a young hypochondriac who is
sent to the deserts of Arizona to recover from imaginary ailments, *Why Worry?* contains basically the same situation, only
Harold Van Pelham is sent to Paradiso, a Latin American nation
that is awash in revolution. There was one original note to Taylor's idea: the picture would feature a giant, a *real* giant. It
seemed easy enough at first. Where are giants found? At the
circus, and at Ringling Brothers they found just what they were
looking for in the person of George Auger, an eight-foot-plus
performer. Auger agreed to appear in the film, but unfortunately dropped dead the day before he was to leave the East for
California.

The great search for a replacement giant began. Publicity
was spread all over the country about the desperate straits in
which Harold's company found itself: no giant, no picture. All
leads concerning tall men were followed up; a false one produced this actual telegram from a city official in Cisco, Texas:

> YOU HAVE BEEN MISINFORMED THERE ARE NO GIANTS HERE AND
> HAS BEEN NONE FOR FOUR YEARS THAT I KNOW OF.

Someone working at the studio read an article in the paper
about the making of a fantastically huge pair of shoes for some-

Production crew for *Why Worry?*, 1923. Newmeyer, Roach, unidentified man, H. M. "Beany" Walker, HL, "Red" Golden, unidentified man.

one in the north. Investigation led to John Aasen of Minneapolis. He was Norwegian, eight feet nine and a half inches tall, with a soft, high-pitched voice. He weighed 503 pounds and was in every sense of the word the equivalent of the ship that Buster Keaton used in his *Navigator* of 1924. When Keaton discovered that the S.S. *Buford* was bound for the wrecker's ball, he persuaded his producer, Joseph Schenck, to buy it for him. The ship became the central gag around which could be constructed a variety of gags. Now, with the imposing physique of John Aasen as a jumping-off point, Harold's gag writers were free to improvise a superb series of situations based on his sheer bulk. Foot for foot, *Why Worry?* probably contains more gags than all the rest of Harold's films.

Harold Van Pelham is a wealthy young eccentric who is convinced he is at death's door. He suffers from all the imaginary ailments, and reads medical encyclopedias ceaselessly. His doc-

Why Worry?, 1923.

tors recommend a sea voyage with a stay in a warmer climate. Accompanied by his beautiful young nurse, who is obviously in love with him (and he with her—he just doesn't know it yet), Harold arrives in the politically unstable land of Paradiso. Coming down the ramp at the pier, his wheelchair goes out of control and smashes its way into the hideout of the American renegade who is about to overthrow the local government. Harold abandons his wheelchair and astonishes the armed-to-the-teeth revolutionaries by nonchalantly ignoring their truculence; he is impervious to danger. He downs the renegade leader's drink in order to pop a pill, dusts himself off with the hat of a lieutenant, hands his umbrella to another for safekeeping. Leaving them openmouthed, Harold walks through the city streets in a series of beautifully orchestrated gags, the point of them all being that in the midst of a violent revolution he sees only peace and harmony. A pretty girl gracefully picks up her

wounded lover; Harold applauds the artistry of their dance. A
man is knocked unconscious and staggers back to fall in a sitting position with his hat in his lap; Harold tosses some coins
into it.

The revolutionaries throw him into the local jail, where he
shares a cell with the giant, Colosso, who is suffering from an
agonizing toothache. Using Colosso's enormous body as a
human battering ram, the two escape. Harold now begins the
great task of pulling the giant's tooth, a deliciously complicated
enterprise which taxes his ingenuity to the utmost. When Colosso's tooth is finally extracted, he becomes Harold's grateful
slave for life. The two then proceed to quell the revolution by a
series of brilliant maneuvers, one of which involves Colosso's
huge back serving as the mobile carrier for a cannon. The

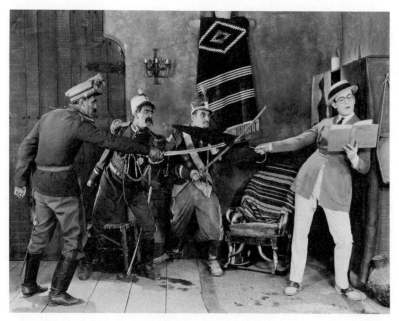

Why Worry?, 1923.

Why Worry?, 1923.

pretty nurse is abducted, and, again, as in *Grandma's Boy*, Harold is the weakling who becomes strong when he is in danger of losing his girl.

The character of Harold Van Pelham in *Why Worry?* displays many of the attributes commonly thought to characterize aggressive, resourceful Americans of the twenties. Nothing fazes him; he can successfully duel with his umbrella while reading an instructional manual on dueling. As for politics, he isn't interested in either side's point of view. A revolution is simply intolerable: "Tell them to stop it. I came down here for a rest." There have been those who see Harold's characters as merely examples of the pervasive, peculiarly American drive for success. What has been overlooked is that while Harold could deal with these matters seriously enough, as in *Grandma's Boy*, he could also use his characterizations to satirize these concerns brilliantly. It is possible, then, to see his art as operating so that Harold has it both ways: his audiences were free to form their own interpretations as to just *what* he represented. This may in part explain why his work achieved such universal acceptance in the twenties.

Despite its cardboard characters and a thin plot, the film is as delightful today as it was in 1923. But back then there were some who were not amused. Many Mexicans were convinced that their homeland was being lampooned in the film and had their consul-general make a vigorous protest. In October 1923, Harold wrote a letter of apology to H. P. Kirby Hade, the Mexican consul in Milwaukee. He tried to mollify the Mexicans: "I am now taking steps towards eliminating all reference to South America, and substituting therefore 'The Isle of Paradiso, A Mythical Island, Somewhere, In Some Body of Water.' Similar action will be taken to eliminate from all advertising matter any reference to South America." Modern-day prints conform to Harold's promise.

Why Worry? did almost as well as its predecessor ($1,476,-000); only something truly extraordinary could have topped *Safety Last.* In Harold's view, it was merely a "gag picture," and he seldom had much to say about it. But, for the sheer amount of laughter it still generates, it belongs among his best.

CHAPTER 6

"CALL ME SPEEDY!"

1

Please, God, bless grandma and Harold Lloyd, for
Jesus' sake, Amen.
                                    —Richard Thomson, age 9

Hal Roach has always maintained that it was his own idea to
break away from Lloyd in 1923, a view that Harold never particularly disputed: "because he [Roach] had so many other pictures going at the same time that required his attention, and he
couldn't give the time to me. . . . He said, 'Harold, you don't
need me anymore, . . . we might as well just go our own way!' "
Even back in the twenties, Harold was anxious to indicate that
the split was "the friendliest possible severance after nearly ten
years of teamwork." It all sounds amicable enough, but it raises
some questions about Roach's later caustic comments about
Harold. Roach claims that Harold urgently required his services while shooting films. It will be recalled that he was firmly
convinced that "Harold Lloyd hadn't a funny bone in his body."
From Roach's point of view, Harold's biggest problem was always wanting to know, "What can I do that will be funny?" or
"What am I supposed to do next?" Comments like these sug-

gest a situation in which a busy Hal Roach simply has no time to cope with an untalented, fearful comedian. It would be in his own best interests to cut the cord and let Lloyd, his creation, go off on his own.

Harold probably was by far the more eager of the two to make the change, but preferred to go along with the way his old friend chose to relate it. Roach and Lloyd quarreled bitterly over money, percentages, and credits, and were still doing it thirty years after they parted. Harold never concealed the fact that he regarded Hal as an inadequate director, always anxious to finish up his films and get them into the can as quickly as possible. There may well have been an element of jealousy here, which does much to explain Roach's later constant down-grading of Harold as a comedian who didn't know his trade. The truth is that Harold became far more important in films than Hal Roach; the pupil clearly surpassed his master. As for Roach's various claims that Harold wasn't funny and that he couldn't function as a comedian without him, they are easily refuted by the fact that Harold's films didn't suffer a decline after he left Roach; actually, they steadily improved.

While Harold was aware that Hal had definitely made valuable contributions to the early pictures, his role by 1923 was that of a former boss who has become a critic. Sometimes he was a valued critic, as in the case of *Grandma's Boy,* where Roach knew what was wrong with the picture, as well as what could be done about it. But 20 percent of the profits on films earning over a million dollars apiece was a lot of money to pay for critical advice and not much else besides Roach's studio facilities. It was partly loyalty to Roach, and perhaps caution, that kept Harold on Hal's payroll for so long. Harold never liked leaping before he'd had a good look at the situation.

The necessity for going their separate ways was clear. With Harold consuming 80 percent of the profits on his own pictures, it became increasingly important for Roach to diversify his productions. By 1923, with a payroll of over two hundred people, Roach was producing action-adventure serials with Ruth Roland and Edna Murphy, the *Our Gang* comedies, and series of two-reelers starring Will Rogers, Snub Pollard, and Stan Laurel. Roach states that Harold was jealous of the time he devoted to others; as he sees it today, Harold wanted him around all the time. But it's likely that Harold had wanted to be his own boss from the time he first visited Pathé in New York.

There is evidence to suggest that Roach wasn't very happy about Harold's departure. When Harold left, he predictably took with him all the members of his own company, but he also hired a number of Roach's key workers. These included Roach's chief film cutter, T. J. Crizer (who had been with Chaplin), Joseph Reddy, his publicity man, and Jack Murphy, his chief purchasing agent. All these people had to be replaced. But perhaps the biggest loss of all was in prestige: Lloyd was one of the biggest names in American films, and it was not likely that Roach could ever replace him.

Gaylord, Elizabeth, and HL, 1924.

Why, then, all the pious avowals of mutual peace and harmony between the two men about their separation? The most likely answer is public relations; these matters were handled in the twenties very much as they are today.

One sure sign of Harold's desire for independence was his creation of the Harold Lloyd Corporation as early as April 24, 1922, more than a full year before leaving Roach. He had required Foxy's help, as well as that of his mother's brother, William Fraser, to set up a very small family corporation with four stockholders: Harold, Gaylord, Foxy, and Fraser, each of whom was issued one share of preferred stock.* The corporate "offices" were located in Harold's home on South Hoover Street.

The HL Corporation, with a studio on Santa Monica Boulevard, included among its employees nearly all Harold's old production company: Sam Taylor and Fred Newmeyer as directors, Tim Whelan and Ted Wilde as gagmen, and Walter Lundin as chief cameraman. Most of the company's regular performers went along as well: Roy Brooks, Charles Stevenson, and Wally Howe. Among them was a young actress, Jobyna Ralston, who had replaced Mildred as Harold's leading lady in the film just completed, *Why Worry?* Jobyna was being paid $100 a week and, with the exception of Harold, who made $1,000, was the highest-paid performer in the company. The only other salaries of significance were those of Taylor and Newmeyer, both of whom made $300 a week.

When Harold replaced Mildred with Jobyna Ralston in *Why Worry?,* his last film for Roach, it was to be on a permanent basis: Ralston took the lead in his next five HL productions. It is more than likely that Harold was not eager to see Mildred return to films. Harold was becoming increasingly aware that

---

* There were also 5,000 shares of common stock, but these were never sold: the Lloyd Corporation began and ended as a family business.

Mildred was far too limited an actress to appear as his leading lady; her candy-box prettiness had become passé. Jobyna was also quite pretty, but she possessed what many have seen as a low-keyed sexuality: she seemed to be far more of a woman than Mildred, not just a giddy girl with long curls.

Mildred didn't accept this judgment easily. She had her first child, Mildred Gloria, in May 1924, but was not happy to retire and be simply a wife and mother. She was a recognized name in the industry and she began to receive various proposals. None of them seemed right until she was offered the lead role in an independent production of *Alice in Wonderland*. Mildred was quite forthright with the interviewers who asked whether she would accept the role in *Alice*. Her reply was, "Yes, if *he* doesn't queer it!" She was afraid that Harold, with his love of negotiating, would somehow upset the arrangements. Her fears were justified; the film was made with another actress.

In 1926, Harold became involved in a plan to make another film with Mildred as the star, with complete financial backing from an investor, J. G. Bachman. It was a comedy, *Too Many Crooks*, directed by Fred Newmeyer and released by Paramount. This 1927 film marked the end of Mildred's career. It may have been just as well; her talents were ill-suited for the tastes of moviegoers of the mid-twenties: Clara Bow had just made her entrance.

When Lloyd leased space out at the Metropolitan Studios on Santa Monica Boulevard, it was in a Hollywood that had changed drastically in the ten years since his first arrival. Hollywood became a boom town in the early twenties. In 1910 the population was only 4,000; by 1920 it had risen to 36,000, and it would reach 157,000 in 1930. All these gains were directly attributable to the growth of the film industry. Regular moviegoing increased dramatically in these years, and box-office receipts surged. The word that jobs and big money were waiting in California was heard around the world. A never-ending procession of talent began to make its way to the California coast. The population of greater Los Angeles had been 576,000 in 1920; it rose to 1,238,000 in 1930. The greater part of this tremendous increase came in the years 1920–24—a gain of 400,-000 in just five years.

The cost of making films in Hollywood was rising just as fast as the box-office receipts. At the beginning of 1920 it had cost only $17,001 to make *His Royal Slyness;* a year and a half later the cost of *I Do* was $53,812. The increases in the cost of making feature films were far greater. Harold couldn't have escaped noticing that the grosses of his films were almost always directly proportional to the amount of money that had been spent on them:

FILM	COST	GROSS
A Sailor-Made Man	$ 77,315	$ 485,285
Grandma's Boy	94,412	975,623
Doctor Jack	113,440	1,275,423
Safety Last	120,963	1,588,545
*Why Worry?**	220,626	1,476,254

On the basis of these figures, Harold had every reason to expect the trend would continue: the more you spend, the more you make. Hal Roach had paid all the bills for these pictures. Now, with his own money to spend, Harold knew that he was entering a dangerously speculative area. Sane, adequate financing has always been the key to survival in Hollywood filmmaking. The trade magazines of the early twenties are filled with ads and stories about scores of small, inadequately financed companies producing films in Miami, New York State,

---

* *Why Worry?* does not conform to the pattern.

HL and Mildred Gloria, 1926.

and all over California. Aware of the huge sums to be earned, they produced cheap, quickly made films that were as soon forgotten, and the firms were bankrupt within a year or so. But Harold had no intention of cheapening his product. His films had cost far above the average from 1919 on; there could be no reversal now. Along with Chaplin, Fairbanks and Pickford, and (all too briefly) Keaton, Harold was delivering custom-made products to the public at a great and, in time, dangerously high cost.

Besides the business advice of doubtful value given him by Foxy Lloyd, Harold now depended for financial guidance mainly upon his uncle William Fraser, given the title of general manager of the corporation. Fraser had been a supervisor in the Federal Forestry Service, an unlikely background for a man about to enter the business side of film-making. Harold thought of him, however, as "a trained businessman," and relied upon him heavily, trusting him to invest his money in areas not directly concerned with making films. Jack Murphy, known as

"Murph," became Harold's chief of production and also served as a general advisor. Harold usually followed Fraser's instructions about money, but in making films he would listen carefully to all three men, then make up his own mind.

In the early boom days of the film industry, many of the stars spent their money as fast as they made it. Mary Pickford was a notable exception; her observations on why she always held such a tight grasp on the immense sums she earned may throw some light on Harold's similar tendencies:

> I always thought that the public would catch up with me one day and find out that I was too little, too fat, or too something, and I wanted my family to have security. . . . I was a little

Mildred Gloria, 1928.

miser. I'd always go down the price side of the menu to see
what's 20¢ or 25¢—could I eat that?

Harold Lloyd was unusually tight with his money in certain
areas, especially if it involved giving it to other people. He became notorious for his low tips in restaurants, as well as for the
wages he paid his household staff. When it came to his own
pleasures, however, he felt no compulsion to skimp. There was
nothing of the tightwad about him when he built Greenacres,
his monumental estate in Beverly Hills. And at no time did he
stint on money to make his pictures the best he could; he was
always concerned with turning out a product of the highest
quality and was aware that economies here were foolhardy. But
in dealing with people he was convinced wanted something
from him, he became extraordinarily cautious. In this regard he
was totally unlike Keaton, for whom money was something to
be dispensed as rapidly as possible. Lloyd's attitudes toward
money and how it should be spent were very much in line with
Chaplin's. Both men maintained a tight rein over day-to-day
spending, invested wisely for the most part, and built up huge
estates.

Those early, penurious years of growing up with the improvident Foxy and his angry, discontented mother surely left their
mark on Harold. The doughnut diet of 1919 was not easily forgotten. Now there was plenty of money, more than he could
ever foreseeably spend, but what if it stopped coming in? What
do you do when that happens? There was only one answer to
questions like these: save your money for the rainy days that
just might start tomorrow.

One of the first investments of the HL Corporation was the
purchase for $60,000 of fifteen and a half acres of rocky, hilly
land in Beverly Hills that in time became Harold's huge estate,
Greenacres. The property was located in a then-remote area of

Benedict Canyon, in what Chaplin liked to call "the scrubby, barren hills of Beverly." There was only one building on the property in 1923, the old Benedict family home, which Harold had remodeled for his mother; she lived there until the construction of Greenacres was well under way.

Sixty thousand dollars then seemed to be a very high price for real estate in such a relatively inaccessible area. But changes were in the air, which then had a faint odor of sage and alkali. The year 1923 was the year in which Beverly Hills cut itself off from Los Angeles by incorporating itself as a separate entity, surrounded by the metropolis. The population of Beverly Hills had been 634 in 1920; by 1930 it had risen to 17,428. Within a year or so, the race for land there was on. Harold knew his purchase had been a wise one: Beverly Hills real estate began a steady rise that has continued for fifty years.

At thirty-one, Harold was the millionaire owner of his own film studio. Pathé and Roach were paying him as much as several hundred thousand dollars per month as his share of the older pictures he'd made for Roach. He was married to a woman he apparently loved; he was the father of one child with more, it was hoped, to come. The one blight on his married life was his mother, Elizabeth, who was extraordinarily jealous of Mildred, especially when Harold gave his wife a valuable gift. If Elizabeth became aware of it, she would immediately demand that Harold buy exactly the same gift for her. She was used to having her own way and was fully capable of creating nasty scenes. In the interest of peace, Harold usually gave in and bought her a duplicate present. One way out of the difficulty was to hide the fact that he gave his wife *anything*.

Known to his staff as "Speedy" or "Champ," Harold was as athletic as ever and neither smoked nor drank. His obsession, ten and twelve hours a day, was making motion pictures. He

On the courts, late twenties.

sometimes appeared downcast while a picture was still shoot-ing. If asked how it was going, he might respond that it was not going as well as he'd hoped; there were problems, serious prob-lems—maybe tomorrow would be better. His concern was gen-uine: making films with Keaton and Chaplin as your chief rivals was a terrific challenge that meant work, hard unending work.

One escape from work was in the compulsive playing of such games as rummy and Parcheesi; he would play for hours on end. Harold played these games as seriously as he did most things: winning was the only thing, and when, occasionally, he lost, it could affect him strongly for days. He was superb at all of them, but losing produced a powerful feeling of personal inade-quacy. Throughout his life he had few close friends, and it may be that he didn't need them. What he lacked in that area, he more than made up for in his compulsive, even frenzied plea-sure-seeking, not only in winning games but especially, later on, in the pursuit of his various hobbies.

2

> You had to be pretty good at knowing how to use time and space.
>
> —Lloyd

In the first days of the HL Corporation, Harold's publicity man, Joe Reddy, handed out a story to the trade and fan journals in which Harold was quoted as saying, "It is my intention to make each and every one of my productions entirely different in their treatment and appeal." Superficially, his intentions were fulfilled in the next few years: the stories *were* different, although their treatment and the appeal they had for the world public remained basically the same. The quality varied, but it is important to note that there are no truly poor Lloyd feature films of the silent era. His standards were very high, and he was now in a position to keep working until he believed he had a film worth releasing, no matter how much time and money it took. Eddie Sutherland, assistant director on *The Gold Rush*, once said of his boss: "Charlie has the patience of Job. Nothing is too much trouble. A real perfectionist." Harold's standards were like Chaplin's. This obsession with perfection is the main reason their pictures have worn so well.

Throughout the twenties, Harold liked to alternate character pictures with gag pictures. *Girl Shy*, the first of his own productions, was intended to be a character picture, but it isn't a very good one, due in part to the sheer weight of its superlative, even overwhelming, final sequence; everything prior to it tends to be blurred in the memory. Harold plays a timid, stuttering village bumpkin, so terrified by girls that he's the laughingstock of the town. Nevertheless, he has been writing a book called *The Secret of Making Love,* and has included chapters on themes popular at the time; we see him acting out his fantasies of "My Vampire" and "My Flapper."

The story gets under way when Harold takes off for the big city with his manuscript. He finds himself sitting next to a pretty girl, Mary Buckingham (Jobyna Ralston), who boards the train with a tiny dog concealed in her bag. Harold uses all his ingenuity to keep Mary and her dog from being thrown off the train, even going as far as to munch on dog biscuits to disarm the suspicious conductor. He tells Mary about his book; she is quite interested, and he miraculously stops stuttering. As they part at the train station, Harold absentmindedly takes the dog biscuits, while Mary is left with his Cracker Jack box.

At the publisher's, the book is, predictably, laughed at, and Harold endures the miseries of rejection. He meets Mary again by chance in a scene filled with genuine feeling. He can't bear telling her the truth about his book: he lies and says that his previous talk with her had been only a part of his research. Mary is deeply offended and embarks on marriage to a man we know to be a bigamist. The plot quickens: the publisher changes his mind and decides to bring out Harold's book as a work of humor. When Harold gets the good news, he hopes it will clear him with Mary. Alas, it is, in fact, the day of her marriage to the bigamist. Can Harold get to the church in time to stop the wedding?

The great race to the church in *Girl Shy* has been reckoned as among the most inventive ones in American film. Harold starts by missing the train; he hops a ride in a car that promptly turns into a driveway. He steals a car from a picnicking couple, and it dies on him in the middle of a field. His next theft is a car filled with booze—Harold is pursued by cops *and* the bootleggers. He exchanges their car for a truck, which gets hopelessly stuck on a narrow mountain road. He hitches a ride from the police car that is still chasing the bootleggers, then jumps aboard a passing truck. After failures with a frightened horse

Shooting *Girl Shy* in 1924.

and a fire truck, there follows the most memorable series of
images in the film: Harold commandeers a trolley and goes
whizzing off through the city streets at full speed. The current
suddenly fails: the powerhead has become disconnected from
the overhead electric line. Climbing to the top of the trolley,
Harold reconnects the head; the trolley resumes full speed,
with Harold dangling from the line. When he is forced to let go,
he drops into the back of a passing car, abandoning it for a cop's
motorcycle. There is a superb image of an earnest-faced Harold
on the cycle coming directly at you, as a flock of chickens flies
directly at his face. The cycle fails, too; when he arrives at the
church he is riding a horse, bareback. On entering the church,
he has regained his stutter and has great difficulty telling Mary
about her present danger. Action is the only answer for the new
Harold: he picks her up and throws her over his shoulder, stut-

Girl Shy, 1924.

Hot Water, 1924.

tering out his proposal, "WILL YOU?" Her reply was never in doubt.

The sequence has been worked out with clocklike precision. Each transition is sure and logical. Harold and his gag writers have achieved here a symmetrical structure of gags in which each one builds on the one just preceding. The result is a kinetic wonder that never fails to produce a state of hypnotic excitement in audiences. Although it gives a narrow idea of Lloyd's talent, along with the daredevilish *Safety Last,* the climax to *Girl Shy* remains one of his very best.

The magic transformation of a mollycoddled dunderhead, a spoiled rich boy, or an idle loafer into a raging dynamo of energy who can accomplish anything and everything whenever his girl

Hot Water, 1924.

is in danger is a staple in silent films, particularly those of Keaton and Lloyd. It is clear that Harold began it with *Grandma's
Boy* in 1922, but both men continued to turn out pictures featuring the hero transformed into a being who can accomplish
marvels of strength and agility. Keaton used the transformation
theme in *Our Hospitality, Sherlock, Jr., The Navigator,* and
Seven Chances, all written in part by fat, jolly Jean Havez, the
same writer credited with the screenplay of *Grandma's Boy.* It
was the same dramatic device, but Keaton and Lloyd were able
to make highly individual films out of it.

In his later years, Harold had almost nothing to say about
either *Girl Shy* or the film that followed it, *Hot Water.* He obviously did not think of them as among his best work, and was
eager to hurry on to the making of *The Freshman. Hot Water,* a
picture that carried the working title of *Hubby,* began as a satire
on young newlyweds, with Harold's chief problem being his
monstrous mother-in-law ("the disposition of a dyspeptic landlord, and the heart of a traffic cop"). Jobyna Ralston was
"Wifey," the young bride, whose family includes a horrible brat
of a little brother and a ghastly loafer for her bigger brother.
Harold attempted to use these elements to make one of his
character pictures, but there were difficulties in developing a
story line that would sustain a full-length film. The result was a
film that amounts to three separate gag pictures, each of ap-
proximately two-reel length; it ran just under an hour.

The opening sequence is justly famous for what Harold was
capable of in physical comedy. Heavily burdened down with
parcels, he wins an immense, live turkey in a lottery just as he
is about to board the interurban trolley that will take him home
to Wifey. This episode bears seeing repeatedly, as Harold goes
through a series of brilliant confrontations with surly passen-
gers, a furious conductor, and nasty little boys before he is
thrown off the trolley. Walter Kerr is correct when he claims

that Lloyd is an "architect of sympathy"; Harold has hit upon one of those universal experiences found so often in his work.

The second episode, "at home," begins with Harold's discovery that Wifey's dreadful family is there *en masse.* They're aware that this is the day when Harold's eagerly awaited new car, a Butterfly Six, is to be delivered. When it arrives, the family boards the car for a wild ride, at the end of which the Butterfly is demolished. Again, much of this section is brilliantly inventive and funny, but, like the first part, could easily stand on its own as a separate film.

The concluding portion of *Hot Water* is a throwback to Harold's two-reeler days: a sleepwalking mother-in-law, frantic misunderstandings, and fantastic coincidences. It's all very lively, but the film as a whole leaves many with the unsatisfied feeling they have sat through an anthology. Whatever its deficiencies, the public liked it just about as much as *Girl Shy,* which grossed $1,729,636. *Hot Water* surpassed it by a fraction: $1,730,324. Harold's combined share of these two grosses exceeded two million dollars, a huge sum in the mid-twenties, but he was to outdo them both with his next picture, *The Freshman.*

3

If we knew in advance when we made any picture
how it was going to be taken by the public, we'd
have to hire a hall to hold the money. . . . Because
you know the public taste changes like styles in
clothes.

—Adolph Zukor

The Freshman, released in the late summer of 1925, just six
weeks before Chaplin's *Gold Rush,* became the most popular of
all Harold's films. It was a work of collaboration and, as usual,
Harold gave credit to virtually his entire writing staff—Sam
Taylor, Ted Wilde, Tim Whelan, and John Grey—and bestowed
the directorial credits on both Taylor and Fred Newmeyer.*

Part of *The Freshman*'s huge success was unquestionably
due to the object of its satire: college life, a magical subject of
intense interest to nearly everybody in the 1920s. Attending
college was only for the lucky few; those fortunate enough to go
were looked upon as a race apart—people to be secretly envied.
Society often uses satire to cope with what it wants badly and
can't have. Hence all those novels and stories about college students who don't do any academic work, wear raccoon coats, and
drink illicit booze from silver pocket flasks. There were many
novels about college life: Percy Mark's *The Plastic Age,* Warner
Fabian's *Flaming Youth,* Joel Sayre's *Rackety-Rax,* and most
memorably, Fitzgerald's *This Side of Paradise.* The films of the

---

* Clyde Bruckman, Jean Havez, and Brooks B. Harding also worked on the story but
received no screen credit. Bruckman's contributions were of great importance, although they came at the very end of the shooting, from February 23, 1925, through
the middle of April.

period also reflect these views: *Good News,* and Keaton's *College.*

The fraternity system was fair game for the satirists. There was also a feeling that lots of covert sexual activity was going on behind those ivy-covered walls. Besides the social life, college sports were sharply scrutinized. The idea of robust young men running back and forth on arbitrarily drawn lines as part of a "game" played on a huge field before thousands was disturbing to many who had been working ten-hour days, five and a half days a week, since they were seventeen or so. All college sports were satirized, and football more than most.

With at least some of this in mind, Harold one day announced to his staff: "Let's make a football film!" He later recalled that a character comedy about football had been in his mind for nearly a decade, but that other projects had intervened. In the fall of 1924 Harold and his gag writers began work. With very little more than the germ of Harold's idea, they decided to shoot some preliminary football material at the Rose Bowl in Pasadena. What they had in mind was to shoot the concluding episode of the film first, very much as they had shot the climbing sequence for *Safety Last.* On that picture it had been relatively easy to go back and devise ways by which Harold found himself climbing the building. This method of working proved useless for *The Freshman:* "I think we worked about a week out there. . . . Finally, I came in and said, 'It isn't going to work, boys. I haven't got the spirit into it. I've got to know what's going to happen before this, in order to catch the quality and the spirit of wanting to win this game.' " The footage from the Rose Bowl was scrapped, and the crew went back to start at the beginning.

At some time in these early weeks on *The Freshman,* Harold and his uncle and business manager, William Fraser, had a fateful lunch with an old friend of ten years' standing, H. C. Witwer, a film producer and a writer of pulp-magazine stories for Street & Smith—fateful, since what was discussed that day at lunch became the basis of an expensive, long-drawn-out lawsuit that dragged on until 1933. During the course of the meal, Harold and Fraser mentioned that they were working on a college football picture. Witwer proceeded to outline for them the plot of a 1915 magazine story of his, "The Emancipation of Rodney." Briefly, Witwer's story concerned a boy who is anxious to be a successful athlete at school in order to be popular; when he fails, he tells his football coach that he has perfected a magic formula that guarantees winning. When Rodney is placed on the line in a game, he is so frightened that he forgets his formula but wins the game by a lucky fluke.

When Fraser and Harold returned from lunch, they told their gag room crew about Witwer's story. The crew correctly viewed it as poor stuff for a feature film. Sam Taylor later recalled saying, "You were leading the audience to expect some marvelous formula and gave them nothing." That seemed to be that, and Lloyd and his crew went on with the shooting of *The Freshman* in their usual improvisational manner. It now seems astonishing that Lloyd and Fraser didn't obtain a quit claim from Witwer, or even perhaps take the plunge and buy the "Rodney" story for a nominal price, just for protection's sake. There was a superficial resemblance between Witwer's story and *The Freshman*: they both concerned young college students who, in order to attain popularity, take up varsity football, a game for which they display a notable lack of talent, but this was the only real similarity between the two. What became damning in the resulting trial was the talk at lunch and the fact that Witwer had sent over a copy of the story for Harold to read. In dealing with Witwer so casually, Lloyd and Fraser clearly displayed a naiveté that proved to be very expensive.

As the shooting on the picture proceeded, Sam Taylor and Fraser began to worry about Witwer. As Taylor recalled:

We realized that Mr. Witwer had told Mr. Lloyd an idea for a college story and that we had ourselves written a college story. The very fact that he had told him a college story we knew was a dangerous proposition; and [we] decided to get Mr. Witwer out to the studio and lay our story before him exactly as we had it lined up and let him judge whether it was in any degree similar to his story. . . .

Witwer was invited out to the studio to hear their story. After listening to it, Witwer is reported to have said: "That is nothing like my story; it is much better than my story. If you want to use any gags out of my story, you are perfectly welcome to use them." Taylor and the others thanked Witwer but said they had their own writers. On the strength of Witwer's professed admiration for their work, they went on with the shooting, thinking they had cleared up matters. They had, but only until *The Freshman* began grossing millions of dollars. Witwer then sued the Harold Lloyd Corporation for infringement. His first suit was dismissed because he was not the copyright holder. It was not until 1929 that Witwer persuaded Street & Smith Publications to assign him the rights to the story, which he had sold them for seventy-five dollars in 1915. Witwer died shortly thereafter, but his case was pressed forward by his widow, Sadie. A lengthy trial was decided in her favor in 1930; the judgment included paying her the bulk of the film's profits. This decision was appealed, but only in the spring of 1933 was the judgment set aside in favor of the Harold Lloyd Corporation. Seven expensive years were spent in the courts; after this, Harold became extremely cautious when dealing with writers.

Despite the high price of the legal difficulties, however, it is more than likely that Lloyd did profit from Witwer in that from these early talks sprang the idea that Harold's character in *The Freshman* must win his victory on the football field by legitimate means rather than by a lucky fluke. It is this factor that gives the picture so much of its universal appeal. The notion that hard work, with a little luck, will win the prize—any prize—is present in all Lloyd's films of the twenties, as well as those of Keaton. One of the chief attractions of their films is our delight in seeing something attained with difficulty.

4

I'm just a regular fellow—step right up and call me Speedy!

—Harold Lamb, in *The Freshman*

One reason for the excellence of *The Freshman* is the care that was taken to keep a delicate balance between the superb gag material and the character portrayal of Harold Lamb, the boy who wanted to win popularity at school. To achieve that balance, Harold shot many scenes over and over:

> Sometimes I'd take five, six, seven, or eight takes. They'd say, "Oh, Harold, you've got it!" I'd say, "Well, think of something else." Some other little thing would come, and you would ad lib it. Of course, there were times when we did ten takes, and we went back and used the first, because it had a certain spontaneity, a simplicity, maybe, that the other ones didn't have. But generally, the takes we kept building turned out to be the best. . . . By the time you finished, you had ten ideas in the scene, none of which you had even conceived in the gag room.

The hero, Harold Lamb, before embarking on his new life at Tate College, has seen a film called *The College Hero*, starring Lester Laurel, a "Glorious Art Production." In the film Lester dances a happy little jig every time he introduces himself, along with an "I'm just a regular fellow" speech. Harold wants very much to be called Speedy and dutifully practices Lester's routine. Harold's father correctly predicts what will happen to him at Tate if he performs that jig: "They'll break his heart or his neck."

Harold meets Jobyna Ralston on the train, just as in *Girl Shy*. This time her name is Peggy, and she is en route to the town where Tate's campus is situated. Harold is smitten with her, but leaves the train in a rush when they arrive. Once on campus, he quickly becomes fair game for the students, many of whom are portrayed as cruel and sadistic. He is duped into making a welcome speech to the other freshmen in the school auditorium; in his excitement he stuffs a live kitten inside his thick, woolly sweater. As Harold gropes foolishly for words, the kitten can be seen busily moving around inside its new home; the audience is in hysterics. A group of students then talk him into standing treat down at the local soda shop. A lengthy scene was actually shot in which they jovially divest Harold of nearly all his money at the soda shop, praising him to the skies while laughing at him behind his back. Preview audiences hated this painful scene so much that it was removed. A brilliant substitute showed the students en route to the shop, followed by three little kittens, each with its tail sticking straight up behind it.

An intertitle tells us that Harold has spent all his money standing treat at the soda fountain; he then has to move into cheaper quarters. In the midst of cleaning up his new room, he amazedly discovers Peggy's face in the wall mirror he is polishing. Peggy is there because this is her mother's boardinghouse and she helps out with the cleaning. Delight in being reunited with Peggy is short-lived: he has come to Tate to play football and has no time for girls.

Because of his ineptitude, Harold becomes a living tackling dummy for the team's practice session. We see him being smashed and pounded down repeatedly by bodies much larger than his own. His display of sheer courage in putting up cheerfully with this brutality shames the coach into placing him on the team in the role of water boy; Harold, however, thinks he has become a regular team member. By this time, he is the only one who doesn't know that he has become the laughingstock of the entire campus—he's still doing that jig. Peggy is aware of the situation, but can't bear to tell him.

Harold attends the campus Fall Frolic, at which occurs a justly famous scene. He has ordered a tuxedo to be made for him by an ancient alcoholic tailor, who suffers from what he calls his recurrent "dizzy spells." On the night of the dance, the tuxedo is still unfinished, although the major parts have been flimsily basted together. All is not lost: the old tailor agrees to come to the dance and finish up his work there. At the dance that night, his endeavors are slowed down by swigs from his "dizzy spell medicine." Not unexpectedly, Harold's tuxedo

The Freshman, 1925.

The Freshman, 1925.

starts to come apart out on the dance floor, bit by little bit, down to the last seam. This scene is one of the high points in Lloyd's work. But while shooting it, Harold wanted to draw the line:

> I didn't want to pull my pants off. I said, "Everybody pulls their pants off in a scene. Let's not do that old, corny lost-your-pants situation." So the first two previews I never lost my pants. . . . there was something wrong. . . . One of the fellows said, "Harold, you've got to lose your pants." So I did and from then on it went fine.

Later that evening, the campus cad forces his attentions on Peggy, who is at the Frolic working in the checkroom. Harold knocks him down in a blaze of anger. The furious cad has his instant revenge in spitefully telling Harold the truth about what his fellow students think of him: he is a joke. Harold attempts manfully to make them all think he is indifferent to their scorn, but he is devastated and, left alone with Peggy, collapses in her lap and weeps. This affecting scene has been eliminated from

Frame enlargement, *The Freshman*, 1925.

modern prints of *The Freshman*; Lloyd felt the pathos here was excessive. Peggy admonishes him to be himself, to stop pretending, and to permit the students to like him for his own very real qualities. Harold half-heartedly agrees, and pathetically brightens up when he recalls that tomorrow is the day of the Big Game, his last chance to make good.

The game is one of Lloyd's greatest sequences and seems as fresh as the day it was shot. Harold and his crew, especially after his talk with H. C. Witwer, realized that for the scene to work, it would be necessary to devise a way whereby Harold Lamb actually wins the game for Tate by legitimate means. By a series of brilliant razzle-dazzle plays, some of them against the rules (for example, he deflates and then hides the ball behind his back as he innocently glides up the field), Harold's team hold its own, but:

The boy gained most of his success on the playing field by being lucky, and that was not good for the finale of the picture. He had to win something on his own merit. That's why we put the final run in: so that to really win the game, even though he had done this and that through luck, the final thing he did win it through was what you might call determination and pure guts.

Earlier in the film, after some particularly murderous play, a point in the game is reached when the coach simply has no more players left to send in. Seeing his chance here at last, Harold begs the coach to send him in to save the game. With no other choice left, the coach agrees, but levels with Harold, telling him that he is really only the water boy. Harold manfully accepts the truth and joins his teammates. The game concludes with his great touchdown run down the entire length of the field, dodging everyone in his path, crossing the goal line with the ball alongside the tip of his nose. He has triumphed over all:

The Freshman, 1925.

as the picture ends, the whole campus has fondly adopted his little jig, although Harold has given it up.

Many find *The Freshman* to be Lloyd's masterpiece. He himself preferred to express equal enthusiasm for three of his pictures: *Grandma's Boy, Safety Last,* and *The Freshman,* and at the end of his life he was adding *The Kid Brother* to the list. *The Freshman* certainly belongs near the top of his achievements, although there are those who find it just a little predictable compared with the looser style of *Grandma's Boy, The Kid Brother,* and *Speedy.* But there can be little doubt that since 1925 it has remained the popular favorite among Lloyd's films.

It earned more than any of his earlier pictures at the time of its release: with a production cost of $301,681, it grossed $2,651,167. A gross of $2.6 million was among the highest for any film made in the twenties; its only rival would be *The Gold Rush,* which produced over $2.2 million in its domestic gross alone. As far as theater owners were concerned, Lloyd was a godsend: "He will get the business any time," and "Lloyd is the great attraction in pictures today." When Pathé launched *The Freshman* in the trade papers, this was the first page of their four-page ad:

> THE GREATEST BUSINESS GETTER
> THE BUSINESS HAS EVER HAD IN
> THE GREATEST BUSINESS GETTER
> EVER PRODUCED!

There was one catch, however, as an angry theater manager complained in 1925; "You have to give 90 percent of what you get in for them, so Pathé gets the money." Many exhibitors found Pathé's terms difficult, but complaints like these are misleading; if the theaters hadn't been making money on the pictures, they wouldn't have kept on booking them.

By the end of 1924 Lloyd was Pathé's greatest single attraction. That was the year it was taken over by the Wall Street firm of Merrill, Lynch, who made every effort to keep Pathé's most valuable asset. *The Freshman* was to be the last picture made under the contract of June 21, 1923. Now that it was time either to renew with Pathé or go elsewhere, Harold asked for a more flexible arrangement, a picture-by-picture contract. Pathé was not happy with this, and Harold and William Fraser began to listen more attentively to Sidney Kent of Famous Players-Lasky (Paramount) Pictures.

At Pathé, Harold was a very big fish in a relatively small pond. Paramount's pond was far larger and Harold legitimately demanded some guarantees as to his place in it. One of the most significant items offered by Paramount was that the HL Corporation would be given its own sales manager, to be located in New York with a staff of four, and paid for entirely by Paramount, thus assuring him that his pictures would be treated as unique items among their many releases. Paramount also agreed that the HL Corporation would have the right to prepare both consumer and trade ads, paid for by Paramount. The most impressive attraction of all was in the area of advances and the HL Corporation's share of the gross receipts.

Roach's share of the Pathé grosses had been 70 percent up to $250,000, then 50 percent on the next $250,000, and then back again to 65 percent on the excess over $500,000. Paramount was far more generous: after weeks of negotiation, they offered Harold *77½ percent of the domestic gross and 90 percent of the foreign*—unheard-of terms at this time. They were also willing to advance him as much as $500,000 per picture; if he desired this financing, his share of the gross would drop to 75 percent.

The sum total of the Paramount offer was irresistible; Fraser (acting for Lloyd) and Sidney Kent signed a forty-five-page distribution contract on October 1, 1924. It demonstrated Lloyd's supreme power at the box office, second to none in the autumn of 1924. When Pathé ran its full-color trade ads for *The Freshman,* they showed Harold appropriately dressed as a king, sitting on a throne.

CHAPTER 7
THE TRIUMPH OF SILENCE

1

Then we have a topper on the topper—and sometimes we get a topper on a topper on a topper. And,
believe me, the topper that's on the topper is generally the best. . . .

—Lloyd

Ground was broken for the construction of the main house at
Greenacres at the beginning of 1925. It would take another four
years to complete. Lloyd kept up with the progress of his
home—one way to spend what little spare time he possessed in
those days. When making a picture, he would often be away
from home from early dawn until late evening. When not working on a new film, he would pursue his various hobbies with the
fierce enthusiasm he gave to nearly everything in life. One of
these was raising Great Danes, an enterprise he followed so pas-
sionately that he became the owner of over sixty-five of the
dogs. At night, the baying of these huge Danes became so painful for his angry neighbors on South Hoover Street that Harold
was forced to build a vast kennel at Westwood Village on a

One of HL's sixty-five Great Danes in 1926.

forty-five-acre tract of land purchased as the possible future home of the Harold Lloyd Corporation.

Sports was another outlet for his enormous energy. When Buster Keaton and his gag writers were held up on a picture by some problem that defied solution, he and his entire crew would play baseball until someone thought of a way out of their difficulty. With Harold it was handball. Hal Roach had taught him something about the game, but at first Harold had seemed hopeless. Now he took up the game again with far better results. He had courts built at the studio, and few working days passed without a game; most days concluded with one.

There were other outlets. He collected cars the way some people collect works of art. In his early days with Roach, besides the blue Chandler phaeton, he drove a relatively expensive Cunningham, a red Buick roadster, and a closed Pierce-Arrow. He was apparently the first on the West Coast to drive a station wagon, built for him on a Chevrolet chassis. His fondness for fine cars was observed by the executives of the Chevrolet Corporation, who sent him as a present their first six-cylinder model. Later he drove—or was driven in—a Lincoln seven, an elegant Packard roadster, and two Rolls-Royces. At any one time he might own six or seven cars; with cars, as with other good things, there could never be enough.

He still neither drank nor smoked. His aversion to alcohol may have arisen early. Foxy Lloyd told Peggy, Harold's adopted daughter, that several of his brothers were alcoholics and that it was the fear of inheriting a like fate that kept Harold abstemious. But certainly his dislike of alcohol would have been strengthened by what he observed of the drinking habits of Hollywood, where many stars drank themselves into oblivion. The painful examples of John Gilbert, John Barrymore, Buster Keaton, and D. W. Griffith were grim warnings of what could happen professionally if one relaxed with booze persistently over the years. More important, Lloyd was convinced that alcohol would immediately damage his work. In a 1928 interview, when asked why he didn't drink (it was illegal then, but nearly everyone did), Harold concluded his reply with a question: "If a man can handle it—remain healthy and use his ability to the fullest—there is no reason why he shouldn't drink, I believe. But how many men can do that?" Chaplin's views echoed those of Harold as they applied to this capacity for work: "I never cared much for alcoholic stimulus. In fact, when working, I had a superstition that the slightest stimulus of any kind affected one's perspicacity. Nothing demanded more alertness of mind than contriving and directing comedy."

2

*I am not funny. Situations are funny. Gags are
funny. Sequences are funny. . . .*

—Lloyd

When *The Freshman* was completed, Harold and Mildred took a
long vacation trip by rail, starting up the Pacific Coast to Tacoma, where Mildred had grown up. From there they continued
farther up the coast to Vancouver, B.C., and then took the long
six-day railroad trip across Canada to Toronto and New York.
After seeing all the popular plays in New York, they headed
south next, ending with a stopover in New Orleans. There were
welcoming crowds everywhere, not on the scale of those for
Pickford and Fairbanks, but large enough to be wearisome.
Harold was nearly always willing to make personal appearances
in connection with the release of his films. If he chose, however, to avoid the press or any sort of publicity, all he had to do
was remove his glasses. Taking them off gave him instant ano-
nymity: his comic persona was built almost entirely on wearing
them. Without glasses, he had, in effect, disguised himself. He
became invisible.

Even *with* the glasses, he was hard to spot. Ted Wilde, the
nominal director of *Speedy,* which was partly shot in New York
City, doubted this and bet Harold he would be easily recognized
while walking down a crowded city street. Harold took him up
on it and walked two teeming blocks one late afternoon, between Forty-third and Forty-fifth streets on Fifth Avenue. Not
one person recognized Lloyd, although he later confessed that
he had furthered the deception by lowering his eyes. The time
of the day was also critical: at four p.m. there are few casual

strollers on Fifth Avenue; everyone is bound on his or her business.

Without glasses, Harold was an extraordinarily handsome young man who looked a lot more like a leading man than a comic actor. Both Keaton and Chaplin were very small, with the kind of gracefully supple body often associated with dancers. Closer to the average in build, Lloyd's body was as expressive as Keaton's or Chaplin's, especially in rapid motion. And he was just as athletic as they, perhaps even more so.

Harold had earned his vacation: it was his first extended time off in the nearly three-year period during which he had made seven feature-length films, each surpassing its predecessor at the box office. His popularity was now so great that Pathé began to reissue all his older features, as well as the entire run of two-reelers. Unlike so many of his great contemporaries—von Stroheim, Keaton, Chaplin, and D. W. Griffith—Harold Lloyd suffered no major setback in the twenties. His ever-growing popularity rested on so wide a base with the public, from tiny tots to octogenarians, that it successfully resisted any threat. Griffith, on the other hand, never made a truly popular picture after *Orphans of the Storm* in 1922; the same was true of von Stroheim after *The Merry Widow* in 1925. The last of Keaton's own productions to make a profit was *Battling Butler* of 1926. After the enormous success of *The Gold Rush* in 1925, Chaplin released only one more film in that decade: *The Circus* of 1928, which showed a marked falling-off from the previous film in popularity with both critics and public.

Keaton and Chaplin were not the only serious competitors that Harold had to reckon with by 1927. Two fresh comic personalities, Harry Langdon and Raymond Griffith, made feature-film debuts that attracted considerable attention. Harold had noticed Langdon's talents on the vaudeville stage and told Mack Sennett about him, leading to Langdon's first contract with Sennett in 1922. For a year or so it looked to many as if Langdon's curious films, *The Strong Man* and *Long Pants*, both directed by Frank Capra in 1926, would be the beginning of a long and distinguished film career. These hopes proved false, and by 1928 Langdon's popularity had vanished, mostly owing to his mistaken desire to become his own director and producer. Firmly believing he had inherited Chaplin's legacy of pathos, Langdon made sentimental pictures like *Three's a Crowd* (1927), which failed dismally with both audiences and critics.

The majority of Raymond Griffith's films no longer exist, and it is largely on the evidence of *Hands Up!* (1925) and *Paths to Paradise* (1924) that modern audiences have recently become aware of what may have been another major talent. By 1928, for reasons that remain obscure, Griffith had lost his popularity, so much so that Paramount canceled his contract. Griffith made no sound films. Because of his impaired vocal cords, he could not speak above a whisper.*

The competition was stiffening, nonetheless. Many headliners from the Broadway stage, among them Eddie Cantor and W. C. Fields, began to make first-rate feature films. Cantor's *Kid Boots* (1926), with Clara Bow, and Fields's *It's the Old Army Game* and *So's Your Old Man* (both 1926) are lively and charming, clearly proving that neither actor required spoken dialogue to demonstrate his great comic talents.

The HL Corporation reacted to the competition aggressively. With William Fraser as a highly motivated business manager, the Lloyd films were promoted by Paramount with a great deal of vigor. Probably no other independent producer of the twenties paid as much attention to the marketing of his films as Harold did. There exist thousands of pages of interoffice memos, queries, tabulations, protesting letters, and whatever

---

* In *All Quiet on the Western Front* he plays the role of a mute, dying soldier.

Shooting *For Heaven's Sake* in 1926:
HL, unidentified man, Jobyna Ralston.

else Fraser and his four assistants felt like writing to the Paramount executives. Situated in their corporate offices at the Paramount building in New York, the Lloyd sales force kept a close watch on everything that pertained to the marketing of Lloyd's films; their findings were dutifully reported back to Los Angeles. Lloyd had been determined not to become submerged in the huge, endless output of Paramount. With this "inner" sales force working for him, he had good reason to suppose that his treatment by Paramount was second to none. All the Paramount trade ads of the time featured Harold's films first and foremost. When the exhibitors were offered the Lloyd, Valentino, and Clara Bow pictures as the plums on the Paramount schedule, they were a little happier to take the rest of the pictures on that list. This was in the days of block booking, when MGM, with its Garbo and Gilbert pictures (after 1927), or First National, with Colleen Moore's, could presell their entire output, which always included its share of disasters.

Lloyd's first film under his new contract was *For Heaven's*

For Heaven's Sake, 1926.

Sake, which was due for delivery by September 1, 1925. The film wasn't released until April 1926, which perhaps indicates some of the problems connected with it: Harold felt the picture was far from finished and wound up disliking it intensely. Newspapers ran stories suggesting that Harold hated the picture so much he was willing to pay Paramount not to release it. But Paramount, eagerly awaiting its first Lloyd feature, was not to be dissuaded by the worries of its maker: they knew that *any* Lloyd film was bound to make money.

The project began as a picture about big-city gangsters and political corruption. The cost of making such a film was thought prohibitive, and most of the story was shelved to become part of *Speedy* in 1928. What survived was turned into a nearly unrelenting gag picture, with a story line that is just barely recognizable. Harold plays another of his rich, bored young millionaires. Harold Meadows is the kind of wealthy young man who pays $10,000 for a white car to match his white pants, wrecks it and buys another on the spot. He falls in love with the pretty daughter of an evangelist who supervises a mission for derelicts. *For Heaven's Sake* was sold to the exhibitors with this catch-line:

> *A man with a mansion*
> *A miss with a mission*

There is a marvelous sequence in which one of the thugs at the mission, in order to avoid detection, slips a stolen powder puff and a bottle of perfume into Harold's jacket. The bottle breaks, and Harold is seen innocently consuming the soaked powder puff, taking it for a cookie. The episode is similar to the one in *Grandma's Boy* when Harold eats the mothballs under the impression that they are pieces of candy. It's all funny enough, but marks no real advance in Lloyd's development. *For Heaven's Sake* is an anthology of sight gags, culminating in a race to the church that recalls the frantic conclusion of *Girl Shy.*

The film contains, however, examples of Harold's physical comedy at its best. There is a sequence in which he rounds up all the assorted cut-throats, layabouts, thugs, and other seedy characters for the benefit of Brother Paul, who runs the mission. Here we see a Lloyd of superb inventiveness as he insults, kicks, and provokes every last bit of criminal fauna he runs into on the street. The whole episode is beautifully choreographed; his tormented victims gather their wits to retaliate, and every last crook in the dingy neighborhood pursues Harold, the Pied Piper who will cunningly lead them all to the mission.

When the picture was completed, no one could think what to call it. One late afternoon, after hours of ever more hopeless suggestions, one of the gagmen wearily exclaimed: "Oh, for heaven's sake, I think—" Harold interrupted him, shouting, "Stop! You've got it. *For Heaven's Sake.* You've got it!"* The film was far below *The Freshman* in quality. A trade paper printed this blunt opinion: "Harold, you slipped terribly on this one, Harold, better watch your step on the next one or it will be, Harold, all over for you." Nevertheless, at $2,591,460 it nearly outgrossed *The Freshman,* with Harold's share amounting to $1,685,036. Lloyd's popularity was now powerful enough to ensure that virtually anything he released would be hugely successful.

---

* Kevin Brownlow informs me that "For heaven's sake" was one of Lloyd's favorite expressions.

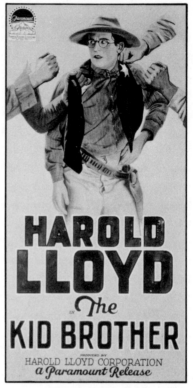

Trade ad for *The Kid Brother*, 1927.

3

"The town meeting's no place for boys."
—*The Kid Brother*

There was almost no film criticism in the twenties. Perhaps this was a blessing. In those days the movies were allowed to be simply the movies, and there was little opportunity, Chaplin excepted, for film-makers to become self-conscious about their work. Comedy fared badly with the critics, and what little serious criticism there was concentrated on the ostensibly serious directors—D. W. Griffith, Erich von Stroheim, and Rex Ingram in America and Fritz Lang and F. W. Murnau in Europe.

Chaplin was clearly the darling of "serious" film critics. It was commonly believed that he was the single true artist of dedication and scope among those appearing in films made for laughter. Robert E. Sherwood, Edmund Wilson, and Gilbert Seldes are the best known of these critics. They saw in Chaplin a master of pantomime, which he was, but they also saw something else that they believed distinguished him from Keaton and Lloyd. They saw Chaplin as a serious major artist whose tramp character represented the essence of the human condition. James Agee indicated something about the quality in 1936 when he recommended that his good friend Father Flye see Chaplin's just-released *Modern Times*: "It's a wonderful thing to see . . . a lot, to me, as if Beethoven were living now and had completed another symphony."

Chaplin, always vulnerable to flattery, especially if it came from intellectuals, began to believe what the critics said about the quality of his art. The effect on his work was slow in coming, but it eventually proved deadly, culminating in the preachiness of *The Great Dictator, Monsieur Verdoux,* and *Limelight.*

Trade ad for *The Kid Brother*, 1927.

Chaplin also began to take much more time in making his films, releasing them three years apart and, in one case, after nearly five years.

The critics of the day, with the single exception of Robert E. Sherwood, had no such love affair with either Keaton or Lloyd. Funny, yes; artists, no. Neither one had any intellectual pretensions about his work; as Keaton and Lloyd saw it, they were strictly entertainers. The tide of critical esteem for Keaton has changed dramatically in the past two decades or so. Of the three it is Lloyd who has yet to receive the high critical esteem he clearly deserves. Despite their profound differences, all three share the distinction of having made films that remain perpetually fresh.

It is now clear that the quality of films increased steadily worldwide during the late twenties, until the sudden extinction of the silents with the arrival of sound at the end of 1928. The year 1927 was the year of Keaton's *The General,* Eisenstein's *October,* and Murnau's *Sunrise,* while 1928 saw the release of Buñuel's *Un Chien d'Andalou,* Seastrom's *The Wind,* Dreyer's *The Passion of Joan of Arc,* Pudovkin's *Storm over Asia,* Keaton's *The Cameraman,* Vidor's *The Crowd,* and Chaplin's *The Circus.* The quality had not lessened in 1929, the last year in which silent films were made in any significant volume: Vertov's *Man with a Movie Camera,* Keaton's *Spite Marriage,* Eisenstein's *The General Line,* and Dovzhenko's *Arsenal.*

Lloyd's final two silent films, *The Kid Brother* (1927) and *Speedy* (1928), are remarkable. They belong with the very best of his work, although neither has been exhibited as widely as many of his other films. *The Kid Brother,* arguably Lloyd's masterpiece, has for decades received only archival screening. The same is true of *Speedy*: for every viewer of these films there are fifty who have seen *The Freshman* and *Safety Last.* Part of the trouble stemmed from Lloyd himself; he kept a firm grip on what he would release for distribution in the last years of his life.

It is remarkable that many of the outstanding films of the late silent period are relatively unknown. One of the main reasons is that the film industry began to regard their products of this time as something of an embarrassment: those pictures closest in time to the advent of sound seemed the most dated to them. There were financial reasons as well; many of the silent films made at the end of 1928 or in the early months of 1929 did not perform at all well at the box office. Moviegoers were waiting impatiently for films that talked and passed over those that didn't. Keaton's *Spite Marriage* fits into this category of relatively unknown films. Ernst Lubitsch's *The Patriot* (1928), von Sternberg's *The Story of Lena Smith* (1929), and Murnau's *Four Devils* (1928) are three films which were forgotten so quickly that no prints have survived.

The Kid Brother is the most perfectly organized of all Lloyd's films. It orchestrates the gags and the story line in an ideal proportion that none of his previous features had quite attained. It brings together a number of themes that had concerned him in films going as far back as *Grandma's Boy*. Here, they have been triumphantly united. More important, *The Kid Brother* contains a genuine warmth of feeling for its central character, the physically weak but brainy son of a rugged, brawny mountain family. A common criticism of Lloyd's work asserts that his films are mechanical and devoid of deeper human feeling and points to Chaplin and Keaton as richly possessing this virtue; *The Kid Brother* is easily Lloyd's best refutation of this charge.

Bearing the working title of *The Mountain Boy,* it was made as carefully as were all his films, but took longer than any of the rest: a total of eight months in production. A great deal of it was shot in the open country around Placentia, California, which furnished the mountain terrain the story demanded. Other sequences were shot near the Santa Ana Canyon and on Catalina Island. With his current gagmen, John Grey, Tom Crizer, and Ted Wilde, Harold worked out a story line that critic William K. Everson believes was based on a 1924 Hal Roach film, *The White Sheep*. Brawny Sheriff Jim Hickory has sired two muscular young giants and a much smaller son, who makes up in cleverness what he lacks in physique. The opening sequences include some marvelously worked-out gag routines to demonstrate Harold's ability to perform the farm chores with a minimum of physical effort. He places the family wash in the butter churn, whirls it around until clean, and then sends it aloft to dry on a line fastened to a kite. Dishwashing is accomplished by putting the dirty dishes in a fish net which, when wound up tightly enough, unwinds itself rapidly in soapy water. The clean dishes are then placed to dry on a shelf directly on top of the stove. The laden shelf is later replaced intact on the wall.

Like Keaton's *The General, The Kid Brother* is a serious work, containing many elements not usually found in film comedies. After an ominous opening shot which shows us the rotting hulk of an abandoned vessel in a desolate bay at sundown, we are immediately introduced to three members of a horse-drawn traveling show, the Original Mammoth Medicine Show. Mary Powers (Jobyna Ralston) is the daughter of the founder, and runs it with the aid of Sandoni (Constantine Romanoff), the menacingly ugly strong man, and the PR man, Flash Farrell. Their wagon stops at the Hickory farm. Harold has donned his father's shirt and sheriff's badge, as well as his holster and gun—with his father and brothers safely away from the farm, he has begun acting out some of his frustrations as the weakling of the family. Fear of total humiliation prevents him from revealing the truth of his lowly status as a male Cinderella. Convinced that Harold must be the sheriff, Farrell persuades him to give them permission to perform in town that night.

Once the show is set up for the night, Mary leaves for a solitary walk in the woods, where she is followed by the lustful strong man. Fleeing Sandoni in panic, she bumps into Harold, who comes to her defense armed with a heavy stick. Sandoni takes one horrified look at Harold's weapon and stupefies the couple by running away. He has seen what they haven't: a deadly snake coiled around the neck of the stick. After thanking her rescuer, Mary starts on her way back to the show in town. Tremendously taken with her, Harold can't bear her departure. As she slowly begins her descent into the woods, he begins to climb a tall tree in order not to lose sight of her. He continues their conversation as he climbs, going ever higher at each question. By the time she has become a tiny speck in the distance, Harold has reached the top of the tree. From there he shouts "GOOD-BYE" to her; her faint "Good-bye" appears on the titles in tiny, four-point type. It is a sweet and innovative sequence, one that epitomizes so much of the film's charm. Not unexpectedly, Harold falls out of the tree after the farewells.

When Sheriff Jim Hickory discovers the truth about the opening of the medicine show that night, Harold is sent to town wearing his father's badge, with orders to close it down. In shame and misery, he sets out for the show, where Sandoni and Farrell proceed to make a fool of him. Mary repays her debt to Harold by rescuing him from Sandoni. The show is shut down, demolished, in fact, by an accidental fire. Harold offers to take Mary home with him to spend the night on the porch, knowing full well that her presence must be kept secret in this Calvinist family of God- and women-fearing men.

Harold's two brothers have caught a glimpse of pretty Mary, and next morning they begin to court her as she presumably lies sleeping on a couch shielded by a curtain Harold has rigged up. But, unknown to them, a neighbor woman has taken Mary away during the evening, claiming that it wouldn't be decent for her to spend the night "with all those men." Having spent the night behind the curtain himself, Harold delights in the luxury of having each of his brothers serve him a complete breakfast in bed. To enhance the deception, Harold occasionally displays a braceleted arm through a crack in the blanket curtain. The two brothers are not at all pleased when they discover the recipient of their cooking.

All of this material has served to set the scene for the story proper, which now begins. The townspeople, a rather nasty, narrow-minded bunch, have entrusted Sheriff Jim Hickory with all their savings, with which they hope to build a dam for the town. When Jim discovers that the money has disappeared, his neighbors are convinced he has stolen it and they proceed to arrest and imprison their own sheriff. Harold wishes to join his brothers in the quest for the missing money but is forbidden to do so, on the old familiar grounds that he might get hurt "doing men's work." Now, and for the first time, Harold tells Mary the truth about his lowly place in his father's household. She tells him that if he will only have confidence in himself, he can't lose. These are the words he has needed to hear; when he summons up the courage to ask her if she really believes in him, she replies with a kiss.

Harold's determination to recover the lost money and his father's honor is thwarted at the outset. He is knocked unconscious by an old-time enemy, a young bully who also has designs on Mary. The blow knocks Harold into a rowboat, which drifts slowly down the river toward the bay in which we earlier saw the rotting, sinister hulk of a derelict ship. It is, of course, here that Sandoni and Farrell have hidden their stolen money. After Harold climbs on board, he becomes aware of the killing of Farrell by Sandoni in a quarrel over splitting the money. There follows a brilliant series of evasive nonencounters between Sandoni and Harold on the deserted ship, a sequence that has strong affinities with one in Keaton's *The Navigator* made three years earlier.

Sandoni has brought aboard the troupe's performing mon-

The Kid Brother, 1927.

key. Suddenly the startled Sandoni hears the clattering above him of many feet. Harold has placed his own shoes on the monkey in order to convince Sandoni that a goodly number of outraged townspeople have boarded the ship in pursuit. The talented monkey here is the same Jocko that Keaton employed the following year in *The Cameraman.* It is probable that Keaton, after seeing *The Kid Brother,* realized that a lot more could be done with the monkey's awesome power of mimicry and decided then to use it as the *deus ex machina* for the conclusion of *The Cameraman.* There was a great deal of this kind of borrowing among the silent comedians, and they would often use a rival's device in order to top it if they could.

The trick with the monkey fails,* and Sandoni finally corners

---

* Harold chose to cut the monkey episode in later years, believing that he didn't need a monkey to compete for laughs.

The Kid Brother, 1927.

Harold in the rotting ship's hold, half of which is immersed in water. After a furious fight, Sandoni pins Harold against the wall and is about to bludgeon him to death with an iron bar. Lloyd always loved to talk about this scene, as it demonstrated the perplexing question of how much the audience should know in advance:

> This one piece of business was with an iron bracket that was fastened to the side of the ship—one part was fastened to the ship, and there was a prong that came out. He grabbed me, and in my getting away from him, I went up against the ship's side, and this iron bracket fitted right into my hair, on top of my head. You couldn't see it. So he had one of these big iron belaying pins, and he came over and grabbed me by the chest, . . . he wanted to crush my skull, so he hit me over the head with it—but of course he didn't hit my head, he hit this iron prong that was in my hair. Of course, he didn't know it, and he gives me this terrific blow, and all I do is blink my eyes. And he can't imagine what's happening. He hits again. And again I don't do anything. He should have killed me. Of

course, I get away then, and as I . . . run, the audience sees why I wasn't hurt. . . .

Now, one way would have been to . . . let the audience know . . . that he didn't know what it was but they did; and the other way was to surprise both the audience and the assailant. We previewed it both ways, and this particular scene, they both got laughs, but we thought the surprise [was] the best.

Sandoni has an Achilles heel: he can't swim, a fact that Harold discovers when the two roll their way down into the dark water. By managing to submerge his enemy repeatedly, Harold finally reduces Sandoni to helplessness. Harold then makes his conquest complete by ringing Sandoni's body from toes to neck with life preservers. Using the body as a flotation device and a broom as a paddle, Harold returns to town to be hailed as a hero. His vindicated father finally pays his son the supreme compliment by telling him, "Son, you're a real Hickory." A new and radiantly confident Harold walks off with Mary, who made it all possible.

There is a sure sweetness of tone throughout *The Kid Brother,* a charm that may be in part due to the work of its nominal director, Ted Wilde, one of the three writers who worked on the story. Although claims have been made concerning Lewis Milestone's contribution to the direction, we now know that the Russian-born director of *All Quiet on the Western Front* worked on *The Kid Brother* only four days. But even granting Wilde his just due, the film is clearly Harold's own, bringing to a triumphant conclusion many of the themes that had fascinated him from the time he invented his glasses character.

As Richard Schickel has pointed out, one of the great virtues of *The Kid Brother* is that its basic story is a good deal more complex and convincing than any of the previous Lloyd features, causing the gags to flow more naturally from the given situations. Here there is no dependence on the magical properties of an umbrella handle, as in *Grandma's Boy*. Nor is there any dependence upon daredevil stunts, a characteristic so frequently associated with Lloyd's films.

Keaton's *The General* was released just three weeks after *The Kid Brother*, early in 1927. Neither Keaton nor Lloyd had the satisfaction of receiving critical acclaim for the film that stands arguably as his best. Keaton's was severely castigated by the majority of the New York critics: *The General* wasn't funny, it was hard to follow and, worst of all, it was *dull*. The public listened, stayed away, and the film was a complete financial disaster. Lloyd fared far better with the critics: they liked his film well enough, but not one singled it out for any special distinction. The *New York Herald-Tribune* was typical in saying that, "all of Lloyd's other pictures have been perfect and so is *The Kid Brother*." Since Lloyd hadn't cared much for *For Heaven's Sake*, the reviews of the new and far better film must have been especially disappointing. Far more important, the movie-going public did not take to *The Kid Brother* as strongly as they had to the earlier film, and this was reflected in both domestic and foreign receipts:

	For Heaven's Sake (1926)		*The Kid Brother* (1927)	
	GROSS	NET	GROSS	NET
Domestic	$1,752,111	$1,161,377	$1,608,825	$1,035,075
Canada	70,468	41,006	66,238	38,534
Foreign	768,882	482,653	728,067	439,364
TOTAL	$2,591,461	$1,685,036	$2,403,130	$1,512,973

When he began working on *Speedy* in the late spring of 1927, he may well have had some doubts about the project. If the public seemed to like the loosely structured, thrill-and-stunt *For*

Heaven's Sake so much, wasn't *Speedy* likely to repeat the relatively disappointing history of *Kid Brother* at the box office? Nevertheless, in *Speedy* he managed to produce a film that comes very close to his best.

CHAPTER 8
THE DEATH OF AN ART

1

I do not believe the public will want talking comedy.
Motion pictures and the spoken arts are two distinct
arts, and when you try to unite them, I am skeptical
of the result. . . . It is action, and little else, that
counts in comedy.

—Lloyd

When Harold and his production crew arrived in Manhattan in
June of 1927 for the shooting of *Speedy,* he had no inkling that
this would be his last silent picture or that the days of the silents were numbered. It was early in October that Al Jolson in
The Jazz Singer told an easily convinced audience, "You ain't
heard nothing yet!" They hadn't heard very much talk in that
picture, but Jolson had awakened their appetite for talkies, or
talkers, as they were called in their early days.

Speedy was expensive to make, costing nearly a quarter of a
million more than *The Kid Brother.* The increased cost was almost entirely due to shooting three thousand miles from Hollywood with the crew of thirty-five that Harold brought along.
The entourage also included Mildred, her mother, "Gaga," and

three-year-old Mildred Gloria. Harold and the family, as well as the most important members of the company, stayed at the Ritz-Carlton Hotel; the lowlier members made do at the far cheaper Shelton on Lexington Avenue. Jobyna Ralston was not among them. Very much concerned with her career, she preferred to have Harold lend her out to Cecil B. De Mille for a thousand a week. She never appeared again in a Lloyd film. Her replacement was the rather vapid Ann Christy, who had a relatively insignificant role in the picture.

Shooting feature films in New York was not uncommon in the twenties, and Harold's presence in the city attracted large crowds wherever he went. Scenes were shot all over the city: at the old Penn Station on Seventh Avenue, at the Queensboro Bridge, up at Yankee Stadium, and down at South Ferry. One of the great pleasures of this film is seeing the vanished buildings of New York as they appeared in 1927. A good deal of ingenuity was often required to get the desired effects. A hidden camera photographed Harold and his girl buying their tickets at Luna Park in a real Coney Island crowd. Occasionally, Harold's ingenuity backfired. He used a Mrs. Parrish, a character actress, to play the part of an irate woman who attacks him at Luna Park with her umbrella. The gag was set up so that Mrs. Parrish could hit Harold repeatedly on his right hand. Since he was wearing his prosthetic device he would be indifferent to the blows. But Mrs. Parrish misunderstood and kept hammering away at Harold's *left* hand until she was restrained. The actress was the mother of the film director-to-be Robert Parrish, who appeared as an extra along with his sister Helen.

Speedy and *The Kid Brother* possess the same sweetness of tone, as well as a sustained balance between plot and gags that distinguishes both films from the earlier ones. Here Lloyd is Harold "Speedy" Swift, who is distinctly not the go-getting world-beater of *Why Worry?* and *For Heaven's Sake*. Speedy has a fatal obsession with baseball, so much so that he can't

Shooting *Speedy* at the Plaza Hotel, New York City, June 1927.

Under the Queensboro Bridge. Ted Wilde next to HL.

With Babe Ruth at the old Yankee Stadium.

hold any sort of job for long. As the picture begins, we see him desperately trying to fulfill his duties as a drugstore soda jerk and still manage to keep his friends in the kitchen posted on the latest Yankee game. He does it by arranging the various pieces of pastry on the counter into numerical shapes. His employers are not amused, and Speedy walks off the job.

Speedy's despair over being jobless is something he prefers to celebrate with a trip to Luna Park and the Steeplechase with his girl, Jane (Christy). There is a great deal of vitality in these Coney Island scenes, which were photographed beautifully by Harold's regular cameraman, Walter Lundin. They are remarkable in their semidocumentary approach, convincing us that these are, in fact, ordinary people having a good time on a Sunday afternoon in the New York of the late 1920s.

Shooting *Speedy*, 1927.

At Luna Park in Brooklyn; Mrs. Parrish at HL's right.

At the end of the day, heavily laden with all their various prizes, Speedy and Jane discover they have spent all their money: there isn't even enough to get on the subway back to Manhattan. But luck is still with them, for they are picked up by the friendly driver of a moving van. Once inside the back of the van, Speedy and Jane realize that all the home furnishings they might require for their future life together are right here in the truck. They quickly rearrange everything in sight, and in a few minutes the couple set up housekeeping in the back of the bouncing van, with a HOME SWEET HOME sign over their improvised fireplace. They've won a cradle at Luna Park and, as Speedy stares down into it, he imagines it filled with twins, both wearing horn-rims. Again, as with his weeping sequence in *The Freshman,* Lloyd cut this entire moving-van section from *Speedy* in later years, believing that modern audiences of the fifties and sixties would find it excessively sentimental, a doubtful view.

Jane is the granddaughter of Pop Dillon, who operates the last horse-drawn trolley in New York. The local street railway magnates want to buy up Pop's franchise for their own greedy purposes. Old Pop can retain the franchise only if he can operate his dilapidated vehicle at least once every twenty-four hours. Speedy is concerned about the old man's ability to perform, but even baseball dreamers must eat and so he is soon driving a cab for the One Only Cab Company. Speedy has as much difficulty driving a cab as he had jerking sodas. Things keep happening to him, mostly funny ones, but they include picking up criminals fleeing from the law, as well as the detectives hot on their trail. The great Babe Ruth himself is a nervous passenger on a wild ride in Speedy's cab up to Yankee Stadium in the Bronx. The temptation to see his famous passenger in action on the baseball diamond is irresistible. Speedy procures himself a choice seat directly behind his boss at the cab company. As he leaves Yankee Stadium, Speedy wonders what he will be doing on the following day, since he won't be driving a cab for One Only.

The demands of the plot quicken, and we see Speedy taking up Pop's fight against the traction magnates who steal his trolley as part of their plan to take over the franchise. Speedy manages to steal the trolley back again and begins an epic ride to Pop's neighborhood around Sheridan Square in Greenwich Village. In a sequence reminiscent of the final race to the church in *Girl Shy,* Speedy finds it necessary to change horses as he gets closer and closer to his destination. He steals a pair and, with the aid of a clothes mannequin made up to resemble a cop, thunders on through the teeming streets as traffic makes way for him.

Down at the Brooklyn Bridge, Speedy, his horses, and the trolley smash head-on into the steel elevated pillars adjoining the bridge. This smash-up was quite accidental and was left in the film with very little editing; it reinforces the documentary feeling of the early scenes shot in Coney Island. Speedy arrives just in time to avoid the penalties of the nonperformance clause. He demands a hundred thousand dollars for Pop's rights to the route, thus defeating the machinations of the evil magnates. Pop gets his price and Speedy his Jane.

Both *The Kid Brother* and *Speedy* are marked by a tender nostalgia for the recent past—the past of a disappearing rural America and a surviving bit of the horse-driven age. In both, Lloyd proves equally resourceful under stress, although his male Cinderella of *Kid Brother* is far from the jaunty, flip city boy of *Speedy*.

Speedy was quite successful, although its domestic gross was about $150,000 less than that of *The Kid Brother*. *Speedy*'s foreign grosses, however, earned enough abroad to produce a total gross of $2,287,798.

Wall Street; Barbara Kent on scale.

At the beginning of both 1927 and 1928 all exhibitor polls showed Lloyd as the number-one box-office attraction in the United States. His films were regularly grossing (worldwide) between two and a half and three million dollars per picture. On the threshold of the sound era, Lloyd and Chaplin (along with Pickford and Fairbanks, and Colleen Moore) were undoubtedly the most successful actor-producers in Hollywood. Chaplin continued to be Harold's only real competition, despite his scant output. After *The Gold Rush* of 1925 came *The Circus,* not released until early in 1928; then *City Lights* in 1931. In that same period Harold released six features, two of them sound films. In dollar volume *per picture,* Chaplin always remained ahead of Lloyd, with Keaton running a very poor third. The comparative world-wide earnings for their mid- and late-twenties releases are revealing:

1925

Chaplin	*The Gold Rush*	$4,000,000*
Lloyd	*The Freshman*	2,651,167
Keaton	*Seven Chances*	590,280
	Go West	589,504

1926

Chaplin	no release	
Lloyd	*For Heaven's Sake*	$2,591,460
Keaton	*Battling Butler*	749,201

1927

Chaplin	no release	
Lloyd	*The Kid Brother*	$2,403,130
Keaton	*The General*	474,264
	College	423,808

1928

Chaplin	*The Circus*	$3,500,000*
Lloyd	*Speedy*	2,287,798
Keaton	*Steamboat Bill, Jr.*	358,839
	The Cameraman	797,000

Nineteen twenty-eight was the last great year for the silents. Just ahead were the sound films that threatened everything these men had accomplished.

2

> If you're not talking, something's wrong.
>
> —Lloyd

> There will be silent films when talking pictures are forgotten. The trouble with the whole industry is that it talked before it thought.
>
> —Joseph M. Schenck

> No, there is positively no sentiment of any kind in this business.
>
> —William Fox

The coming of sound in 1928 has been customarily regarded as an inevitable step in the development of film. Inevitable, yes, but at a terrible cost for some, for sound literally meant the death of the art of Chaplin, Lloyd, and Keaton, so masterfully

---

* These are estimates: worldwide figures for Chaplin are not currently available. The domestic gross for *The Gold Rush* was $2,255,599, and for *The Circus* $1,911,400.

created in less than a decade. In none of their sound films did these three men ever rise to the heights they reached in the silent era. Their art had nothing to do with words: all three lost their unique magic the moment they opened their mouths.

Many leading film-makers were dead set against sound from the beginning. Eisenstein punned that "it was fundamentally unsound to develop screen stories through the medium of dialogue." He did not even bother to take along recording equipment when he went to Mexico to make his ill-fated *Que Viva Mexico!* at the end of 1930. F. W. Murnau displayed complete indifference to the radical changes imposed by sound in 1928 and 1929. His final film was the silent *Tabu,* released in 1931, the year of his death. Chaplin remained mute until he sang a gibberish song in *Modern Times* in 1936, and it was not until *The Great Dictator* of 1940 that he produced a real sound film.

There was general uneasiness about the effect of sound on film-making. It may now seem bizarre that so many knowledgeable people could have been as bitterly opposed to the abandonment of the silent picture as they were in 1928. One of the best ongoing accounts of the rapidly changing feelings of the Hollywood film community can be found in the editorial pages of *The Film Spectator*, an idiosyncratic film journal edited and published by Welford Beaton. Founded in 1926, *The Film Spectator* was widely read in Hollywood as an objective, tough-minded, slightly highbrow account of current film-making. To guarantee objectivity, the film studios were not permitted to buy advertising space. Beaton was bluntly outspoken in his opinions, and his magazine soon began to be read as far east as Baltimore, where H. L. Mencken read it regularly, and in New York, where Robert E. Sherwood became a fierce adversary of Beaton's views on sound.

Beaton started off by approving of sound. In November 1928, just as the first wave of talkers arrived, Beaton was convinced that the introduction of sound was going to be a great thing for films and defended these early, experimental ones against their detractors. In this early honeymoon period, Beaton was convinced that it was not only possible but infinitely desirable that film producers continue to make silent films along with their talkers.* But Beaton was soon worrying about what might happen if they didn't: "The silent drama has become a great art and I hope the advent of sound is not going to arrest its development."

The change came about very rapidly, as studio after studio began the great shift. With the exception of Warner Brothers, where he maintained an ongoing feud with Jack Warner, Beaton had complete access to the product being turned out by nearly all the Hollywood studios at the time. Sitting day after day in studio projection booths, he would often see both the silent *and* the sound versions of a number of films in this experimental period, when producers wanted to have it both ways until all their theaters were wired for sound. It may have been these experiences that caused his growing disenchantment with the talkers, because by the end of 1928 he had hardened his position, claiming that the virtue of silent film art was that it created "a world of shadowy make-believe far removed from the world of flesh and blood humans. . . . " Although he displayed great admiration for Mary Pickford's first sound film, *Coquette*, he correctly surmised that this was truly "a different Mary," and that she would now probably appeal to a different audience.

Beaton's basic quarrel with the sound film was this sudden abandoning of what he called the "shadow world" of the silents for the harsh, crude, everyday realities of the spoken word. He was convinced that audiences would shrink from the task of

---

* This notion was not as farfetched as it may now seem. Sidney Kent of Paramount, writing to Harold's uncle, William Fraser, in November of 1928, was also convinced that it was possible: "Personally, I believe the time will never come when the outstanding silent pictures will be out of the market. We are trying to work out the best possible combination of sound and silent."

coping with the "intellectual content" in all those words coming from the screen at them. His reasoning about the lack of intellectual content in silent films is false, and Beaton did not see
that it would be the great comic talents of the silent era who
would suffer the most from the coming of sound.

The sheer *amount* of talk in these early sound films was
especially irritating to him when the picture became simply a
filmed stage play. His comments on pictures of this kind were
often shrewd and quite prophetic:

> Audiences never will accept stage plays transferred to the
> screen, but before all this dawns upon them, the producers
> will have wasted many millions of dollars, will have continued
> to drag out this utterly ridiculous period of confusion and will
> have disgusted the public with sound pictures in general.

By early 1929 Beaton had adopted a no-retreat position in his
opposition to sound films, using these scare headlines on the
cover of his journal:

TALKIES WILL NOT
CONTINUE TO BE
SUCCESSFUL

PUBLIC DOES NOT WANT
TO HEAR VOICES

But they did, and in ever increasing numbers.

Beaton's complaints were based on fact. Anyone who has
ever seen a single example of a primitive talker will agree with
Joseph Schenck's verdict that the film industry failed to think
before it talked. The early sound era saw the release of some
truly awful films, of which Warner Brothers' *The Lights of New
York* was the most successful. Perhaps the most hilarious scene

in the film features four gangsters sitting around a table while discussing the upcoming fate of a fifth. All four actors look terribly uneasy as they try to keep their eyes away from the bowl of flowers on the table which contains the microphone they are all so anxious not to appear to notice. They speak in stilted, measured tones that bear no resemblance to any speech known outside of a beginner's class in English. The chief gangster tells his associates that if the police don't find their friend, "it will clinch everything for us. Don't you understand . . . ?" Aghast, a mobster replies: *"You . . . mean . . . ?"* His boss tells him: *"Take him . . . for . . . a . . . ride. . . . "* The phrase caught on and swept the country, creating an enormous word-of-mouth appeal for the film.

One of the reasons some of these pictures were so terrible was that the actors and actresses were attempting to make the most of their voices, many of them for the first time in their lives. But the trained stage performers also had problems: they were all doing something new, and many of them thought there must be a *special* way to do it, that talking in films was an art that could be mastered by attending voice-culture schools. The fan magazines helped create waves of uncertainty by conjecturing what favorite stars would sound like: the term "mike fright" became popular. Many performers, especially those without prior stage experience, were deeply troubled about their careers: suppose their voices were "wrong" for sound films. Would they ever work again? The major studios began to schedule "voice tests" for their principal performers. Almost everyone believed that voices registering a certain general tone of culture and refinement were what the filmgoing public wanted to hear.

By late summer of 1928 a feeling of panic descended over Hollywood. Some major studios, Paramount and Warner, took the plunge at once, abandoning all silent production and switching over completely to sound. Others, notably MGM, waited until September before embarking on their first sound films. In these frantic, hurried months, many films were released with only one spoken reel. To satisfy the craze for sound, nearly all films were given sound tracks carrying hurriedly written theme music. It was at this time, in August 1928, that Harold began work on the film that became *Welcome Danger.* He began it as a silent.

3

No spoken words ever reached the heights of Chaplin, Lloyd and Keaton. If they go in for humorous dialogue they will lose something that is priceless and irreplaceable . . . for they have achieved by means of grotesque physical actions, an eloquence that is far beyond the limitations of any language.
—Robert E. Sherwood

I think we're at the point where we have no choice. We've got to make a sound picture.
—Lloyd

While waiting for the completion of their new home at Greenacres, the Lloyds continued to live at their old house on South Hoover Street. Under construction for five years, Greenacres was not ready for occupancy until late summer of 1929. In January of 1928, a year before they moved to Greenacres, a fire broke out in the South Hoover Street house. Mildred suffered painful burns, requiring a brief stay in the hospital. It seems possible that it was her injuries at this time that made Harold and Mildred believe they could not have any more children. In any case, they began soon after to think seriously about adopting a playmate for four-year-old Mildred Gloria. As for Mildred, she had by now abandoned hope of returning to films. Furnishing Greenacres now occupied all her time.

Harold also spent a great deal of his free time overseeing the work in Beverly Hills. His quest was for perfection: he wanted everything in his mansion to be the very best, whatever the price. With his 1920s income of at least a million a year, he had no difficulty pleasing himself. Despite his own genuine misgivings about the future of sound, he furnished Greenacres with RCA Photophone projection equipment, the best and most expensive variety then on the market.

Like so many prominent film-makers of the day, Lloyd was extremely uneasy about the impact of sound. His initial attitude may have been close to Chaplin's, who clearly saw that his tramp character could never speak. Lloyd's various "boy" characters were not as inexorably bound to silence, but a sound film would require a shooting script, a tyranny Harold's company had always avoided. If there were to be scripts, what would happen to the immensely rewarding technique of working out things in the gag room and then trying them while shooting the picture, essentially an improvisational-mosaic method by which bits and pieces of the story were developed with precision? How could a single scriptwriter, or a dozen scriptwriters, ever come close to achieving the superb results Harold and his co-workers had developed during the decade? With perhaps such thoughts as these, Lloyd decided to continue with what he knew best and began shooting *Welcome Danger* as a silent film at Metropolitan Studios in August 1928.

In July he had been interviewed by the doyenne of film gossip columnists, Louella Parsons. He told her that he felt *sound* "was doomed," but that he wasn't going to be rigid about it:

First he will spend five to seven months producing a silent picture. He will go ahead and make a complete silent version before he so much as considers dialogue and then after he previews his picture and makes his changes he will make the sound version with synchronization (music) and dialogue.

The effects of all the tension in the air concerning the arrival of sound must surely account for the kind of film that Harold and his crew shot in the next six months. Carrying working titles of *The Butterfly Collector* and then *T.N.T.*, the film finally ran to sixteen reels, or about two hours and forty-five minutes, at a time when the typical length was under an hour and a half. Lloyd later claimed that this sixteen-reel silent version went over extremely well with preview audiences, but that he realized a film of this length would be commercially unfeasible. Ted Wilde was the director for the first month, until he was replaced by Mal St. Clair, one of the leading comedy directors of the late twenties. With the help of St. Clair and the rest of the staff, Harold began cutting the film by at least a third, but with unforeseen results. The new preview audiences became increasingly cool as the picture grew shorter. This was after only three or four reels had been cut, but by the time they had reduced the film to ten reels, "she started to perk up again . . . I don't know why." It was at this point, with a successfully previewed *Welcome Danger,* that Harold began to worry about what might happen to *any* silent picture in the fall of 1929. He had good reason to worry.

On April 20, 1929, Creed Neeper of the Harold Lloyd Corporation's New York office wrote a long letter to his boss in California, William Fraser, setting forth the fact that, as of that week, pictures containing dialogue and sound effects of some sort amounted to 89 percent of all pictures then in release. With reference to playing time in theaters, the figures were even more impressive: silent pictures accounted for only 4 percent of the total. He concluded his letter with what could have been taken as a warning: "for the leading theaters the silent picture is almost obsolete."

On one of the last nights of the previews of the silent version, Harold saw a now-forgotten two-reel sound comedy:

> . . . and they howled at this. . . . They had the punkest gags in it, but they were laughing at the pouring of water, the frying of eggs—it didn't matter—the clinking of ice in a glass. We said, "My God, we worked our hearts out to get laughs with thought-out gags, and look here: just because they've got some sound in it, they're roaring at these things."

Now convinced that *Welcome Danger* was doomed to failure if he released it as a silent, Harold told his crew: "I think we've got to convert this into a sound picture, some way." They did, but only by an enormous amount of work and money. Mal St. Clair's services were not retained. His successor was the legendary Clyde Bruckman, who had written the story for Keaton's *The General*.

Clyde Bruckman appears in American film history as an almost mythical creature, a strangely elusive figure about whom little is known. He regularly performed writing and directing assignments for several major performers. The few facts we have fail to explain the richness of his varied contributions to silent film comedy. Born in San Bernardino, Bruckman embraced a brief career in journalism before beginning to write stories for Monty Banks, a now-forgotten film comedian of the early twenties. He soon began writing for Buster Keaton: *Our Hospitality* (1923), *Sherlock, Jr.* (1924), *The Navigator* (1924), and *Seven Chances* (1925). His services increasingly in demand, Bruckman then worked as a writer on Harold's *The Freshman* for seven and a half weeks at the beginning of 1925. Later that year he worked on *For Heaven's Sake*.

Truly a chameleon, Bruckman easily adjusted his talents to such diverse personalities as Lloyd and Keaton. He had the

seemingly magic power to bring out the best work from whom-
ever he worked with. The extraordinarily wide range of Bruckman's abilities is attested to by the fact that he directed some of
the best of Laurel and Hardy's silent comedies: *Putting Pants
on Phillip* (1927) and *Battle of the Century* (1927). In discussing his contributions to the two-reelers, William K. Everson
praised Bruckman's editing powers: "The cuts all come at such
'right' moments that editorially it almost has the rhythm of an
Eisenstein or Griffith work." That sense of rhythm is nowhere
better demonstrated than in *The General,* which Bruckman co-
directed with Keaton.*

Both Lloyd and Keaton found in Clyde Bruckman a man they
could rely on whenever they needed him—which was often. He
had only one major flaw: he drank, so much that there were
times when he was unable to show up for work. Lloyd put up
with this, and so did his other employers, because when Bruckman was good, there was no one better. The drinking was especially serious when Bruckman was directing a picture: Lloyd
recalled: "He had a little difficulty with the bottle and we practically had to wash him out and I had to carry on." The picture
was the 1932 *Movie Crazy*; Lloyd generously gave Bruckman
complete screen credit as director. He continued to work on all
of Lloyd's pictures from *Welcome Danger* through *Profesor Beware* in 1938; the single exception was *The Milky Way* (1936).

Bruckman's fortunes fared badly in the nineteen-forties and
fifties. His alcoholism made steady work impossible. In despera-
tion, he sold Universal Pictures a number of the gag situations
he had created for Harold during the shooting of *Movie Crazy* in
the early thirties. The gags appeared in one of Joan Davis's
films, *She Gets Her Man* (1945). Harold sued Universal and
collected heavy damages for the appropriation of his property.

---

* Bruckman also directed W. C. Fields in some of his best sound comedies: *The
Fatal Glass of Beer* (1933) and *Man on the Flying Trapeze* (1935).

The suit made Bruckman unemployable and in 1955 he borrowed Buster Keaton's pistol and killed himself in a telephone booth on Santa Monica Boulevard.

What Bruckman advocated for *Welcome Danger* was to scrap at least half of it and to dub the remaining half, a piece of surgery that left its mark on the structure of the sound version. Lloyd found the dubbing experience nightmarish:

> In those days no one knew very much about dubbing. . . . When we tried to dub the one-half that had been shot silent, it was like an insane asylum. We had seven or eight different people that were all making different effects. One man was walking upstairs and back down, another one was rattling, another one was hammering on this, another one was coughing. . . .

The dialogue was inserted directly on the new soundtrack created for the silent footage: "Oh, the dubbing was horrible. We didn't know what we were doing. We had a screen up there and we'd run the picture with "x" marks on it. . . . " This cumbersome process was intended "to tell us just when to get ready to anticipate when we were going to talk. . . . "

The subject of this frantic endeavor was a picture radically different from Harold's other films. Besides its awkward structure (the story doesn't surface until one-third of the picture is over), *Welcome Danger*'s hero has none of the charm of Harold's previous ones—in fact it is impossible to like him. The son of a police captain, Harold Bledsoe is a tiresome monomaniac obsessed with tracking down "The Dragon," an archfiend of San Francisco's Chinatown drug trade. By profession a botanist, Bledsoe attempts to catch his culprit by drearily mastering the art of fingerprint detection. In the film's endless two hours, countless skulls are noisily crushed, while trapdoors and secret panels squeakily open and close with tiresome regularity.

At one point in the sound version, Bledsoe and his incredibly

Sound recording in 1929: *Welcome Danger.*
Clyde Bruckman on far right.

Shooting *Welcome Danger* in 1929.
Noah Young in policeman's uniform.

thick-witted sidekick, Officer Clancy (Noah Young), are left in darkness in the basement of a Chinese opium den. As they grope their way around, they begin an animated chattering that drags on, minute after agonizing minute, a stream of words coming at you from a black screen. It's as if Lloyd and Bruckman were saying, "Sound, you wanted sound? Here it is, plenty of it, just like on the radio!"

The film abounds in what rapidly became known as "smart dialogue," or what Irving Thalberg called "smart lines": On arriving at the town of Newberry, Harold's response is "Newberry? Well, I've heard of strawberry and raspberry, but this is a new berry on me." When asked, "Have an accident?" Harold

Welcome Danger: Barbara Kent on HL's right.
His prosthetic device can be noticed here.

replies, "No thanks, just had one." In nearly every scene Harold has become a "comic," a comedian loaded down with an endless supply of unfunny quips: a 1929 Bob Hope.

As the sound version was about to open in New York in October, Lloyd appeared happy with the results: "We were afraid that the addition of dialogue would slow up the action considerably, but we got around it very nicely. . . . We ran off the silent film time and time again, *figuring out just how we could add dialogue and keep the pace. . . .* "* Thirty years later, Lloyd was still convinced he'd achieved a contradiction in terms: "the pace and quality of a silent picture in a sound film." What he had made was a composite picture, and only toward the end of his life would he grudgingly admit its faults: "It didn't turn out to be one of our best pictures, but it has its good points."

Although there were some good reviews, not everyone was pleased with *Welcome Danger.* Martin Dickstein of the *Brooklyn Daily Eagle,* the only New York critic who had admired *The General,* dismissed the talking Lloyd by asking the question, "Should Harold Lloyd have stuck to pantomime in the first place?" Dickstein expressed his distaste at hearing any of the three great silent comic artists:

> Harold Lloyd is one comedian whom this department would rather see than hear. Chaplin, by all means, is another. And of course, Buster Keaton. . . .

Even more interesting, some of the Paramount salesmen who previewed it in their New York screening room indicated pretty much what present-day critics William K. Everson and Andrew Sarris found wrong with the picture in the late 1970s:

> Harold Lloyd is essentially a pantomimist and when he starts to talk, his stuff does not go over so well. . . . There is too

---

* Emphasis added.

much repetition of comedy gags—for example, knocking people down by hitting them on the head, so much so that it becomes monotonous and reaches a point where some people
will resent it. . . . The first part of the picture is very slow and
the entire production would be improved by further cutting.

One Paramount executive had an even more drastic solution:

I suggest that before this picture is released, we screen it before an audience both in the dialogue version and in the silent
version. If the silent version is up to the standard of previous
Lloyd pictures, I feel certain that it will please the public
much better than the dialogue version.

Another was equally grim:

I think the talking slowed up the picture, I don't think Lloyd is
as funny talking as he is silent. . . . I am nearly one hundred
percent certain that the critics in New York are going to say
Lloyd is much less effective talking than in his old silent pictures.

These negative reports created something of a crisis at Paramount. One executive asked Fraser if he could preview the silent version in Yonkers to see whether the audience preferred
it; he was apparently rebuffed. But all the criticism was in vain.
The film became enormously popular: the wide public couldn't
wait to hear their favorites talk. *Welcome Danger* obtained a
worldwide gross of nearly three million dollars, making it
Lloyd's most successful film since *The Freshman,* although not
the most profitable. Starting off with preliminary costs of $147,-
000, the silent negative cost was $521,000. The sound version
cost another $289,000, bringing the total up to $979,828, but
still leaving a profit in excess of a million dollars.

Lloyd might well have told Chaplin, "You see, sound isn't so bad after all. Look at some of these reviews. Just look at these grosses!'' Chaplin wouldn't have agreed; he continued working patiently on *City Lights* as a silent film and released it with a musical track early in 1931. *Welcome Danger* is now of interest only to those morbidly curious about how bad an early talkie can be. Its huge success marked the beginning of Lloyd's undoing as a significant film-maker—he was now, truly, a talking comedian.

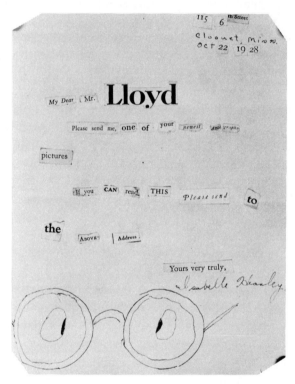

CHAPTER 9
THE MAN WHO TALKED TOO MUCH

1

You know, Harold, this is the only place I've been to
outside of Hearst's San Simeon where I felt I wasn't
slumming.

— Townsend Netcher

There isn't a corner anywhere on this property
where you can't hear the sound of water.

— Lloyd

Greenacres was finally ready for occupancy in August 1929. In
the previous two years, the Lloyds had spent virtually all their
free time selecting the thousand things thought necessary for a
home of this size. When it was time to move in, Harold and
Mildred must have had a strong feeling of anticlimax: here it
was at last and what were they going to do with it? One of their
first acts was to give a gargantuan housewarming party that
lasted for days. It then took several more days to get rid of the
last of the stragglers. This was an experience that was seldom
repeated; the Lloyds preferred their guests to arrive and depart
in small groups.

Greenacres: general view of the main house.

Much has been written about the splendor of the huge Italian Renaissance mansion Lloyd built 120 feet above Benedict Canyon. The sheer opulence of Greenacres served to confirm a widely held view that Lloyd built it not so much as a home to live in but rather as a monument to himself and his career—a modest San Simeon. The impressive physical grandeur of the Lloyd estate instantly became a part of Hollywood folklore. Now that it is mostly gone, much about Greenacres has taken on the quality of legend. That Lloyd intended it to be a showplace admits of no doubt, but it is clear that he hoped it would be more than that.

Lloyd's first biographer, Richard Schickel, expressed a hearty dislike for almost everything about Greenacres. His objections were wide-ranging, but it was plainly the sheer size of the place that galled him so powerfully. His tone was determinedly moralistic—by what right does a man living in Southern California in the twentieth century *dare* to build an Italian Renaissance palace? In addition, Lloyd was given low marks for his taste. On inspection, Schickel discovered that "nothing has any true distinction," and that the attractions of the estate were impressive only for their obvious costliness. He described Greenacres as cavernous and gloomy, rendering a dismal verdict that the whole place was "one of Lloyd's playthings that didn't work out."

Lloyd hadn't been seeking a plaything in 1925. He had wished to build a home that would reflect his position in the motion-picture world of the time, a position second to none. He was not alone in such a wish; this was the time of Valentino's famed Falcon's Lair, and the even more famous Pickfair of Mary Pickford and Douglas Fairbanks. It was also the time of Keaton's Italian Villa, though that was built at the request of his wife, Natalie Talmadge. Chaplin had also succumbed to the building fever in Beverly Hills. He designed his own mansion, which boasted forty rooms set down on a modest six-acre plot of land. One of the chief distinctions of major screen stars in the Hollywood of 1925 was the possession of a stately mansion.

One of HL's classic cars at Greenacres.

Lloyd's, however, became the stateliest of them all.

Why did Lloyd want Greenacres to be so overwhelmingly monumental? There are those who are convinced that displaying his huge earning power by building a Greenacres indicates a deep-seated anxiety. Lloyd's early, insecure years of wandering in poverty from one small town to another with his improvident father and resentful mother might have been sufficient reason for him to build a monument to his achievements. His three children, as well as his grandchild, Suzanne, referred to Greenacres as "The Mausoleum," a name that stuck.

The main house with its thirty-two rooms stands today pretty much as it did in 1929. There is a huge sunken living room with a sixteen-foot ceiling adorned with gold leaf, and a massive pipe organ with forty-five ranks, the kind normally found only in theaters. The auditorium, designed for film showings, seats one hundred. The formal dining room can accommodate twenty-four, although it seldom did. Even at the full height of Harold's popularity, the Lloyds were never as social as their contemporaries Chaplin and Pickford and Fairbanks.

Nearly everything in the house was custom-made, including all the furniture, rugs, and drapes. The walls were eighteen inches thick. The structure of the main house was built directly into the rock below, as if the house were designed to survive the last judgment of a California earthquake. Deep down in the bowels of the house, a long pasageway led to the game room and cocktail lounge. The corridor had been hewn out of the bedrock far below. It was decorated with hundreds of autographed photographs of all the celebrities who had ever visited the Lloyds. The visitors were supplied with a recent picture of themselves and asked to write something. Nearly everyone obliged, and the collection of photographs is still intact in a warehouse on Santa Monica Boulevard.

The grounds were as imposing as the house they sur-

Gloria Lloyd's Tudor playhouse, 1929.

1929: Gloria Lloyd presenting Tommy Armour with a watch for breaking the "Safety Last" golf course record with a play of 30-29-59.

rounded. The pool was Olympic size, framed by a large pavilion
where the Lloyds did most of their entertaining. A 110-foot wa-
terfall, illuminated at night, descended from a hillside adjoining
the main house into an 800-foot lake that could be used for can-
oeing. There was a vast reflecting pool. The huge, formal
gardens required the attention of—at least in the early days—
eighteen gardeners. There was a nine-hole golf course. Since
Lloyd's estate adjoined that of Jack Warner, who had built his
own nine-holer, it was possible for guests to play eighteen holes.
Many of the famous golfers of the day, Tommy Armour and
Bobby Jones among them, played the course with delight.
There were handball and tennis courts; Lloyd frequently con-
ducted tournaments in both sports, with the contestants drawn
from his friends in the industry. In these early days, the Lloyd
estate was usually a festive place, especially on weekends.

At Greenacres: Joseph M. Schenck, HL, unidentified man,
Bobby Jones, Douglas Fairbanks, unidentified man.

Greenacres was a palace and Lloyd was king.

Young Gloria Lloyd's Tudor thatched-roof playhouse is located not far from the main house. Only five at the time her family moved in, she found herself the solitary mistress of a miniature cottage, fully equipped with real plumbing, electric lights, and a cooking stove that worked. The house was furnished with beautifully scaled-down furniture. A joy, perhaps, but a lonely one for an only child on a sixteen-acre estate. A Shetland pony was no substitute for what she so desperately needed—a playmate of her own age.

With this in mind, the Lloyds proceeded to adopt a child: Gloria Freeman, who had been abandoned by her mother only one hour after her birth. The child had been placed in the custody of a Mrs. Louise Sullivan, who operated a foundling home in Pasadena. After some severe financial reversals, Mrs. Sullivan was forced to put most of the children up for adoption. Four-year-old Gloria paid a trial visit to Greenacres in August 1930. A month or so later, she was legally adopted and renamed Marjorie Elizabeth, or Peggy, as she has been known for most of her life. Peggy was at first homesick for Mrs. Sullivan and the children at the foundling home and would call her in secret, begging to be taken back. But in time she seems to have adjusted to becoming Gloria's younger sister and playmate. The two little girls were always dressed identically until their mid-teens. Today, both women say they hated looking alike and put up with it grudgingly.

Within a few months both girls, as well as the parents, had a pleasant surprise: Mildred's unexpected pregnancy in the early summer of 1930. She gave birth to her second child, Harold junior, in February 1931. Born prematurely in the seventh month, an incubator baby, Harold weighed only three pounds. He remained a weak and fragile child during his early years, but in time attained normal health. Lloyd was extremely pleased to have a boy at last.

At thirty-seven, the father of the young heir looked at least ten years younger. His universal popularity had been recently reconfirmed by the financial success of *Welcome Danger*. When he began shooting his second talker, *Feet First,* in the summer of 1930, there were objective reasons for Lloyd to believe he had mastered the sound film.

2

His individuality is being submerged in a sea of dialogue.

—Welford Beaton

The great danger in a movie is to be boring. Without a story, even with the most incredible artistry, you will be boring. Without a story there is no movie. . . .

—Milos Forman

Welford Beaton, the publisher of *The Film Spectator*, continued to display his contempt for the talkers. In a negative review of Keaton's *Free and Easy,* Beaton left no doubt what he thought of a talking Keaton:

In putting him in *Free and Easy,* his first talker, Metro made the mistake of giving Keaton a vehicle in which he had to gain laughs by the things he said, not the things he did.

In the transfer to sound, Lloyd's foundation for his various comic characters was undermined by talk. The swiftly moving Lloyd, who told it all with his body, had disappeared, to be replaced by an argumentative young man who kept assuring you how nice he really was. This was precisely what had been

Peggy Lloyd, Harold Lloyd, Jr., and Gloria.

wrong with *Welcome Danger*. Lloyd knew perfectly well that he couldn't possibly hope for a success with another picture of that quality. Once, yes, but not twice. It had been only the sheer novelty of hearing him speak that had brought in the three million dollar gross.

After nine months of deliberation, Lloyd and his writers decided to go ahead with their next film, *Feet First*, portions of which were shot on board the S.S. *Manola* en route to Hawaii in June 1930. As he did with *Speedy*, Lloyd brought along his entire production crew, but outside of a single shipboard scene, the only visible signs of the Hawaiian trip are the authentic shots of the docks in Honolulu.

Feet First contained a lot less talk than *Welcome Danger* and attempted to resurrect the thrill factor that had contributed so heavily to the success of *Safety Last*. The result was a curious mixture of the old and the new that has dated very badly and is now rarely shown. More important, *Feet First* permanently established the public's perception of Lloyd's talking character in very much the same deadly way that Keaton's was fixed by his

(*Above*) Clyde Bruckman and HL on center platform. (*Left*) Shooting *Feet First* in 1930. Shooting platform and false facade in downtown Los Angeles.

Harvey Parry climbing the facade.

(*Above*) Harvey Parry sitting on windowsill of facade; Bruckman, in white shirt, standing on platform below.

Free and Easy of the same year. Despite the many differences, both films present their stars as doltish young men who possess not one bit of the poetic charm they displayed so strongly in their silent films.

The extremely weak story of *Feet First* concerns Harold Horne, a young shoe salesman in Honolulu, who strives mightily for the success he's sure will soon be his. There is a girl in Harold's life, in the person of Barbara Kent, the same leading lady he used in *Welcome Danger.* She is no better here, and one of the film's biggest weaknesses is the asininity of their romance. Falsely believing that his Barbara is the daughter of the shoe magnate whose favor he seeks (she's actually the secretary), Harold Horne is required to pretend that he possesses both wealth and sophistication. The deception finally leads him into stowing away on board the liner bringing Barbara and her boss back to California. What Lloyd and Clyde Bruckman were really concerned with in the first half of *Feet First* was how to get Harold into a situation that would justify a reprise of the great climb in *Safety Last.* Harold is required to deliver a manufacturing contract to the mainland by seaplane, in order to gain favor with the magnate. Just about to be placed in irons (they've discovered his stowaway status), he hides in a mail bag, which is flown ashore and accidentally placed on a scaffolding that immediately starts ascending the facade of an office building in downtown Los Angeles. Cutting his way out of the bag, Harold begins his climb to the top. After what seems an eternity, Harold leaves the building unscathed, to win the girl and the approval of his boss.

In *Safety Last* it was success that spurred Harold into continuing the climb; here there is no motivation whatever—it's only by chance that Harold winds up in the mail bag. This is climbing for the sake of climbing. The photographs on page 226 show in some detail how the shooting of the climb was accomplished. Although the facades were a little fancier, the techniques did not differ significantly from those used in *Safety Last* seven years earlier. The photos clearly demonstrate that at no time was Lloyd in the slightest danger from the heights so skillfully suggested by his technicians. The camera platforms and the false building facades needed to suggest the exaggerated heights were again erected on the roofs of several buildings in downtown Los Angeles. In the long shots, Harvey Parry performed Lloyd's climbing chores. As Parry now recalls it, there was then nothing terribly secret about his standing in for Harold. As a professional stunt man, he was expected to be reasonably discreet about the nature of his work, especially when it involved a star of Lloyd's importance. Since publicity shots like those on page 226 were being taken as the picture progressed, it was clear there was no possibility of keeping his presence in the picture a total secret. In the late seventies, Parry told Kevin Brownlow, "[I] never mentioned that I doubled Harold Lloyd until Harold passed on." Despite efforts to credit him for work on the earlier film, today Parry wants it understood that he doubled for Lloyd in *Feet First* but not in *Safety Last.*

While this 1930 climb is technically superior in every way to the one in *Safety Last,* it creates a rather different effect on its viewers. Here, Lloyd's every grunt and gasp can be clearly heard as he goes through his antics on the side of the building. It is likely that the harsh, labored sounds of Harold's fearful progress were dubbed in after the completion of shooting. But with the addition of sound, this climb is *too* real. The fun is only intermittent: Lloyd's desire to surpass *Safety Last* resulted in a picture that surely and powerfully terrifies but offers little more in the way of entertainment—it's almost too excruciating to watch:

[At the preview] I think the climb was about two and a half to three times as long as we intended to leave it. In other words,

the climb must have been at least three reels [thirty min-
utes], if you could *imagine* that. Well, we wore the audience
out. They were in one state of horror all the way through. At
first they got great fun out of it, but finally they got to the
point where they were tired, they couldn't stand any more of
it. . . .

One astute theater manager in Berlin coped with the situation
by deciding to turn off the sound track for the duration of the
climb. His audiences were reportedly pleased with the silent as-
cent.

Other factors worked against the film. Lloyd had picked the
worst possible time to make a film about success; most of the
audience saw the film in 1931 and 1932, the first years of
the Great Depression, in which the notion of success in the
business world contained an irony that few appreciated. Aside
from this unfortunate timing, Lloyd's character had undergone
a marked change from all its earlier incarnations. As the critic
Adam Reilly has indicated, Harold Horne obtains all his ideas
about how to succeed in business from the pages of a textbook.
All of Lloyd's previous heroes had eventually discovered (as in
Grandma's Boy and *The Freshman*) their *own* inner strength.
In *Feet First* and the films that followed it, Lloyd lost touch with
the basic motivating force that made these earlier characters so
likable.

This loss of what had been his unique quality began slowly to
undermine his popularity. The domestic gross for *Feet First* was
$1,068,098, nearly three quarters of a million less than for *Wel-
come Danger*. Things were even worse in the foreign market.
Here the film earned only $461,914, less than half that of
its predecessor. The picture produced worldwide grosses of
$1,589,263, barely half the total for *Welcome Danger*. The profit
margin was also sadly shrunken. At a production cost of $647,-
353, Lloyd's share of the Paramount grosses was $983,089,

leaving him with a profit in excess of three hundred thousand dollars but far below that of his previous films. Some of the blame for the falling-off can be attributed to the ever-worsening rigors of the Depression, but it is also clear that Lloyd had begun to lose some of his audience and that the relatively slow erosion of his hitherto solid popularity started here, at the beginning of the 1930s.

The appetite for talk was still voracious. The most successful film of the year 1930 has been almost forgotten, because it contains almost nothing *but* the endless talk of the popular radio team Amos 'n' Andy. But *Check and Double Check* was a one-time aberration. Tastes in film comedy were changing rapidly; the Marx Brothers, Eddie Cantor, and W. C. Fields were far more formidable rivals in their early sound films. After the Marx Brothers' debut in *The Cocoanuts* of 1929, the early thirties saw the four in their extraordinarily successful *Animal Crackers* (1930), *Monkey Business* (1931), and *Horse Feathers* (1932). Here there was a lot more than just talk. The mad logic of both their stories and their dialogue was something genuinely new in films, a quality never rivaled. After a superb appearance in the silent *Kid Boots* of 1926, a new, singing and talking Eddie Cantor returned to far greater acclaim in his first three sound films, *Whoopee!* (1930), *Palmy Days* (1931), and *The Kid from Spain* (1932). Despite their excellence, W. C. Fields's silent films, particularly *It's the Old Army Game* and *So's Your Old Man* (1926), were never outstanding successes at the box office. Like Cantor, sound gave Fields a brand-new audience, although it never became as big as one would have thought. He often required the support of an "all-star" cast, as in *Million Dollar Legs* (1932), *If I Had a Million* (1932), and *International House* (1933). The wonderful films in which he appeared as the central character, *You're Telling Me* (1934) and *The Man on the Flying Trapeze* (1935), were never as successful; Paramount dropped him in 1937. By that time, Cantor's career as a star had also largely run its course, as would soon that of the Marx Brothers. Everything these new talking attractions made after 1937 was simply a repetition of what they had done far better in earlier years.

A soundless bombshell suddenly exploded in this sea of talk. Just three months after the domestic release of *Feet First,* Chaplin's *City Lights* opened up to what many people in the industry thought would be an indifferent audience. His own releasing organization, United Artists, thought so poorly of the picture that they refused to meet his usual terms on the gross. Chaplin then released the film himself in New York City as a road-show attraction. The people in the industry were wrong, as Welford Beaton of *The Film Spectator* was happy to note.* In a world of endless talk, Chaplin's silent film managed to gross two million dollars domestically—twice as much as Lloyd's *Feet First.*

Chaplin's smashing success was startling in the face of all the predictions of sure disaster awaiting a completely silent picture made more than two full years into the sound era. In hindsight, while *City Lights* is one of his greatest triumphs, it is clear that only Chaplin could have succeeded with a silent picture at the beginning of 1931. His stunning confidence in his audience, plus his complete financial independence, made it possible for him to maintain his silence until *The Great Dictator* of 1940. Lloyd, on the other hand, was already committed to sound and couldn't turn back, but he believed there just might be a way to combine the best of the silent techniques with those

---

* Beaton had not lost his hostility to the talkers: "I frankly admit they are here to stay. They have neither the art nor the real entertainment value that the best silents had, but they have been forced upon the public, and there is no escaping them." He was still railing away at the sound film as late as 1941, the year that *The Film Spectator* suspended publication.

of the sound film. The result was *Movie Crazy,* generally regarded as his best talking picture.

3

> With everyone everywhere rushing into sound, I wanted to stage a last-ditch struggle for the silent film. I knew talkies would win when it was all over, but I wanted to hold off until the end so as to show how good silent films could be.
>
> —Yasujiro Ozu*

> That's one of the good things about my kind of comedy—all you have to do is look.
>
> —Lloyd

Movie Crazy was undoubtedly shaped by Lloyd's desire to win back his huge audience of the twenties, the one that now seemed to be rapidly leaving him. His solution to the problem was simple but effective: make a sound film interspersed with "islands" of silent, physical comedy, filled with all the visual gags that had always been Harold's strong point. He may have been influenced in his decision by Keaton's *Parlor, Bedroom and Bath* of early 1931, an otherwise dull film enlivened by a scene involving Buster in a sequence he lifted bodily from his *One Week* of 1921. Forced to abandon his Baby Austin car on a

---

* Ozu regarded Lloyd's work very highly, even going so far as to lift some of Harold's gags from *A Sailor-Made Man* and *Girl Shy* for his 1929 film *Days of Youth.* Ozu's college hero wears horn-rimmed glasses to complete the homage.

railroad track, Buster is delighted to observe that the fast express bearing down has come through on a parallel track. The reprieve for the Austin is momentary; a second train on the other track immediately smashes the car to bits. In an all-talk film, the sequence is a complete throwback to his silent techniques, and it is one of the few scenes in the picture possessing the slightest interest today. Made on relatively small budgets of about $250,000, Keaton's MGM sound films were grossing nearly three quarters of a million. If Keaton could get by with including silent spots in his films, why couldn't Lloyd?

But the triumph of Chaplin's *City Lights* was probably the major factor that induced Lloyd to return to some silent techniques in *Movie Crazy*. Harold Hall has come to Hollywood seeking success in the confusing new world of the talkies. As if to convince his viewers that a great deal of the old Lloyd was back, the opening shots feature him apparently riding in the

Shooting *Movie Crazy* in 1932: HL, Bruckman, and Constance Cummings.

plush back seat of a huge Rolls-Royce, recalling the beginning of *For Heaven's Sake.* As the camera comes a little closer, the car leaves the frame to the left, now permitting us to see Harold pumping away on his trusty old bike, which had briefly been keeping up with the Rolls. Recalling the opening sight gag at the railroad station in *Safety Last, Movie Crazy* proves to be a *Merton of the Movies* story, with moviestruck Harold being invited out to California because his father has inadvertently mailed a fan magazine a picture of a young man far better looking than his son. The mistake results in the offer of a screen test. Upon his arrival at the old Union Station in downtown Los Angeles, accident-prone Harold wreaks havoc upon everything connected with the picture being shot there. This is also the occasion when he meets the girl who is at the center of the most peculiar romance in all of Lloyd's films. She is performing in the picture, heavily made up as a sexy, dark-haired Latin. The actress is Constance Cummings, the only first-rate leading lady in Lloyd's sound films. Immediately smitten, Harold fails to recognize her as the same girl when she gives him a lift home that afternoon in her tiny car. Now she is blond, Waspish Mary Sears, who chooses to keep her two identities separate, alternately encouraging and repulsing Harold's advances in order to "test his sincerity." Her perverse behavior makes little sense and should have weakened the picture; oddly enough, it succeeds in strengthening it.

Perhaps aware that *Movie Crazy* would be taken as his "stand or fall" sound film, Lloyd and his staff came up with superb gag sequences that are fully as good as those in his silent films. One of the best involves Harold's presence at a gala social function attended by movie brass, with all the guests wearing formal evening dress. He manages accidentally to exchange dinner jackets in the men's washroom with a professional magician. When Harold returns to the dance floor, he discovers very slowly (and painfully) that "things started to happen. A little

Movie Crazy, 1932.

child's laundry came out of my sleeve and eggs came out of my sleeve and a pigeon flew out from under my coat and eggs came out of my sleeve and a rabbit was found. . . . '' There is something special about his boutonniere: it begins squirting a stream of water into his hostess's eye. With the room a shambles—there were white mice in that coat—Harold is booted from the party, another defeat in his search for stardom. The scene has been compared unfavorably with the one in *The Freshman* when Harold's dress suit comes apart on the dance floor. The argument usually asserts that there the scene was carefully motivated, while here it's all due to pure chance. In the long run it doesn't make much difference: they're both funny.

So is an extended sequence in which Harold ruins at least a dozen takes during his screen test. All he has to do is pick up a ringing phone and speak a few simple lines of dialogue. In dazzling bursts of invention, Lloyd manages to bungle the test again and again, each occasion differing from all the rest. Truf-faut may well have recalled this scene in *Day for Night,* which also contains a lengthy series of botched takes. Many of the scenes in *Movie Crazy* have a warmth of affection for the tech-niques of moviemaking, a love for the form itself that is rarely found in American films.

The picture concludes with a lengthy fight scene occurring again, as in *The Kid Brother,* deep in the hold of a ship. But this time we're on a movie-set ship with the cameras turning. After a violent confrontation with Mary Sears's drunken boyfriend, Harold is knocked out. When he awakes, he sees Mary being menaced by the drunk and flies to her rescue, not aware that he is now part of the film being shot. During the course of the struggle, the film's director is knocked unconscious, with a silly grin adorning his face. The cameramen keep right on shooting, convinced that his grin is a sign of approval for the authenticity

HL and Constance Cummings.

of the fierce conflict in the water. After subduing his enemy by repeated immersion, Harold is acclaimed for his "performance" as a brilliant comic actor and given the contract he's been striving for, as well as a single, undivided Mary.

Still taken with the value of trying out his films on audiences before releasing them, Harold screened *Movie Crazy* for a group of deaf people. They were baffled only twice during the picture. Although not up to the standard of his best work of the twenties, *Movie Crazy* is a minor triumph; many of its scenes have not dated and can still be seen with delight. Its relative failure at the box office was due to a combination of factors. When the picture was released in September 1932, it was the very bottom of the Depression; twelve million people were unemployed and in many areas of the United States movie admission prices had dropped to a dime. It was often difficult for distributors to collect the revenues earned by their films. A number of the leading Hollywood studios were either in receivership (Fox and Lloyd's own Paramount) or on the brink of bankruptcy (Universal, RKO, and Warner Brothers).

The excellent reviews *Movie Crazy* received were of little help, although they were the best he'd had yet for a talkie. Owing in part to the chaotic state of the industry, the picture grossed only $675,194 in the domestic market. The foreign revenues were a bit higher at $719,169, bringing the total gross to $1,439,182, a distinct falling-off from *Feet First*. Actually, the domestic gross of *Movie Crazy* was only about one half as much as its predecessor's. With a negative cost of $675,353, Lloyd's profit on the picture was a small one compared with the millions of the late 1920s.

Fully aware that he was now on what seemed to be an irreversible downward track, Lloyd and his business manager, William Fraser, tried to place the blame on Paramount. If the reviewers liked *Movie Crazy* as much as they said they did, why didn't the box-office receipts show it? It seemed obvious that the poor showing couldn't be *entirely* due to the Depression. It wasn't: when *Movie Crazy* opened in New York, the new Marx Brothers film, *Horse Feathers* (a Paramount picture), out-grossed it there by more than two to one. So, too, did Eddie Cantor's 1932 film, *The Kid from Spain.* It is clear now that if an impoverished audience was going to see a new comedy, it would be Cantor and the Marx Brothers who received the lion's share of the business. Even Buster Keaton's mediocre, cheaply made MGM films were earning grosses approaching three quarters of a million against negative costs of less than $300,000. Tastes were changing, but someone had to take the blame for the falling-off of Lloyd's popularity, and the Lloyd Corporation placed it squarely on Paramount's doorstep.

George Schaefer, the man who gave Orson Welles his contract to make *Citizen Kane* at RKO in 1940, was running the distribution arm of Paramount in 1932. It was to him that Lloyd and Fraser addressed their questions and complaints. Schaefer's reply to Fraser gives an insider's picture of what was plaguing the film industry at the end of 1932:

> Conditions haven't changed and if anything, they have become worse. Many of the important key situations throughout the country find it very difficult to do any downtown business. Chicago is simply deserted at night and in New York you are lucky to get three weeks on a [first] run picture at the Rivoli or Rialto. There is no such thing as a [first] run in Boston, Philadelphia, Pittsburgh or Washington; and in other important cities such as Denver, Birmingham, Dallas, Houston, etc. one of the first-run houses in each city named has gone into a split week policy. . . . Neighborhood and suburban houses are cutting their prices fast, some of them going as low as 10 and 15¢. My opinion is that you cannot stop that trend. . . .

Confining his letter to the economic crisis of the industry, at no point did Schaefer entertain the idea that Harold's pictures were becoming outmoded—that despite the genuine excellence of *Movie Crazy* it remained to some a bastard creation, half old and half new. More important, he avoided the painful possibility that Harold Lloyd had lost the thing that had made him unique.

Schaefer offered Lloyd and Fraser some advice about the making of Harold's next picture:

> The only "out" that you have is to make a severe cut in negative costs. I am as certain as I am of sitting here, that the time is past when outstanding pictures costing more than $500,-000 can make a profit. I think that we have to get back to an average negative cost of $200,000 or $250,000, and that only when we have a picture like A FAREWELL TO ARMS or a Chevalier or Dietrich, can we go to $500,000. Negatives costing $750,000 and $800,000 are out for many many years to come. . . .

(*Above*) On board the *Bremen* in 1933: HL with Primo Carnera and Irving Berlin.
(*Left*) HL in 1933 with Sonja Henie and unidentified man.

Harold's production costs were exactly in the area that Schaefer thought dangerous, but he was not about to take Schaefer's advice. From the very beginning, Harold had found his profits in products that *looked* expensive; he was not about to reverse himself in the middle of the Depression.

In the nineteen-twenties and early thirties, it was fashionable for the major stars to display themselves to their fans by traveling far to meet them. It began with Pickford and Fairbanks's triumphal tour of Europe in the mid-twenties that took them as far as Russia. Chaplin was ecstatically greeted by huge crowds in Europe in 1921 and again in 1931, when his trip became a worldwide, year-long odyssey. MGM treated Buster Keaton to a relatively brief European trip in 1930. In the early fall of 1932, convinced that *Movie Crazy* was his best sound film, the one in which he had integrated the best of his silent skills with talk, Harold took his family for a long vacation in Europe. When he began the trip he was unaware that *Movie Crazy* would be only a qualified success.

They spent six months in Europe, accompanied by some of Harold's staff: Joe Reddy, his publicity man, and Jack Murphy functioning as an aide de camp. The trip took them to England, France, Germany, Hungary, and Switzerland, where Harold met Sonja Henie, then a young prize-winning skater. Taken with her charm and vivacity, Harold told her what she might hope for in the way of a screen career in Hollywood, an expectation that became real when Darryl F. Zanuck saw her for the first time. After several weeks of skiing in Switzerland, Harold and Mildred left the two girls in school in Cannes while they continued their tour of Europe. They were entertained wherever they went; there was no doubt of Harold's continuing popularity on the Continent. Europeans may not have liked his sound films as much as the silents, but the silents were still close enough in time to be recalled with immediate pleasure.

When the Lloyds arrived back in New York in March 1933, they returned to a frightened America filled with long breadlines, banks that had only recently reopened, and a motion-picture industry whose current receipts were 20 percent lower than those of the year before. It was a land of foreclosures, salary cuts, and permanent layoffs. Closer to home, the cruel statistics about the relatively poor showing of *Movie Crazy* were waiting to be endlessly examined. The big question in Lloyd's mind that spring may well have taken this form: "If a first-rate composite film like *Movie Crazy* can make only a tiny profit, what am I going to do next?"

Although still unaware of Lloyd's faltering popularity in 1936, Welford Beaton accurately pointed out what had happened:

> Charlie Chaplin and Harold Lloyd are the only two comedy headliners who have retained their box office standing throughout the talkie revolution. Chaplin in a greater degree because he has kept his technique intact, has kept his silent appeal on the borderline of tragedy. Harold has gone over wholly to talkie technique, and only the mirth-provoking quality of his pictures, his reliance upon physical situations for their comedy values, make us overlook the fact that anyone of a score of comedians could play his part as well as he does and I could name half a dozen who could play them better.

Half a dozen is stretching it; Beaton was probably thinking of Cantor in 1936.

CHAPTER 10
HARD TIMES AT GREENACRES

1

If we have corned beef for dinner one night there has got to be corned beef hash for luncheon the next day.

—Lloyd

Harold fired himself on May 31, 1932. Considering the steadily decreasing income of the Harold Lloyd Corporation, he cut off his weekly salary of $5,000,* electing to live on his savings and investments, which now amounted to several million dollars. His investments had always been conservative, a blessing at a time when many business firms' stocks and bonds had become worthless paper. In August, he drastically cut the salaries of his major employees: William Fraser was cut from $1,000 a week to $700; Jack Murphy from $500 to $350; his brother, Gaylord, from $125 to $100. The Depression was at its deepest, and Lloyd was becoming apprehensive about its effects on the motion-picture industry. By the following spring, his worst

---

* A few years later, Harold was to resume paying himself a salary—this time $1,000 a week.

imaginings had become a reality. Paramount, by then in receivership, was having great difficulty collecting money from its exhibitors—there would be little or nothing coming in on *Movie Crazy* in 1933. On March 9 that year Lloyd made further salary cuts. Fraser went down to $350, Murphy to $175, and Gaylord to $50 a week.

For the press at least, economies were to be effected in his home in keeping with the general plight of the nation. With an establishment as grand as Greenacres, however, it was next to impossible to impose any significant reduction in expenditures. The indoor house staff consisted of nine: a cook and an assistant, a "major-domo" and his assistant, two nurses for the children, two upstairs maids, and a houseboy. Personnel outside the house included a pool boy, two chauffeurs, and eighteen gardeners. The fan magazines were eager to inform their readers how Harold was weathering the Depression and carried stories which included the grim details of his new austerity at home: "I want to know why we have used four dozen more eggs this month than we used last." The stories about Harold's frugality concerning the eggs and corned beef served at his table seem particularly silly if one recalls those eighteen gardeners.

Charge accounts had always been a vexing subject in the Lloyd home; Mildred had once run one up to $18,000. Now, in 1932, they were all canceled and her monthly allowance was fixed at $300. Christmas was to be celebrated that year with "cheap toys for the children." In actuality, the Lloyds celebrated a merry Christmas at St. Moritz in Switzerland. Neither the corned beef nor the cheap toys made the slightest sense in the real world of young Gloria's playhouse, where everything worked, and her birthday parties, at which Miss Shirley Temple became a regular guest. The austerity was mostly sham for the fans. Harold was still earning his reputation for being tight with money but, as always, he did not exercise thrift in the area of his own pleasures.

2

So we put two pieces of paper into a hat, "the old way," "the new way"—and we drew out "the new way"—and we abided by that.

—Lloyd

Still half-convinced that the failure of *Movie Crazy* was due to Paramount's problems, Harold began to look elsewhere for distribution. This was a major decision. He'd been Paramount's star attraction for seven years and finding a replacement would be difficult. Since *Movie Crazy* had come dangerously close to the line between profit and loss, he toyed with the idea of outside financing for his next film. Joseph M. Schenck, now on his own after resigning as president of United Artists, offered Harold $350,000 to make a new film—presumably Schenck would arrange for its distribution through United Artists—an indication of his continuing faith in Harold's strength at the box office. But Harold was also talking with his old friend Sidney Kent, the man who had given him his 1924 distribution contract at Paramount. Kent had left that badly stricken firm in 1932 to become president of the Fox Film Corporation, a firm with its own share of troubles, as Harold would shortly discover.

By 1933 the moribund Fox Film Corporation had been in receivership for three years. Its founder and president, William Fox, had been deposed by the banks and the American Telephone and Telegraph Company. Winfield Sheehan was chief of production for a firm whose films were negligible in box-office appeal, despite their generally high quality. A number of Fox's better directors had already left the studio or were soon to do so, including Raoul Walsh and Frank Borzage. There were two notable exceptions to the general mediocrity at Fox: the two lead-

ing box-office attractions of the mid-thirties, Shirley Temple
and Will Rogers. Without them, Fox would not have survived
for long. As a stellar attraction himself, Harold could demand
guarantees that his pictures would be booked on terms at least
as favorable as those accorded to Rogers.

Kent reiterated his belief that the failure of *Movie Crazy* was
simply one of distribution and that Fox could remedy that situation if they had a chance to handle Harold's next film. Fox,
however, was not willing to finance the film. Despite considerable worries about getting his money back, Lloyd turned down
Schenck's offer and borrowed $250,000 from a Los Angeles
bank at the now incredible interest rate of 3 percent. With this
money and a Fox distribution contract that was not quite as lucrative as Paramount's (Harold was to receive 75 percent as
opposed to 77½ percent), he began to think seriously about
beginning his new film. It was clear to Harold that it was time
to change his go-getter characters of the twenties. He began to

Peggy Lloyd, Shirley Temple, Harold junior, and Gloria.

Hollywood preview, 1933: Mildred, Carmen Pantages, and HL.

think about ways of making that character more believable in the harsher realities prevailing in the America of the early thirties.

Lloyd bought the rights to Clarence Budington Kelland's new novel, *The Cat's Paw,* which had appeared, as had most of Kelland's novels, in the old *Saturday Evening Post.* This was the first time that Harold had bought a literary property as the basis for one of his films. In choosing a novel upon which he could base the script of his next picture, Lloyd had reason to hope that he was now in the mainstream of the talkies, whose success or failure, many thought, ultimately rested on the quality of the *source* of the film. The evidence around him, however, was wildly conflicting. Two of Paramount's biggest hits in 1932 had been *A Farewell to Arms,* based on Hemingway's novel, and the Marx Brothers' *Horse Feathers,* a picture loosely assembled

Shooting *The Cat's Paw* in 1934.

The Cat's Paw, 1934.

from the four brothers' old vaudeville and Broadway routines. But Harold was not alone in thinking that the Marx Brothers were the exception that proved the rule and that one needed a strong story line to support a talking film. Kelland's novel had another attraction: MGM had bought the author's previous work, *Footlights,* which they transformed into Keaton's *Speak Easily* (1932). The result was a poor film but one that grossed over three quarters of a million dollars. Harold had wanted to buy *Footlights* but had been outbid by MGM. This time he won, obtaining the film rights to *The Cat's Paw* for $25,000, a handsome price in 1933 for a work of lightweight fiction.

Harold was apprehensive about embarking on his new film at the end of the summer of 1933. The perilous state of the economy, as well as his own steadily downward slide at the box office, made him hedge his bets. When he hired Sam Taylor, his frequent collaborator in the twenties, to prepare the script and direct the film, Taylor's contract, at $1,500 a week, contained a cancellation clause in case Harold decided to stop production by the end of the third week of shooting. Clyde Bruckman, the most talented of all Harold's "regulars," spent an uncredited twenty-one weeks working on the script. The shooting was to take place at the General Service Studios, with the addition of some exteriors shot at Harold's Westwood property.

A major decision had to be made at the outset, and it was then that Harold resorted to picking "the new way" from the hat, recalling the tossing of a coin back in 1912 when the decision concerned where Foxy and he should go—east or west. This time the choice was about how to make a film from Kelland's book:

> There were two ways we could do it; we could do it the old way that we'd always made all of our pictures, with business and gags, along the same lines; or we could do the picture the way

Kelland had written it . . . do it straight, let dialogue more or
less take the prominent place in the picture, and then just let
the business into wherever it belonged.

This decision became the death knell for the gag in Lloyd's pictures—the word had finally triumphed.

Despite the immense difference in their relative popularity
and consequent ability to pick what they would appear in, both
Keaton and Lloyd were by 1933 performing in exactly the same
kind of picture—plot films based on plays or novels in which
the humor was to be extracted from the situations created by
the scriptwriters. The improvisation of their silent days was
now mostly gone, replaced by the rigidities of the shooting
script. The irony here is that Keaton actually had no choice at
all; MGM thought it knew best what to do with the talents of its
major comedian. Lloyd, on the other hand, quite free to make
any kind of picture he wished, made the choice all on his own,
motivated by much the same kind of thinking that prevailed in
MGM and most of the other studios. In comedy films, story and
dialogue were the two absolutes of the day; the only exceptions
were the Marx Brothers' films, which lacked strong story lines,
while Chaplin's *City Lights* dispensed with dialogue.

By bowing to the demands of Kelland's book, Lloyd and his
writers were forced to abandon everything they'd learned in
nearly two decades of film-making. For the first time Lloyd is
not a Harold; he is Ezekiel Cobb, a missionary's son who has
been raised in China according to the philosophical principles
of one Ling Po. Upon his arrival in a graft-ridden California
town, Ezekiel is persuaded to run for mayor by the gang of
thieves who control it; they're convinced he'll surely lose.
Elected by a fluke and faced with the corruption all around
him, Ezekiel resorts to the principles of the ancient leader Fu
Wong, who took the law into his own hands by executing all the
known criminals in the Chinese nation. His modern disciple

accomplishes this task by putting on an impressive black magic show that is so well done that the criminals and all their supporters, seeing an apparent decapitation, are convinced they are in the hands of a fanatic who will stop at nothing. The criminals freely consent to their arrest, Ezekiel gets his girl, and all is well in a predictable end.

In 1958 Lloyd had no illusions about *The Cat's Paw*:

> I think if I had it to do over again, I would have done it the old way, and I think we'd have gotten more out of it. But a great many people thought this was fine and liked it that way. By doing it the new way, we didn't collect the amount of laughs that we had in some of the previous ones, but the story end of it was better. . . .

Lloyd was correct, the majority of the reviews were quite favorable. There are some genuinely funny moments, but at no time does the picture exhibit any of the brilliance of the silent Lloyd. The terrible truth of the matter is that it would probably have been a more interesting (and profitable) film starring either Eddie Cantor or Will Rogers. As a "straight" actor, Harold lacked the warmth of character that Rogers especially displayed in his films and that many American filmgoers now obviously preferred.

Sidney Kent of Fox repeatedly urged Harold to cut his production costs on the new film, pointing out that the Will Rogers pictures cost only $350,000 to produce (roughly the same amount as the Shirley Temple vehicles made in the next year or so). But Harold was adamant in his decision not to cheapen his films. Few economies were effected: he assembled a cast of expert players with Una Merkel as his leading lady and with George Barbier, Grace Bradley, and Alan Dinehart for support. There was even a musical production number for Grace Bradley to appear in, singing a song especially written for the picture. All this ran the production costs up to $617,000, not much less than for *Movie Crazy*. To begin to show a profit, *The Cat's Paw* would have to gross at least double its negative cost. But with a domestic gross of only $693,000, the picture wound up as a dead loss for both Lloyd and Fox. Even the foreign revenues were down, 20 percent less than for *Movie Crazy*. This was the first time that Lloyd had lost money on one of his productions.

Fox had even worse news for Harold at the end of the year. *The Cat's Paw* had been booked by the exhibitors on the same terms as those for the Will Rogers pictures. When Frank Harris of Fox wrote to William Fraser on December 31, 1934, he attempted to explain the exhibitors' hostility:

> This means that an exhibitor who grossed $1,000 on the last Rogers picture grossed roughly $700 on our picture. When he paid 30% for the Rogers picture he had $700 left for himself. When he paid 30% for our picture he had $490 left for himself. This . . . has brought many of the men to the point where they are willing to take the position that *it is all right to distribute Lloyd pictures but that they cannot get and do not deserve Rogers terms.* *

In plain English, Fox would be unwilling to grant Lloyd the same distribution terms on his next film. This meant that he must look for another distributor, as well as perhaps someone else to participate in the financing. The losses incurred on *The Cat's Paw* were not crippling, but they promised to be only the first in a series. By the beginning of 1935 Harold was aware that he had lost a great deal of his popularity and that only a miracle could arrest his decline. But he was not going to give up without a fight.

---

* Emphasis added.

3

The only trouble was that his character could not age; he concentrated so much on the dopey but likeable young man who always wins out in the end that he just could not carry it over into middle age.

—Hal Roach

By the spring of 1935 Harold must have known that his days as a major Hollywood star were, if not over, then perilously close to being so. Many of his old friends from the early silent era had already vanished from the screen. Mary Pickford made her last picture, *Secrets,* in 1933, while her former husband Douglas Fairbanks made his farewell appearance in the British-made *The Private Life of Don Juan* of 1934. Buster Keaton had been fired by MGM in 1933 and was now making a living by appearing in cheaply made two-reelers at Educational Films. Nineteen thirty-four had been the year when Gloria Swanson and John Gilbert, two of the greatest romantic stars of the period, made their last attempts at comeback pictures, *Music in the Air* and *The Captain Hates the Sea.* Both films failed badly with the public. Gilbert died in 1936 and Swanson did not re-establish herself until *Sunset Boulevard* in 1950. Among the major stars, only Garbo, Chaplin, and Ronald Colman emerged from the talkie revolution unscathed.

The problem of "unsuitable voices" had little to do with the fading of these stars: alcoholism (Keaton and Gilbert), changes in public taste (Pickford, Fairbanks, Swanson, and Gilbert), and aging (Pickford, Fairbanks, and Swanson) were the main reasons. In 1935 Harold was forty-two but physically still capable of playing characters a decade younger. But they were characters that audiences were finding harder and harder to admire. The talking Lloyd lost thousands of his old fans every time he released a new film. His performances were more than adequate, but his talking-film *persona* was relatively drab and colorless. He lacked that special magic of personality required to compete against the performers in the best comedy films made in the Hollywood of the mid-thirties. Many of these performers demonstrated that magic just as richly in their comic roles as in their dramatic ones: James Cagney (*Boy Meets Girl*), Cary Grant (*Topper* and *Bringing up Baby*), Gary Cooper (*Mr. Deeds Goes to Town*). The last of these pictures must have been especially painful to Harold, because it was based on a Clarence Budington Kelland novel, *Opera Hat,* written just after *The Cat's Paw.* But it is doubtful if Lloyd could have succeeded in filling such a role.

As Lloyd was his own producer, it was relatively easy for him to keep the fact of his eroding popularity largely to himself. Perceiving him in his public role as the smiling millionaire master of Greenacres, few would have suspected that each one of his films since 1929 had made less than the one before. While his output had now ground down to one new film every two years (he'd made two a year in the twenties), stories about Harold and his three children continued to appear regularly in the fan magazines. Although social life had gradually tapered off from the first flush of the early days at Greenacres, Harold and Mildred were still seen at all the fashionable openings in town. So far as the general public was concerned, as well as a good part of the film community, Harold Lloyd was one of the very few stars of the twenties who had managed to survive.

The secret was not as easily kept from the financial powers in the business. Unwilling now to gamble any more of his own money to make another film, Harold discovered that others shared his fears. Back in 1933 Joseph Schenck had been ready with the production money for *The Cat's Paw*; by early 1935, as the president of the new Twentieth Century Pictures, which

HL in 1936.

was about to merge with Fox, Schenck was not willing to advance Lloyd any money—certainly not the huge sums Harold required. Nor, apparently, was anyone else in Hollywood.

The money for Harold's next picture came from Adolph Zukor, and Lloyd was hired as a salaried actor for the first time since 1923. In the Paramount production of *The Milky Way*, Harold was paid $125,000 for his role as the lead and, perhaps as a concession to his former status as a major producer, the Harold Lloyd Corporation would receive 50 percent of the net profits. Despite the obvious comedown in status from being his own producer, Harold regarded the Paramount deal as a good one. He would be the star in a high-budget film without risking a penny of his own money. As a virtual guarantee of the new

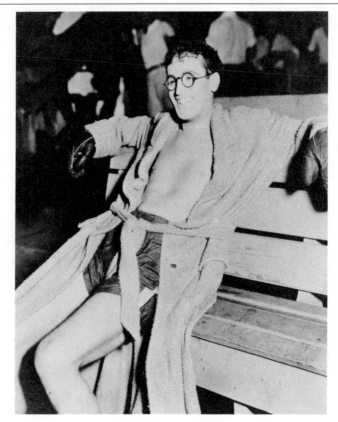

The Milky Way, 1936.

film's success, Harold's contract specified Leo McCarey as the director. By 1935 McCarey was the reigning director of comedy films at Paramount. After an apprenticeship with Laurel and Hardy for Hal Roach, McCarey directed Eddie Cantor in *Kid Millions*, the Marx Brothers in *Duck Soup*, W. C. Fields in *Six of a Kind*, Mae West in *Belle of the Nineties*, and Charles Laughton in *Ruggles of Red Gap*—all of these in a three-year period.

In McCarey, Harold was probably getting the best comedy director then working in Hollywood—a director of considerable range, as his impressive tragic film about old age, *Make Way for*

Tomorrow, clearly demonstrates. One reason for Harold's deep regard for McCarey's talents was his willingness to use silent techniques, as in the famous scene in *Duck Soup* in which Groucho is baffled by a Chico pretending to be his mirror image in a nonexistent mirror. This mime sequence was brilliantly performed in complete silence. In a world of endless talk, the scene seemed a blessed momentary return to the joys of physical comedy.

When Paramount bought *The Milky Way,* a short-lived 1934 Broadway play by Lynn Root and Henry Clork, they undoubtedly had Harold in mind for the leading role of Burleigh Sullivan, a timid young Brooklyn milkman who inexplicably becomes the middleweight boxing champion. At forty-two, Harold was saddled with his likable-young-man character, who was beginning to seem more and more of an anachronism. There is no evidence to indicate that Lloyd ever thought seriously of giving up his basic character entirely, as Chaplin finally did in 1939, when he began making *The Great Dictator.*

The timid milkman has only one dear one outside of his beloved horse: his young sister Mae, who works as a hat-check girl in a Manhattan nightclub. Beautiful young Mae is harassed one night by two drunken customers who are smitten with her charms. As is his custom, Burleigh arrives to take Mae home, but finds her warding off the combined assault of the drunks. Not caring for Burleigh's remonstrances, one of the brawlers swings at him. Burleigh's only defense against all opponents is ducking, a practice he adopted when too young to protect himself from his schoolmates. It is Burleigh's ability to duck that results in one drunk knocking the other out cold. When the police arrive, a puzzled young milkman is standing over the unconscious body of Speed McFarland, middleweight boxing champion of the world.

The fluke knockout becomes the springboard from which Burleigh is carefully launched to become a contender for

McFarland's crown, through a series of crooked bouts arranged by the champ's manager, Gabby Sloan. Sloan, an insomniac nonstop talker, is played superbly by Adolphe Menjou. Lionel Stander, in one of his early screen appearances, portrays the champ's dumb bodyguard and trainer. Verree Teasdale is Gabby's sharp-tongued mistress, who teaches Burleigh to box by playing waltz records, with the punch *off* the beat: one, two, *boom-boom*! The pioneer film critic Otis Ferguson observed at the time that Lloyd had the sense not to try to steal the show; it would have been a difficult task against such accomplished comic performers as Menjou, Stander, and Teasdale.

McCarey included a number of excellent sight gags, including a sequence in which Harold, as part of his fight training, bravely jumps over a hedge to find himself abruptly waist-deep in a stream we haven't noticed. There are several tantalizing moments, similar to those in Keaton's sound films, when the old, physical Lloyd is present, as when he instructs a society matron in the finer points of ducking. Burleigh wins the championship by an assorted variety of tricks, including knocking out the champ by giving him Gabby's sleeping medicine.

When Harold began work on *The Milky Way*, he had not performed in front of a camera for two years. He felt quite rusty:

> The first two days were a *tremendous* effort. You didn't feel at ease and you didn't do things in the way you should do them, and Leo [McCarey] came around and he said, "Harold, I can tell from the way we've run this stuff in the projection room, you're not too happy with those first two days, are you?" "Oh, no," I said. "They're pretty bad. They're horrible." He said, "Would you like to make them over?" and I said, "Oh boy!"

Otis Ferguson found *The Milky Way* to be a first-rate example of contemporary comedy at its best—the kind that became known as "screwball comedy": "Just as fine and crazy as anything that had ever been called by a new name for pure dumb lack of knowing the venerable branch of the family it honored." Ferguson, the first regular film reviewer for *The New Republic*, was not alone in his enthusiasm. His generous views were echoed by the popular press—the reviews for *The Milky Way* were among the best for any of Lloyd's sound films. His performance was praised by many and slighted by none. On the strength of his reviews, Harold had good reason to think that he had finally made a film that succeeded in bringing his old silent character unscathed into the sound era. In the first few weeks after the picture's release, Lloyd began to think that *The Milky Way* marked a revival of his fading popularity.

The painful truth only became clear later that summer. While *The Milky Way* was a great critical success, it could never hope to show a profit. The worldwide gross was $1,179,-192, but since its total production cost slightly exceeded a million dollars, the result was a loss of $250,000 for Paramount; there would be no profits to share with the HL Corporation. The film would have had to gross nearly twice as much to show a profit. Lloyd blamed the high production costs on Paramount (a lot of shooting time was lost because of the illnesses of various cast members, a factor that did escalate the final cost).

These explanations, however, avoid the complete truth about the financial failure of the picture: Harold had lost just enough of his old audience to tip the balance between profit and loss, and he was not picking up the new audience that he required to change the situation. Looked at today, Adolphe Menjou's performance is clearly far superior to Lloyd's; his superb comic style makes Harold seem relatively dull. Lloyd is more than adequate, but he's now playing a role similar to those being enacted by performers who could easily muster far more dash and style. Either Eddie Cantor or Bob Hope might have portrayed Burleigh Sullivan with a great deal more vivacity; the box-office receipts confirm this view.

4

The Milky Way was stolen by Adolphe Menjou. Harold didn't want a picture like that. . . . He wanted an old-fashioned silent picture formula, with dialogue.

—Elliott Nugent

There is conflicting testimony about Lloyd's family life at this time. The smiling side is recalled by British-born Kitty Lippiatt, who became Harold junior's governess in 1935, at about the time when *The Milky Way* was in production. Kitty worked at Greenacres until her "retirement" in 1943, but returned again in 1955, when she reassumed her governess position for Lloyd's granddaughter, Suzanne, a job she held until Lloyd's death in 1971. Kitty Lippiatt recalls a rather idyllic existence at Greenacres in the mid- and late thirties. There wasn't much entertaining; people came to dinner only two or three times a month. Chaplin came once; so did Maurice Chevalier. On weekends, Harold played a lot of handball with his photographer friend John Meredith. Most evenings at the house were spent playing games; Harold and Mildred played endless Parcheesi, rummy, and, later, Monopoly and Scrabble with the two girls, Gloria and Peggy. Bridge and poker were conspicuous by their absence.

Old Foxy Lloyd spent as much time at Greenacres as at his own home; his main task for the HL Corporation was taking care of Harold's fan mail and "autographing" pictures for him. Elizabeth Lloyd's visits were far less frequent. As a reward for her work with the Columbian Society, she had been appointed to the California State Board of Labor Arbitration. Proud of her younger son's fame as a film star, she indulged her "*grande dame*-ism" to the fullest by holding expensive and elaborate fancy-dress parties at her house on Roxbury Drive. In addition to his brother Gaylord, Harold's old retinue from the early days with Roach was still in regular attendance, especially Jack Murphy, who held the title of chief of production, and William Fraser, who attended to finances.

Harold's only close friend in these years, other than John Meredith, was Wally Westmore, the famous makeup artist who created the cosmetic firm that bears his name. In his forties, Harold was no more open to deep friendships than he'd been in his twenties. For a man with his energies and with an ever-increasing number of hours to kill, the result was an intense, feverish pursuit of pleasure. He became an incessant movie-goer, occasionally viewing two or even three new feature films in the same evening, usually in the company of young Gloria and Peggy. This would mean a tight schedule: racing from one theater to another in Westwood, Santa Monica, or Hollywood, and having his chauffeur stand by outside the premises. At the end of the picture, Harold would dash to his car and speed off to the next screen. Peggy Lloyd recalls this practice vividly, but not much about the films, for she and Gloria would often be sound asleep not very far into the second one.

Peggy is convinced that the emotional lives of all three Lloyd children were strongly influenced by Harold and Mildred's overindulgent behavior as parents. She recalls that she and Gloria took turns sleeping with their parents until they were at least twelve (in different beds; the adult Lloyds maintained sep-arate bedrooms), and Harold junior slept regularly in his mother's bed until he was thirteen. Peggy believes that these constantly changing sleeping arrangements confused the chil-dren and made them far more dependent on Harold and Mildred than they should have been. There is no question of Harold's genuine love for his children, but, as with so many other things in his life—the grandeur of Greenacres, the sixty-five Great Danes, the hobbies he pursued so vigorously—he had little sense of proportion.

Mildred Lloyd was often lonely at Greenacres. If Harold wasn't shooting a picture he was usually planning one; their time together was spent playing games. A need for company may have been the reason for inviting her best school friend from her youth in Tacoma to take up more or less permanent residence on the estate. This was Roy Brooks, a bald, six-foot-four former actor, who had appeared with Mildred in Harold's two-reelers. Witty, well-educated, and openly homosexual, Roy became Harold's social secretary, as well as the actual writer of all his correspondence. Harold's ability to write had not improved since his early school days.

Those relatively few people invited to the house were most often directors like McCarey and Elliott Nugent or comic actors like Lionel Stander and Sterling Holloway. Stander loved to argue for hours with Harold, from a consistently left-wing position, about the current political situation, while Harold retaliated by regularly beating Stander at Chinese checkers. Lloyd was invariably a genial, affable host, who never betrayed any evidence of worry to his guests, especially any concern about the decline of his career. Always determinedly cheerful, he outwardly displayed full confidence; since few knew the truth, concealment wasn't difficult. But by early summer of 1936 Lloyd knew that he had really lost the battle to remain a major star: only a miracle could have arrested his decline. It is to his great credit that he didn't simply give up, that he was willing to try once more, even if it did cost him his own money.

CHAPTER 11

PRODUCED, WRITTEN, AND DIRECTED BY PRESTON STURGES

1

From then on it was all Lloyd's money.
—Elliott Nugent

It took only a few months for Harold to discover the commercial failure of *The Milky Way*. By the end of the twenty-ninth week of release, it had earned only $614,500, even less than *The Cat's Paw* in the same amount of time. If Paramount had been aware that *Milky Way* would do that badly, it is doubtful that they would have contracted for another Lloyd film. But, on the strength of his extremely fine reviews, Harold was able in June 1936 to gain financing for *Professor Beware*. Fraser and Lloyd worked out an unusual cooperative scheme with Paramount for the production of the film. Paramount agreed to advance the HL Corporation $600,000 for the production, while Lloyd would supply any additional financing he might require for completion of the film. Paramount wanted a guarantee that if Harold went over his budget, he alone would pay the excess. Instead of drawing a salary, he would receive 15 percent of the gross receipts earned by the film, up to the first million. This money was to be paid him before any other deductions could be made.

Cameraman Archie Stout, Elliott Nugent, and HL on
the set of *Professor Beware*, 1938.

He was thus sure of obtaining a sum commensurate with his
normal pay scale.

Harold chose Elliott Nugent to direct the picture. A New
York stage director and later the coauthor with James Thurber
of the play *The Male Animal,* Nugent had started off in Hollywood as an actor (*The Last Flight*) but then turned to directing
films, including *Three-Cornered Moon* and *She Loves Me Not.*
Though scarcely in McCarey's class as a director, Nugent was
capable enough to direct Bob Hope in the 1939 version of *The
Cat and the Canary.* For his supporting cast, Harold picked a
number of the best comic actors working in Hollywood, among
them Sterling Holloway, Franklin Pangborn, Raymond Walburn, William Frawley, Cora Witherspoon, and, for the second
time, Lionel Stander. Within just a few years several of these
performers became regular members of Preston Sturges's stock
company.

The cost of making *Professor Beware* proved to be far higher
than anticipated. Still a perfectionist, Lloyd found the budget
problem oppressive. Aware that Paramount's $600,000 could
only be stretched so far, he knew that if he stuck within their
limits he would be starring in a cheap-looking film. Eventually

he began to invest his own money in the picture. Elliott Nugent recalled what happened, going out of his way to praise Harold's efforts to make the best film he could:

> We ran out of Paramount's money, and from then on it was all Lloyd's. Lloyd would say to his business manager, "All right, I'm not going to ask Elliott Nugent to make extra takes any more. We're going to be satisfied as soon as he's satisfied. We'll cut down, and we'll finish this as soon as we can."
>
> He'd stick to that for about one day and then go back. . . . When I got one or two takes that satisfied me, Harold would say, "Let's do it a couple of times more, because I'd like to try something different." Then we'd print about four takes. Then when we cut the picture, and made the selected take—which was sometimes his, sometimes mine, usually mine—he continued to cut it for about two months afterwards, going back and looking at all the outtakes and improving it—and he *did* improve it.

During his steady decline in the thirties, Harold had gradually divested himself of the creative group that he'd functioned so well with in the twenties. Although Sam Taylor had been brought back to direct *The Cat's Paw* in 1934, only Clyde Bruckman among Harold's original gagmen was working for the HL Corporation by 1936. With his production slowed down, it became impractical to keep the group on the payroll. Ted Whelan and Fred Newmeyer went off on their own, becoming unsuccessful directors. The absence of these technicians does much to explain Lloyd's ever-growing uncertainty about what to do next. When he'd been genuinely successful, as in *Movie Crazy*, he had the collaboration of Vincent Lawrence as screenplay writer, as well as the gag contributions of Clyde Bruckman, John Grey, and Lex Neal. *The Cat's Paw* had nearly dispensed with gags and made the old crew obsolete. In *The Milky Way* Leo McCarey attempted with some success to revitalize the old Lloyd formula, but this was a one-shot proposition. In making *Professor Beware,* Harold put his faith in the basic story line, just as he'd done with the Kelland novel that became *The Cat's Paw.*

His faith was again misplaced: what doomed *Professor Beware* from the start was the story devised for Harold by his three writers. Not even all the efforts of Clyde Bruckman, who adapted their story, nor Delmer Daves, who wrote the screenplay, could do much with their tall tale of a young Egyptologist who believes his fate has been foretold on an ancient tablet which relates the story of Nefurus, entombed alive because of his passion for a beautiful woman. Harold is the twentieth-century reincarnation of Nefurus who finds himself fleeing from a young woman bearing an unearthly likeness to his female nemesis in the past. The result is a cross-country chase picture which consists almost entirely of the chase. Some of the episodes are funny enough, as when, after a frenzied race, Harold hides his car in a tent. About to be discovered by his pursuers, he drives the entire tent down the road. But this is a return to the sight gag with a vengeance; the scene has nothing to do with the story.

There is a good sequence in which Lloyd, Stander, and Walburn are riding the rods on top of a fast freight train; a tunnel looms up ahead and the three men begin a mad dash for life toward the rear of the train. The main trouble with these gags— excellent in themselves—is that they seem just thrown in to salvage an insipid story. Or at least this is what the general public thought. The major critics weren't as harsh, but the press consensus was that *Professor Beware* was a tiresome collection of old sight gags.

The few really good sequences in the picture came out of Harold's determined need to *get it right,* the same need that he demonstrated in all his films. His determination was expensive: by the time the picture was completed in 1938, Lloyd had invested $220,275 of his own money. This amount, plus the $600,000 from Paramount, brought the total production cost up to $820,275. Within only a few weeks, the fate of *Professor Beware* was clear. In its initial worldwide engagements, the film earned only $796,385, or $25,000 *less* than its basic production cost, which did not include distribution costs, printmaking, or any of the other usual costs. The loss was mainly Paramount's, because they were supposed to recoup their investment from 85 percent of the first million earned. Their estimate of their own loss was a quarter of a million dollars.

Harold didn't fare much better: although he received his 15 percent off the top of the gross ($119,400), this still left him with a loss of a hundred thousand dollars. His repayment scheme called for him to recoup his expanded production costs only after Paramount had been paid back their original $600,-

Bowling night with family, 1939.

Supervising *A Girl, A Guy, and A Gob*
at RKO in 1941.

000 investment. It took another twenty-five *years* for *Professor Beware* to earn $933,063 (mostly through TV rentals), or enough to return most but not all of his investment. With figures like these, it was obvious that Harold Lloyd was no longer a star who could command the outside financing necessary to make his own pictures. It was equally clear that he wasn't going to invest any more of his own money in them. All the facts pointed to the immediate dissolution of the HL Corporation.

2

Hobbies must possess you to really let them do what
they can for you.

—Lloyd

When he understood the complete failure of *Professor Beware,*
Harold did exactly the same thing he'd done back in the fall of
1932: he reduced the salaries of everyone working for the HL
Corporation, starting off by cutting his own from $1,000 a week
down to nothing. Besides the fate of *Professor Beware,* there
was another good reason to cut back. He discovered that the

With Desi Arnaz and Lucille Ball, 1941.

combined expenses of Greenacres and the HL Corporation amounted to $157,000 per year. Since the corporation earned only $77,000 in 1937, this left a deficit of $80,000. Most of the expenses were entailed by the upkeep of Greenacres—$8,000 a month or nearly $100,000 a year. To absorb some of these expenses, Harold sold for $175,000 the forty-five acres of Westwood property that he'd bought in the 1920s to build his own studio.

Although reason dictated otherwise, Harold was determined not to give up the HL Corporation. For the next few years he kept hoping that the time would come when he could resume his own production. His staff, Fraser, Murphy, Foxy, and Joe Reddy, were just as loyal as they'd been in 1932. They accepted their 50 percent salary cuts and continued with their routine tasks. Creed Neeper, for example, continued to work in New York at the Paramount building on Times Square, sending back the latest figures on the older Lloyd films.

After spending several months on a film project based on the romance between King Edward VIII and his American friend Wallis Warfield, Harold gave up the idea when he realized that the king's abdication had destroyed the situation's comic possibilities. His next effort was to create Harold Lloyd Productions, a new firm that would make films starring other people—if the fans didn't care for Harold Lloyd as much as they once had, perhaps they might care more for some of the up-and-coming comic talents. The films were to be distributed by RKO, with Harold putting up most of the production money. The first of them was *A Girl, a Guy, and a Gob,* starring Lucille Ball and George Murphy. Harold had been right in assessing the talent, but his timing was off by a decade; it took television to make a major star of Lucille Ball. The second film was *My Favorite Spy,* with the orchestra leader Kay Kyser. Neither film was particularly successful. By the time he finished the second, America was at war, and Lloyd gave up producing films.

By 1942 Harold must have known that his career was finished. At the age of forty-nine, with his energies scarcely diminished, he had received a terrible blow, which he discussed with no one. In the past he had always been able to occupy himself with the current project; now there was nothing. He began to curtail his social life after 1938; fewer and fewer people were invited to Greenacres. To fill the time, Lloyd threw himself into the pursuit of his hobbies with his customary energy. He began to spend small fortunes on painting and stereo photography. In order to paint, Lloyd decided to study the nature of color, amassing a library of several hundred volumes. The results, mostly abstractions, are plainly awful by any standard, but he was able to arrange one-man shows in Los Angeles and New York. Harold couldn't paint, but his work in that field achieved its real purpose—to keep him busy.

The stereo photography went on for decades. Lloyd's photographer friend John Meredith estimates that Harold must have spent close to half a million dollars taking pictures. Some of these were pretty views of landscapes—he regularly entered them in competitions throughout the country, occasionally winning prizes. But the vast majority of his pictures, hundreds of thousands, were of beautiful young women, all of them naked. Harold's stereo slides have all been preserved. His nudes are of the type once described as "tastefully artistic," or perhaps more accurately as cheesecake of the 1960s *Playboy* variety.

It is likely that Harold had sexual relations with many of the young models who posed for him. John Meredith, who arranged for many of the shooting sessions, has no doubt about this. In these later years, Harold's sexual appetite was as vigorous as ever, although sex itself was perfunctory. He was apparently not interested in starting any kind of serious relationship with a woman. How much Mildred knew about Harold and his models is conjectural.

Stereo photography in the forties.

Harold was not particularly secretive about the nude pictures or his continuing interest in young women, especially when his picture-taking took him to Paris. Poking gentle fun at him in a 1962 *New Yorker* interview, the "Talk of the Town" writer noted that Lloyd was still using the same boyish vocabulary he'd had in the 1920s, filled with exclamations of "gosh!" "gee!" and "say!" Queried about his forthcoming trip to Europe, Harold responded by remarking that "a fellow can have a lot of fun in Paris." The remark prompted the interviewer to comment, "We got the perhaps erroneous impression that he was thinking of a trip to the top of the Eiffel Tower or an hour's rowing in the *Bois*."

While Harold immersed himself in his hobbies, Greenacres became progressively more isolated from the outside world. It could be a lonely place, especially in the long afternoons. As Kitty Lippiatt, Harold junior's governess, put it, "After 1939, the telephone didn't ring very often." By the beginning of the 1940s, Mildred Lloyd had embarked on her own hobbies, particularly the collecting of rare china. She maintained friendships with a number of women her own age (including Julie Brigham), who were invited over regularly for tea. She also spent a great deal of her time talking with her old friend from Tacoma, Roy Brooks, who continued to live over the garage at Greenacres. When Harold was making his last films, Roy was employed as an advisor on the costumes.

By the beginning of the 1940s Mildred had become an alcoholic, and the malady plagued her for many years. Her drinking was unpredictable. After long periods of abstinence, she would suddenly immerse herself in a period of heavy, solitary drinking up in her bedroom. These drinking bouts cast a pall over the house. But despite their occasional outbursts of rage over the drinking, Mildred and Harold remained fond of one another. When sober, she was still very much the woman he'd married in 1923—warm, impulsive, still girlish in her forties.

Gloria and Peggy Lloyd were raised on extremely strict lines. Both use the word "Victorian" when they recall growing up at Greenacres. Drinking was always forbidden; when they began going out on dates, Harold would insist on smelling their breath when they returned home at the end of the evening. Despite the grandeur of their surroundings, Harold was determined to teach the girls the value of money. They were both given an allowance of thirty dollars per month during the time they attended UCLA at Westwood; they traveled there and back on their bicycles. They were expected to purchase all their clothing from the allowance money, a next-to-impossible task.

Lloyd's daughters recall these years at Greenacres with mixed feelings. Harold's rigid standards of behavior were especially irritating to two good-looking young women. Since Mildred and Harold were obsessively concerned with the *kind*

of young men their daughters were seeing, the girls were sub-
jected to a running critique of their dates' personal appearance,
personality, and financial background. Besides his fear of alcohol, Harold was also wary of permitting the girls to drive; cau-
tionary lectures always preceded the use of the cars. There
were problems about dress; only after the age of sixteen were
the girls free to dress as they chose.

In their teens neither Gloria nor Peggy thought of herself as
the daughter of a famous film star: "We didn't know a movie
star from a plumber," as Peggy puts it. Harold's enforced idle-
ness after the failure of *Professor Beware* left him with a lot
more time to become an active father to his children. Despite
his playing the role of a Victorian *pater familias* to the hilt, both
Gloria and Peggy felt closer to Harold than to their mother;
Mildred never seemed mature enough to them. It was always
Harold's approval they sought, but he could be a difficult parent. Although normally ebulliently affable, he could become ill-
tempered or indulge in temper tantrums, especially if he hit a
losing streak in one of his favorite games. Then he might sulk
for days. But his powerful charm would soon break through, accompanied by his unquenchable energy. He had retained his
youthful appearance; at his fiftieth birthday in the spring of
1943 Lloyd appeared to be in his late thirties. Despite his continuing passion for ice cream, he kept his weight down,
through daily swimming and handball.

Harold's mother, Elizabeth Lloyd, died in August 1941. It is
perhaps significant that Harold fired her brother, William
Fraser, his business manager for twenty years, within a year
after her death. Lloyd became convinced that Fraser had been
inept in investing his money. An ultraconservative, Fraser had
placed Harold's millions in Depression-proof stocks and bonds;
as times improved, this form of overly cautious investment became less and less profitable. Harold took over his uncle's job
himself, but displayed equally poor judgment in his invest-

ments. Not until the 1960s, when he met wealthy businessman Richard Symington, Sr., did Harold, with the help of his new lawyer, Thomas Sheppard, finally get his investments into appropriately lucrative form.

As the war advanced, Harold became increasingly anxious to get back into films. Although it was clear that he was finished as a star, he could easily have obtained secondary acting roles in other people's films, but this course of action was out of the question for him. Early in 1943, he signed a $25,000 contract with Columbia to develop and write a screenplay for them, but the project never went further than its earliest stage. His rescuer from enforced idleness was to be an early admirer of *Grandma's Boy*, *Safety Last* and especially *The Freshman*.

It was Preston Sturges who succeeded in bringing Harold out of retirement when they made *The Sin of Harold Diddlebock* together. By 1944 Preston Sturges had created a screen world of his own in the series of comic films that made him famous: *The Great McGinty* (1940), *Christmas in July* (1940), *The Lady Eve* (1941), *Sullivan's Travels* (1941), *The Palm Beach Story* (1942), *The Miracle of Morgan's Creek* (1943), and *Hail the Conquering Hero* (1944). Sturges wrote and directed all of them, earning the reputation of being the "wonder boy" of the 1940s; he even got first billing in the ads. Unlike the films of Orson Welles, who came to prominence at the same time, Sturges's films were profitable, thus ensuring (all too briefly) his freedom to continue making them. A total eccentric and nonstop talker, Sturges operated his own restaurant in Hollywood while indulging his hobby of inventing Rube Goldberg gadgets. He had started off in Hollywood as a writer and, despite a successful foray into directing his own work, remained a writer to the last.

Sturges has been accurately described by the critic Manny Farber as "the only legitimate heir of the early American film, combining its various methods, adding new perspectives and

developing the whole in a form suitable to a talking picture."
What was especially significant in his relationship with Harold
was Sturges's joy in returning to the long-abandoned devices of
slapstick comedy. As Farber notes, he regularly combined these
with a kind of dialogue new to American film:

> Although it has been axiomatic . . . that the modern film talks
> too much and moves too little, Sturges perversely thought up
> a new type of dialogue by which the audience is fairly
> showered with words. The result was paradoxically to speed
> up his movies rather than to slow them down, because he
> concocted a special, jerky, spluttering form of talk that is the
> analogue of the old, silent-picture firecracker tempo.

With Ronald Reagan and Jane Wyman, 1944.

HL and Mildred with Ken Murray and Preston Sturges.

Contrasting Sturges's work with that of Capra, Wilder, and Wellman, Farber indicates that the last three "take half a movie to get a plot to the point where the audience accepts it and it comes to cinematic life. Sturges often accomplishes as much in the first two minutes, throwing an audience immediately into what is generally the most climactic and revelatory moment of other films." A doubtful conclusion, but one that clearly demonstrates Farber's passion for Sturges.

All of Sturges's films are satires on nearly every aspect of the values held dear by many Americans: business, patriotism, and motherhood. Many contain scenes of a bizarre madness unequaled by any other film-maker of his generation. In *The Palm Beach Story*, we encounter the aging millionaires of the Ale and Quail Club. Excited by the unexpected presence of young Claudette Colbert on their private Pullman coach, the members begin to drink away their inhibitions. Their hunting dogs are released to run wild through the train, shotguns are discharged, and complete chaos reigns aboard the train as it roars on through the night. In the midst of it all, the unfortunate Pullman conductors reproach the errant clubmen with shrill, piping cries of "Misdemeanor!" in a vain attempt to restore order to the stricken train.

Harold had been in Sturges's office at Paramount one day in 1944 when the newly famous director-writer was asked to be the host of a radio program to be modeled on Cecil B. De Mille's popular show, *Lux Radio Theater*. This was to be *The Old Gold Show,* hour-long dramatizations of current films, with the M.C. filling in details about the stars of the program, usually the ones who had appeared in the films. Sturges was far too busy for the undertaking but recommended Harold, who jumped at the chance to be in front of an audience again, even if it was going to be largely invisible.

Harold's brief radio career played an important role in the rehabilitation of Buster Keaton. By the end of the 1940s, Keaton was reduced to working as a gag consultant at MGM, earning a salary of $300 a week. Harold and Buster both employed Ben Pearson as their agent—Harold primarily for his radio work. When Pearson began to muse about the future of this new medium, television, Harold excitedly told him, "It's Buster Keaton that ought to be on television with all those sight gags of his!" Pearson agreed and Buster was soon starring in his own TV show in Los Angeles, one of the first steps in his slow but ultimately successful attempt at a comeback.

Admiring each other's work, Harold and Sturges quickly became friends. When he visited Greenacres, Sturges was taken aback by the somewhat dilapidated state of the mansion. After nearly twenty years of hard use, the house furnishings were beginning to look just a bit shabby—"the house began to look like a shopworn mausoleum," Peggy Lloyd recalls. Unless it was absolutely necessary, Lloyd refused to replace anything on the estate that had worn out. His refusal arose from a reluctance to spend money on something that was sure to outlast him. Sturges found the once-beautiful floor-to-ceiling drapes in the living room so horrendously tacky that he generously offered to buy new ones; Harold accepted his friend's gift with no hesitation.

Sturges had been eager to be independent of Paramount for some time; he resented their power over the fate of his unconventional film projects. The money for that independence soon came from another, even greater, eccentric, Howard Hughes, who believed Sturges was the most original talent working in Hollywood. Hughes created California Pictures for Sturges, who decided that his very first film would be a project involving the favorite comedy star of his youth, Harold Lloyd. A lifetime admirer of *The Freshman,* Sturges thought it might be fun to find out what happened to Harold Lamb after he won the big game for Tate College at the end of the picture. The film would be a sort of homage to Lloyd and his work. What made the idea especially attractive to Harold was Sturges's decision to include the final reel of *The Freshman,* the touchdown sequence, at the beginning of the film, thus perhaps assuring a new audience for the silent Lloyd. At the outset, Harold was convinced that "we could make one of the best pictures I'd ever made." On a budget of slightly over a million dollars, Harold was paid $50,000 for his participation as star, plus another $50,000 for the use of the *Freshman* segment.

The working title of the project was *The Saga of Harold Diddlebock,* but Sturges changed it to *The Sin* in order to parody the old Helen Hayes tearjerker film *The Sin of Madelon Claudet,* a joke few appreciated. The sad thing about Diddlebock was his dreary fate after one brief moment of glory on the football field. At the conclusion of the 1925 footage, Harold is accosted in the dressing room by Mr. Waggleberry (Raymond Walburn), who offers him a bookkeeping job in his ad agency. We then see

The Sin of Harold Dibblebock, 1947, with Jimmy Conlin.

a young, idealistic Harold sitting at his desk, surrounded by the cheerful adages that adorn the walls, all of them asserting the joys of hard work. The passing of the years, ever quickening, is indicated by the various presidential faces, Harding to Truman, on the turning pages of the calendar. After twenty-two years in the same job, Harold has not advanced one inch; but his clothing has become noticeably moth-eaten. He has proposed to and been rejected by all seven Otis sisters, who filled the position of office girl over the years. Mr. Waggleberry fires Harold, telling him, "You have not only ceased to go forward, you have gone backward. You have not only made the same mistakes year after year, you don't even change your apologies."

After clearing out his desk and bidding the last Miss Otis good-bye, Harold encounters "Wormy" (Jimmy Conlin), a diminutive racetrack tout who escorts him to a nearby bar for his very first drink. The unique concoction invented there by the bartender (Edgar Kennedy, famous for his slow burn) causes Harold to lose the inhibitions of a lifetime. Now gloriously drunk, and on the threshold of a new life, he purchases a plaid suit that could not be rivaled for loudness. The salesman is prissy Franklin Pangborn, another member of Sturges's regular stock company. With his new identity as a success firmly in place, Harold buys a circus with his entire life savings.

Harold and Sturges apparently had no disagreement concerning the first third of the picture:

> Any scene I had to do, he said, "Harold, how do you figure you'd like to play this?" I'd say, "I'll think it over and bring it to you in the morning." I'd come in the morning with a version of how I thought it should go. He'd say, "That's it." We had no trouble. We just seemed to be in complete harmony.

The ever-increasing trouble between them arose from the final portion of the script; according to Harold, Sturges had worked on the first third of it for three or four months, while "the last two thirds he wrote in a week or less." They differed in two major areas: Sturges fell in love with the idea of Diddlebock's buying the circus, to the exclusion of all the other comic ideas that he and Lloyd had originally projected:

> There were so many themes that could have come in there. But he didn't want gags to come into it, he wanted this dialogue. But this called for business, it just cried for it. I came to him with business, and he said, "Well, the business is too good for my dialogue!" I said, "Preston, this is terrible." He said, "It'll kill the dialogue." I said, "*Let* it kill the dialogue, what are we after? We're after entertainment, laughs."

But Sturges was adamant about his dialogue and Harold gave up looking for "business."

The other point of difference between them lay in the way they regarded Diddlebock. Lloyd was eager to win the audience's sympathy, as he had always sought to do when making his own films: "They must like you. They must work with you, and of course laugh with you, at your idiosyncrasies and your mistakes, but at the same time, they like you and they're with you and trying to help you." But Sturges preferred to treat Diddlebock in the way he usually treated the objects of his satire—as a half-mad dolt, caught up in a whirlwind of chance events. Both men had foreseen the possibility of differences of opinion about making the picture:

> I had a section in my contract that if I didn't like it, I could play it the way I wanted. . . . That meant that in the projection room, we had to argue it out, and we didn't fare any better in the projection room than we had on the set. For about two weeks, we made two versions, two scenes, each way.

At the heart of their quarrel was an irreconcilably different approach to making films. Preston Sturges was not about to give up one second of the dialogue that had made him internationally famous. While Lloyd's rendition of Sturges's lines in the picture is faultless, he knew instinctively that the Sturges script's virtue lay only in its opening scenes; the central idea of what became of Harold Lamb had not been sufficiently developed. There just wasn't enough material in the script to sustain a ninety-minute film. Harold attempted to convince Sturges that the addition of some physical comedy routines might save the day, but Sturges's only concession in this area was for Harold to perform what amounted to a reprise of the "danger at great heights" idea from *Safety Last*.

Harold and Wormy take a lion along with them on a fund-raising trip to the offices of a Wall Street banker. The lion decides to take a stroll along the window ledge thirty stories above the yawning chasm of the street. Within a short time, Wormy and Harold are dangling over the street, held back from falling only by being fastened to the chain around the lion's neck. But it's clear that the sequence was filmed against a process background, and it lacks any of the art that Harold displayed in *Safety Last* and *Feet First*. Harold rightly objected to this sequence: "He'd have you put to a height, and then if you wanted to go any higher, you couldn't, you were already up there. You don't leave any space to reach a climax."

After a superb beginning, Diddlebock became a film in which characters scream their way through an increasingly silly plot. Shooting scenes in two different versions caused the picture to exceed its original budget. The total cost ran to $1,712,959, with Harold earning another $40,000 in addition to his original $50,000. Shooting began on September 12, 1945, and was not completed until January 29, 1946; the picture had been scheduled for completion in 64 days but took 116. All of Harold's fears about the fate of the picture were realized by a generally apathetic reception at the hands of the critics and the public. Although all the decisions were Sturges's, he had duplicated Harold's policy on *Cat's Paw, Milky Way,* and *Professor Beware* by spending far too much money. A $1.7 million *Diddlebock* would have had to do remarkably well at the box office to show a profit; the relatively mild reaction to it caused it to lose money. After its initial opening in early 1947, Howard Hughes removed the picture from circulation, cut it again, added a terrible ending with a talking horse, and reissued it in 1951 through RKO as *Mad Wednesday*. This version encountered an audience even more unresponsive than the first.

Luckily for his continuing friendship with Sturges, Harold was able to deflect his anger about what had happened by suing Howard Hughes, the California Corporation, and RKO for damages to his reputation "as an outstanding motion picture star and personality." The defendants were persuaded to offer a settlement of $30,000, which Harold accepted, but the whole experience left a bad taste. *Diddlebock,* which had started with so much hope, was Harold's farewell to films.

CHAPTER 12

"JUST CALL ME HARRY!"

1

I just don't like pictures played with pianos. We never intended them to be played with pianos, . . . that's not the way the public saw them.

—Lloyd

I'm just turning forty and taking my time about it.

—Lloyd

A smiling portrait of Harold adorned the cover of *Time* in the summer of 1949. The occasion was his election as the Imperial Potentate (or "Pote") of the Ancient Arabic Order of the Nobles of the Mystic Shrine, a fraternal organization then claiming 75,000 fez-wearing members. Shriners must be top-echelon Masons, either Knights Templar of the York Rite or thirty-second-degree Masons, which is the highest rank for the parallel Scottish Rite. Freemasonry sprang up in the eighteenth century as a secret society in England, quickly spreading its doctrines of fraternity, equality, and enlightenment to continental Europe and eventually all over the world. Mozart was a Mason, and Pierre Bezukov in *War and Peace* becomes an avid one. Masonic ritual is based on biblical stories. The white lamb-

skin apron worn by members signifies innocence; trowels sig-
nify brotherly love. In contemporary America, as elsewhere,
men often become Masons because they feel it may aid them in
their business or political careers; more than a dozen American
presidents have been Masons, including Theodore Roosevelt,
Franklin D. Roosevelt, and Harry S. Truman.

Foxy Lloyd had urged Harold to join the Masons with him in
1924*; they became Scottish Rite practitioners. Over the years,
Harold advanced through all thirty-two degrees: Grand Master
Architect, Prince of the Tabernacle, Grand Inspector, and In-
quisitor Commander. With his customary thoroughness, he
then started all over again with the York Rite and advanced to
the top grade of Knight Templar. In the Imperial Divan of the
Shrine, Harold made use of all his considerable charm against a
sea of contenders for the post of Imperial Potentate or chief officer. He told his friends that winning the job had given him
more satisfaction than anything he'd done in the past ten years.
It was gratifying to be a celebrity again.

During Harold's long involvement with the Shrine, his time
was largely spent as a national trustee in administrative work
connected with running hospitals for crippled children built
and financed by the organization. A great deal of his time in the
fifties and sixties was devoted to this work, about which he
modestly remarked, "When you do those things for children
you can't help get a great satisfaction. . . . You can't help a little
crippled child uphill without getting closer to the top yourself.
And that's the joy that I have had out of working with the
Shrine." Not normally drawn to philanthropic enterprises,
Lloyd seems to have been attracted to the Shrine as an outlet
for his huge energy. He spent so much of his time on Shrine ac-

---

* Foxy died in Palm Springs in 1947 at the age of eighty-three. He continued to write
letters to his "Speedy boy" to the end.

tivities that his granddaughter, Suzanne, believed for years that Harold's occupation must surely be hospital administration.

By the end of the 1940s silent films and their makers had been largely forgotten. A generation had grown up completely ignorant of the power and beauty of silent film. Only a tiny band of dedicated collectors did much to preserve the past, most of it now perilously close to extinction because of nitrate disintegration. Among the great silent comedians, Langdon was dead, a forgotten Keaton was working at MGM as a gag consultant, in addition to doing bit parts, and Lloyd was now familiar to many only as an Imperial Potentate. Chaplin alone was still making

The Grand Potentate on the boardwalk in Atlantic City.

films, although much of his fame at this time was due to the public outrage over his continued British citizenship, a paternity suit, and his support of left-wing causes. His only film in these years was *Monsieur Verdoux* (1947), which he quickly withdrew from circulation after a disastrous reception—most of it based on acrimony toward its maker.

When James Agee published his famous *Life* magazine essay "Comedy's Greatest Era" in 1949, he singled out Lloyd's work for high praise, along with that of Chaplin, Keaton, and Langdon. Agee's article, later reprinted in *Agee on Film*, was one of the earliest essays in film criticism to point out accurately the great achievements of the silent comedians and the tremendous losses incurred by film comedy because of the arrival of sound. Agee's article was the first significant step in the revival of interest in silent comedy, although Chaplin had reissued *The Gold Rush* in 1942. This was a shortened version, containing a musical soundtrack in addition to Chaplin's own commentary about the antics of what he now liked to call "the little fellow." Despite this weakening of the original, the 1942 *Gold Rush* was quite successful in wartime America. Until the beginning of the 1950s, Chaplin was the only silent-comedy star to attempt a revival of his pictures.

Lloyd began his reissue program with caution. Rather than start with a silent film, he chose in 1949 to reissue *Movie Crazy*, a picture he correctly felt had never really been given a chance. The only alteration he made was to cut the picture by twenty minutes. Although not at all in the *Gold Rush* class, the shortened version was reasonably successful. If it had fared as well as Chaplin's, Harold might then have embarked on a reissue program for all his major silent films. But he was apprehensive about the way they might be received:

If I thought there was a demand with the public for the pictures, I would love to release a great many of them. I feel very loathe to release any of them unless I feel they're really wanted and desired. . . . That's the reason I took it to Hollywood High down here. . . . Their whole response was tremendous because they didn't miss a gag; even anything that was a little subtle, they got it right away down there.

Harold took several of his best silent films to colleges around the country (Purdue, Ohio State, and the University of Illinois), in order to get reactions from the students. He had one doubt about the considerable enthusiasm displayed:

The question is: are they [the general public] going to come and see it? Now, what's the use of releasing pictures in the theaters if they don't know you and they don't know what they're going to see? Therefore, they don't come to see it.

Lloyd went on to demonstrate that his pictures were guaranteed to be successful with modern audiences "if they could be conditioned." What he meant was that his audience should know in advance they were coming to see a silent Lloyd under optimum conditions—new prints projected at the correct speed and accompanied by a pipe organ or an orchestra. The dilemma, as he saw it, was how to achieve these conditions with a mass audience; without it, he saw only failure. As late as 1969, he had found no solution to the problem.

The possibility of selling his films to television came up frequently in Lloyd's later years. He told a Beverly Hills audience what his terms were:

I've had many offers. My price is a little high. . . . I don't mind telling what I'm asking. They've come close to it, but they haven't come up. I want $300,000 for two showings. That's a high price, but if I don't get it, I'm not going to show it. That's it.

Lloyd's prices were outlandish, quite unreal even by 1960 standards. It is clear he had no real desire ever to see his films shown in chunks fitted into prime-time TV slots. He would have no control over the speed at which they were shown—in those days always at sound speed—a fate he dreaded with good reason.* In the late fifties and early sixties a popular TV program, accurately enough called *Fractured Flickers,* took special delight in showing silent films at the faster sound speed for the sake of the cheap and easy laughs desired by its producer. In addition to being shown at the wrong speed, the films were accompanied by the dreadful kind of music identified as "rinky-dink." TV was clearly not yet a medium for showing silent films.

Lloyd had taken his career seriously from the beginning. Oddly similar to F. Scott Fitzgerald in this respect, Lloyd preserved anything about it that he thought might be of interest. Both men were concerned with documenting their careers; the huge amount of material concerning Fitzgerald has been attracting scholars to Princeton University for years. Harold went further with his documentation because there was considerably more to document. He employed a small army of people over the years to clip out anything that appeared about him in print and to paste it down in huge ledger-size scrapbooks. This practice

---

* Silent films shot prior to 1925 and projected at sound speed (24 frames per second) appear ludicrously speeded up. The situation worsens on TV, where the speed is increased to 25 frames per second. Silent films were originally projected at a variety of speeds, determined by several factors, including the projectionist's feeling about the film and, more important, the instructions contained in the musical cue sheets distributed with the film. Modern equipment usually permits only two choices: "silent" speed at 16 to 18 frames per second (far too slow) and "sound" speed (a little too fast). Neither alternative is satisfactory, with the ideal speed somewhere in the neighborhood of 20 to 22 frames per second. This condition can only be realized with equipment utilizing adjustable controls, a solution now possible with the latest technical advances.

Kevin Brownlow suggests that sound speed is satisfactory for most silent films made *after* 1925, when motor-driven cameras replaced the hand-cranked ones. This solution does not work equally well for all films: *The General* seems to flow by far too fast at sound speed. Variable control is certainly preferable.

began in 1919 and continued until the very last of Harold's own films in 1938, *Professor Beware*. All seventy-eight scrapbooks have survived; they stand in stacks about five feet high, along fifteen feet of wall. Vanity may have played a large part in this endeavor, yet it surely attests to Lloyd's conviction that a future generation would be interested in him.

All three of Lloyd's children were eager to enter show business, with Gloria Lloyd coming closest to success. Her great beauty brought her a contract with Universal Pictures just after the war; she appeared in 1946 as the second female lead in a Merle Oberon film, *Temptation,* followed by small roles in several other pictures. In 1950 she married William Guasti, son of a wealthy wine merchant. A daughter, Suzanne, was born in 1952, but Gloria's marriage foundered and she obtained a divorce the following year. In fragile health for many years, she spent a large part of the next decade traveling in Europe, causing Harold to change her nickname affectionately from "Glo" to "Global." Harold and Mildred, now nearing sixty, found themselves raising young Sue as if she were their own daughter.

Gloria's adopted sister, Peggy, married Almon B. Ross not long before Gloria's wedding. After bearing a son, Peggy found her marriage a failure. She divorced Ross, remarried him, then divorced him a second time. In the mid-fifties, Peggy married the actor Robert Patten, by whom she had another son; this marriage also ended in divorce. Mildred Lloyd had disapproved of both Peggy's husbands and indicated that she was no longer welcome at Greenacres; as a result Gloria and Harold paid her secret visits. Peggy had economic difficulties in these years, often working as a model as well as doing stand-in assignments for a number of actresses. She eventually concocted a clever nightclub act built around her considerable abilities as a psychic reader. Harold came to the show regularly, telling her, "I don't believe a single word of it, but you're phenomenal." Peggy's adventures with magic may have prompted Harold to revive his own early interest in the art. In the 1950s, calling himself "Clayton the Great" and assisted by Roy Brooks, Harold put on a series of performances for guests at Greenacres, featuring "The Mental Marvels" in "Crystal Gazing Supreme." Harold loved the opportunity to dress up and perform and used his comic abilities to the utmost.

Exceptionally personable, Harold junior attempted both singing and acting careers. Despite a number of major nightclub engagements in New York and Hollywood, his singing career did not advance significantly. Nor did his brief acting career in films, where he appeared in a wide variety of cheaply made science fiction and "youth" pictures. Harold attempted to help his son as best he could by appearing with him on talk

Christmas at Greenacres, 1955. *Front:* Almon Bartlett Ross, Jr., Peggy, HL, Mildred, Gloria and Suzanne, Harold junior. *Back:* Dorothy Davis, Cindy Davis, Howard Davis, Caroline Davis, Roy Brooks, Jean Graham.

Buster Keaton and HL in Rochester, New York,
at George Eastman House in 1955.

shows, but even with this encouragement nothing seemed to
work. Lloyd would try to console "Dukey" by telling him, "It's
not important what kind of a job a man has as long as it's well
done."

When Harold discovered that his son was homosexual, he
was admirably mature about the news—a rare reaction in the
late forties. In fact, Dukey Lloyd and his father remained close
through many difficult periods. Still, the rapport was frequently
brought to the test, for young Lloyd was, like his mother, an alcoholic, and there were limits to Harold's tolerance. He drew
the line when Dukey brought his various lovers to the house;
these visits nearly always wound up in scenes of alcoholic violence. Part of the problem was that young Lloyd had an unfortunate propensity for choosing violent lovers and he would often
return to Greenacres bloody and battered.

Although he frequently quarreled with the children, Harold
maintained close emotional ties with them. He regarded Peggy
as rebellious in her decision to go out with young men who did
not meet with his or Mildred's approval. There were many
clashes over allowances or just when the children had to return

1959: with Suzanne in Nice.

home at night. The results of the quarrels were unpredictable: "You could fight him up to the point where he began to think he'd lost your love—then he might give in," Peggy comments, recalling Harold's struggles with her when she and Gloria were attending college.

As he entered his early sixties, Harold showed no sign of relaxing into conventional middle age. In addition to his continual traveling for the Shrine, he was now occupied by a new role as surrogate father of young Suzanne. His hobbies were as important to him as ever—when *Time* ran a cover story on him in 1949, they observed that he "rides a succession of hobbies with grim preoccupation." Physically he was nearly as trim as ever: bowling, swimming, and handball kept him that way for the next decade.

2

Harold Lloyd was a strange, strange human being.
—John Meredith

That old house came alive again!
—Rich Correll

By the beginning of the 1960s, Lloyd had become convinced that the only way he might find a new audience for his silent films was through the device of assembling their greatest moments in compilations with accompanying musical sound tracks. The first of these was *Harold Lloyd's World of Comedy,* which included some of the high spots from *Safety Last, Why Worry?, Girl Shy, Hot Water,* and *The Freshman.* To demonstrate that he was not entirely a creature of the twenties, Harold also included scenes from *Feet First, Movie Crazy,* and *Professor Beware.* As pure entertainment the film is superb, although some critics have justly observed that it depends far too much on the use of climaxes, without any of the motivation necessary to understand them. The film was first shown at Cannes in the summer of 1962 and received a standing ovation from an audience of perhaps the most sophisticated filmgoers in Europe. It went on to earn several million dollars in bookings throughout the world, enough to encourage Harold to repeat the process in 1966 with *Harold Lloyd's Funny Side of Life.* This time only silent pictures were chosen: excerpts from *For Heaven's Sake, The Kid Brother,* and *Speedy,* but with *The Freshman* virtually complete. As with the previous compilation, special music was written by Walter Scharf. This second attempt did not fare nearly as well and was shown mainly in Europe.

The circulation of these two films did much to reawaken interest in Lloyd. Additional attention was created by the long chapter devoted to him in Kevin Brownlow's *The Parade's Gone By* of 1969, the book that stirred curiosity about silent films more than any other. Until this reawakening of interest, Lloyd's critical reputation had become embalmed in various misconceptions about his work. One of these is based on the assumption that Harold Lloyd was a comedian of the silent era who climbed tall buildings for comic effect and did little else. Another, and a far more misleading way of regarding Lloyd, has been to think of his comic *persona* as the quintessential brash, smart-assed young American of the 1920s—a character now and forever trapped in our national past. Both beliefs are equally false: Lloyd did a lot more than climb, as his films of the twenties, from *Grandma's Boy* through *Speedy*, clearly demonstrate. These films also display a far wider range of characters than is generally believed—including the coward of *Grandma's Boy*, the cocky young cab driver of *Speedy*, and the male Cinderella of *The Kid Brother*. Younger audiences in the sixties

1960: with Harold junior.

March 1961: At the screening room of Twentieth Century-Fox in New York City after a screening of *The Freshman.*

and seventies have become aware that the Harold Lloyd of the film textbooks—the "daredevil"—is not necessarily the one they now encounter. A recent article in *American Film* claims:

> [Harold Lloyd] turns out to be a lot more complicated than anyone thought. [*Safety Last, For Heaven's Sake,* and *The Kid Brother*] amaze college audiences with the dexterity of their gags and intrigue with their perversity. Lloyd's hero greets sexual contact with dumb pride or bolting terror. He revels in embarrassment, and, when all else fails, he is capable of astonishing violence.

Lloyd did a lot of traveling in these last years. The pages of his late-1960s passports are filled with visas from all over the world, including the Middle and Far East. Some of the junkets were concerned with invitations to show his films, but many were just sightseeing trips. After their initial interviews with Harold in New York in 1958, Joan and Bob Franklin ran into Harold in London several years later. Following a pleasantly prolonged dinner, Lloyd seemed reluctant to part with his guests—apparently ready and willing to make a long night of it in the entertainment world of London's West End. They were impressed by his vitality and youthfulness and, most of all, by his eagerness to discuss his films with them, hour after hour.

The television producer Peter Robeck relates much the same story of a man who gave no sign of accepting the fact of increasing age. At seventy and beyond Harold Lloyd loved the pleasures of life and worked hard to secure them. The only slight concession he may have made to aging was to subtract three years from the date of his birth on passports; his new birthdate was April 20, 1896.

His superstitions were just as strong as ever, and now he added a new one. This had to do with absentmindedly hiding odd currency in books; over the years thousands and thousands of dollars were salted away in various volumes around the house. Once the money was discovered, however, it was immediately placed in the safe. Harold was convinced that finding his own money was a sign of especially good luck.

Because of the huge amount of time devoted to his hobbies, Lloyd's social life at Greenacres was relatively scant in the sixties—at least that involving people his own age; Colleen Moore was a notable exception. But he did make some new and close friends, Jack Lemmon and Debbie Reynolds in particular. It was with a much younger group of people, however, that he began to spend much of his time. These were the school friends of his granddaughter, Suzanne, who started in her teens to invite them to enjoy the pleasures of the estate. Richard Correll, the son of one of the creators of radio's *Amos 'n' Andy,* became acquainted with Harold in 1965 through his close friendship with Sue. After his first few visits to the house, he became a regular and eager listener to Harold's stories about his career in

On the set of *The Great Race,* with Blake Edwards and Jack Lemmon, 1965.

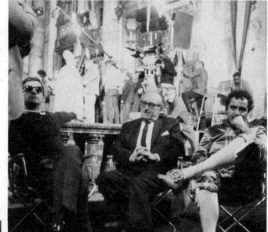

At the Roundhouse in London, October 1970.

the silent era. Lloyd, in turn, greatly admired Correll, who he believed possessed many of the energetic qualities he himself had shown at the same age. With his friends Dave Knoll and Richard Symington, Jr., Correll began to assist Harold in preserving and cataloging the nitrate negatives stored in a vault on the estate. Many of these, mostly the "Lonesome Lukes," had been lost in an explosion and fire in 1943; now, with time running out, it was the last opportunity to ensure that no further loss would occur. Through their combined efforts, all Lloyd's feature films and a good number of his two-reelers are in pristine condition. This work has continued to the present day, and the film career of Lloyd is available to us in far better condition than those of almost any of his contemporaries.

In his long talks with Correll, Harold indicated that he "knew he'd lost his rightful place in the film world because he'd kept his films out of circulation." But, as he explained, he'd really had no choice—if he let them go, what might happen to them? As a film-maker who'd worked harder than most, he expressed genuine pain when he saw his favorite old films on TV brutally cut up for insertion between commercials. On the other hand, Lloyd did not seem particularly taken with the idea of having his films shown exclusively in art houses. He remained convinced that there must be some way to "condition" modern audiences—large ones—to accept his films on their own terms, or at least the way *he* defined those terms: shown at silent speed and accompanied by music, either Wurlitzer organ or live orchestra.

Young Sue Lloyd regularly brought home all her closest friends from school, including Jennifer Edwards and Linda Hoppé, both of whom frequently stayed on at the house for weeks on end. During the last six years of Lloyd's life there was a great deal of strenuous fun around Greenacres, more than in the previous quarter of a century. As Correll puts it, "Greenacres became a big, twenty-four-hour health club!" Most of the

activity involved Harold, who had by now chosen a new nickname for himself: "Speedy" had been replaced by "Harry."
Lloyd's stamina seemed unchanged—he bounded up and down
the stairs with the vitality of a man decades younger. In his
early seventies, he was capable of swimming the entire length
of the Olympic-size pool underwater. Harry could out-bowl and
out-swim nearly all his new young friends. Sex was not a thing
of the past either: Sue Lloyd recalls him cheerily returning to
their hotel suite in Paris at six in the morning after a late
"date."

When John Meredith summed up Harold Lloyd, whom he'd
known for fifty years, he referred to him as a "strange, strange
man." Meredith believes that Lloyd was unlike anyone else
he'd ever known, that he'd been a man with few, if indeed any,
real friends. The Harold Lloyd he'd known hadn't needed
friends: he'd been obsessed with only two things in life: first, his
work and its success, and then the hobbies, which he followed
with the same energy and passion he devoted to his work.
Meredith is convinced that Lloyd simply did not have the requi-
site emotional maturity to deal with the problems of ordinary
family life. He just couldn't see why his adopted daughter,
Peggy, demanded to know the identity of her real parents—a
subject over which they quarreled bitterly. He seemed unable
to comprehend adequately the anguish felt by his son at his
lack of the success that Harold wished so much for him.

Mildred Lloyd aged far more rapidly than Harold. Because of
this she became unreal to him in the later years—and her
drinking worsened matters. She suffered her first stroke in
1968 and died of a heart condition the following year. Harold
seemed overwhelmed by the death of the woman he'd married
forty-six years ago; it undoubtedly made him aware that he
himself wasn't going to live forever. He did not slacken his ac-

tivities, however, and continued to travel the world with his films, showing them wherever they were requested.

By the end of the 1960s the creation of elaborate stereo sound systems had become Lloyd's main interest. Toward the end, he maintained nine separate systems with forty speakers; he possessed over 10,000 long-playing records, all meticulously catalogued. Some of these he played at full blast in the late hours—he was an insomniac and required only five or six hours sleep. The stereo vibrations were strong enough to cause a faint but steady rain of the gold leaf from the ceiling. But Greenacres was so well constructed that the other members of the household were seldom disturbed, even by a new recording of *Le Sacre du Printemps,* played at full volume. His taste in music was completely eclectic, although he claimed that Beethoven was his favorite composer; he placed standing orders for the entire output of several recording firms. Now the living room became a hazardous labyrinth of criss-crossing cables for the components of the stereo equipment that filled it to capacity.

Television producer Peter Robeck recalls that in these last days Greenacres was becoming shabbier than ever; the upholstery was visibly worn and dirty. If Lloyd had paid any attention to the deterioration around him, he would not have found time to do much about it. But despite his preoccupation with his hobbies, Harold became an eager, affable host whenever a caller stopped by to discuss the films he'd made in the twenties. George C. Pratt, Donald McCaffery, and Kevin Brownlow all recall the warm hospitality with which Lloyd greeted them on their visits to Greenacres. Pratt mentions being led by Lloyd at lunchtime into the vast kitchen, where his host carefully prepared tunafish sandwiches for them.

Roy Brooks came into a small inheritance in 1967 and left Greenacres to live in Santa Monica. With his departure there were few members of the original HL Corporation left. The survivors included Jack Murphy, who assisted Harold in putting together the compilation films. He and John McVeigh, who took care of financial matters, both worked in space over the gargage. "Clemmy" Mazoni, after forty years in service, still ran the household, its staff now severely reduced to a few gardeners and a cook. The young people who came to Greenacres now didn't need servants.

In September 1970 Lloyd was a special guest at the Cinema City Exhibition held at the Round House in London under the auspices of the *Sunday Times* and the British Film Institute. Sir Michael Balcon introduced Harold, who, in turn, introduced the audience to *The Kid Brother,* a film not seen in England in over forty years. The British gave the picture a warm response, regarding it as a major rediscovery. While in London, Harold paid one of his customary visits to Bebe Daniels and her husband, Ben Lyon. The Lyons had been living in London since the late 1930s; they had become immensely popular there as the stars of a radio show, "Hi Gang!" Over fifty years after she'd given it to him, Harold was still wearing Bebe's ring. The silent star Colleen Moore, another old friend from the twenties, was also in London that September. The four of them, all now in their mid-seventies, had much to recall about an industry they'd seen grow from infancy.

Harold had begun to lose weight earlier that year and found himself tiring far more easily than usual. His doctors informed him that he had cancer of the prostate, a condition that was quickly remedied by surgically removing the diseased tissues. The operation was a success, and Harold continued to live in much the same style as before.

Shortly after Harold's return from London in October 1970, Dr. John Davis, Mildred's younger brother, who had been "Stinky Davis" in Hal Roach's original *Our Gang* comedies, paid Harold a visit. A resident of Hawaii for several years, Dr.

Davis hadn't seen his brother-in-law for some time. He was shocked by Harold's altered appearance and immediately placed him in a hospital for further tests. His suspicions were correct. Harold's cancer had spread to his legs and chest. Dr. Davis recalls that the cancer raced through Harold's body with ferocious speed. After a short regimen of cobalt treatments, which weakened him considerably, Harold was told by his doctors that there was no hope of recovery. He took the news calmly, went up to his bedroom and waited for the end, which came exactly three weeks later, on March 8. He died with the conviction that his best work would continue to charm future generations—a hope based solidly on the permanent worth of his achievements.

HL in the Rogue's Gallery at Greenacres.

AFTERWORD

When Harold died he was convinced that Greenacres would become a museum devoted to the art and history of motion pictures. His will expressed this intention in creating the Harold Lloyd Foundation, but that same will mysteriously failed to provide the necessary funds. With the help of borrowed money, obtained with the main house as collateral, the Lloyd estate became a tourist attraction in the early seventies, with busloads of visitors arriving daily from all over the world, but insufficient revenues brought this method of fulfilling Harold's will to an end within a year or so. In the event that the museum idea failed, the will also contained a provision that Greenacres should be given to any one of the following institutions that would accept it: the City of Los Angeles, the City of Beverly Hills, the University of Southern California, the University of California at Los Angeles, the State of California, or the federal government. All the institutions turned Greenacres down: none of them knew what to do with it. The main house was then sold at auction to an Iranian buyer for the extremely low price of $1.4 million. The money from the sale of the house went to the Harold Lloyd Foundation, which annually bestows funds to organizations connected with the study of film, at UCLA and elsewhere.

After extensive negotiation, Harold's films were leased to Time-Life Films in 1974. Time-Life prepared horrendously edited musical-sound-track versions of the silent films, which are intended to be shown on TV at sound speed, and which represent everything that Harold had feared would happen to his best films. A framing device now surrounds the reduced image in order to give the pictures a "family album" quality. A spokesman for a prominent American film distributor informs me that the Time-Life versions of Lloyd's films are "unplayable" in theatrical release. However, there are archival prints still available at institutions such as the Museum of Modern Art in New York, where it is possible to see Lloyd's work as he meant it to be seen.

Harold Lloyd died a wealthy man, leaving an estate worth about $6.5 million. His principal heirs were his three children and his granddaughter, Suzanne. Harold junior outlived his father by only a few months. After a forty-year separation, Peggy Lloyd was finally reunited with her natural mother. Gloria, Suzanne, and Peggy continue to live in or near Los Angeles.

FILMOGRAPHY

Harold Lloyd's first appearances on film were as an unbilled extra in a number of Edison and Universal shorts in 1913. He also appeared in a variety of extra roles in a single feature, *Samson and Delilah,* in that same year. After his real debut in *Just Nuts,* he was an extra at the Sennett studio for a couple of months. Since his extra appearances are impossible to list accurately, they are omitted from this filmography, which was prepared by Elizar Talamantez with the assistance of the author.

LONESOME LUKE SHORTS (1915–17)

All films: One reel (unless otherwise noted).

Produced by Rolin Film Co. Released by Pathé Film Exchange.

Directors: Unknown, but Lloyd gives credit in his "Autobiography" to himself, Hal Roach, Alf Goulding, and G. W. Pratt.

Writers: None credited.

Photography: Unknown, but probably Walter Lundin from pretty early on.

Cast: Harold Lloyd, Bebe Daniels (started with fifth or sixth film), Harry "Snub" Pollard (started with Daniels), and the following players, who developed into the Hal Roach Stock Company: Dee Lampton, Gene Marsh, Earl Mahan, Herb Crawford, Mae Cloy, Billy Fay, Charles Stevenson, Edmund "Bud" Jamison, Margaret Joslyn, Harry Todd, Sammy

Brooks, Fred Newmeyer, Ben Corday, Slim Fitzgerald, Marie Mosquiri, Estelle Harrison, Noah Young, Dorothy Terry, Catherine Starter.

* Indicates that the film is not known to exist.

1915
Just Nuts.
Rel. Apr. 19; no copyright.
Cast: Roy Stewart, Jane Novak.

* *Lonesome Luke.*
Rel. June 7; no copyright.
Based on a story by Tad Dorgan.

* *Once Every Ten Minutes.*
Rel. July 12; no copyright.
Based on a story by Tad Dorgan.

* *Spit-Ball Sadie.*
Rel. July 26; no copyright.
Based on a story by Tad Dorgan.

* *Soaking the Clothes.*
Rel. Aug. 9; no copyright.
Based on a story by Tad Dorgan.
The first Lloyd short released under the brand name "Phunphilms."

* *Pressing His Suit.*
Rel. Aug. 23; no copyright.

* *Terribly Stuck Up.*
Rel. Aug. 28; no copyright.

* *A Mixup for Mazie.*
Rel. Sept. 6; no copyright.

* *Some Baby.*
Rel. Sept. 20; no copyright.

* *Fresh from the Farm.*
Rel. Oct. 4; no copyright.

* *Giving Them Fits.*
Rel. Nov. 1; no copyright.

* *Bughouse Bellhops.*
Rel. Nov. 8; no copyright.

* *Tinkering With Trouble.*
Rel. Nov. 17; no copyright.

* *Great While It Lasted.*
Rel. Nov. 24; no copyright.

* *Ragtime Snap Shots.*
Rel. Dec. 1; no copyright.

* *A Foozle at the Tee Party.*
Rel. Dec. 8; no copyright.

* *Ruses, Rhymes and Roughnecks.*
Rel. Dec. 15; no copyright.

* *Peculiar Patients' Pranks.*
Rel. Dec. 22; no copyright.

* *Lonesome Luke, Social Gangster.*
Rel. Dec. 29; no copyright.
Split a reel with "Where the Trees Are Stones."

1916
* *Lonesome Luke Leans to the Literary.*
Rel. Jan. 5; no copyright.

* *Luke Lugs Luggage.*
Rel. Jan. 12; no copyright.

* *Lonesome Luke Lolls in Luxury.*
Rel. Jan. 19; no copyright.

* *Luke, the Candy Cut-Up.*
Rel. Jan. 31; no copyright.

* *Luke Foils the Villain.*
Rel. Feb. 16; no copyright.

* *Luke and the Rural Roughnecks.*
Rel. Mar. 1; no copyright.

* *Luke Pipes the Pippins.*
Rel. Mar. 15; no copyright.

* *Lonesome Luke, Circus King.*
Rel. Mar. 29; no copyright.

* *Luke's Double.*
Rel. Apr. 12; no copyright.

* Them Was the Happy Days!
Rel. Apr. 26; no copyright.

* Luke and the Bomb Throwers.
Rel. May 8; no copyright.
Last short released under the name "Phunphilms."

* Luke's Late Lunchers.
Rel. May 22; no copyright.

* Luke Laughs Last.
Rel. June 5; no copyright.

* Luke's Fatal Flivver.
Rel. June 19; no copyright.

* Luke's Society Mix-up.
Rel. June 26; no copyright.

* Luke's Washful Waiting.
Rel. July 3; no copyright.

* Luke Rides Rough-shod.
Rel. July 10; no copyright.

* Luke—Crystal Gazer.
Rel. July 24; no copyright.

* Luke's Lost Lamb.
Rel. Aug. 7; no copyright.

* Luke Does the Midway.
Rel. Aug. 21; no copyright.

Luke Joins the Navy.
Rel. Sept. 3; no copyright.

* Luke and the Mermaids.
Rel. Sept. 17; no copyright.

* Luke's Speedy Club Life.
Rel. Oct. 1; no copyright.

Luke and the Bang-Tails.
Rel. Oct. 15; no copyright.

* Luke the Chauffeur.
Rel. Oct. 29; no copyright.

* Luke's Preparedness Preparations.
Rel. Nov. 5; no copyright.

* *Luke, the Gladiator.*
Rel. Nov. 12; no copyright.

* *Luke, Patient Provider.*
Rel. Nov. 19; no copyright.

* *Luke's Newsie Knockout.*
Rel. Nov. 26; no copyright.

Luke's Movie Muddle (*Luke's Model Movie,*
Director of the Cinema).
Rel. Dec. 3; no copyright.

* *Luke, Rank Impersonator.*
Rel. Dec. 10; no copyright.

* *Luke's Fireworks Fizzle.*
Rel. Dec. 17; no copyright.

* *Luke Locates the Loot.*
Rel. Dec. 24; no copyright.

* *Luke's Shattered Sleep.*
Rel. Dec. 31; no copyright.

1917
* *Luke's Lost Liberty.*
Rel. Jan. 17; no copyright.

* *Luke's Busy Day.*
Rel. Jan. 21; no copyright.

* *Luke's Trolley Troubles.*
Rel. Feb. 4; no copyright.

* *Lonesome Luke, Lawyer.*
Rel. Feb. 18; no copyright.

* *Luke Wins Ye Ladye Faire.*
Rel. Feb. 25; no copyright.

* *Lonesome Luke's Lively Life.*
Rel. Mar. 18; © Mar. 16, 1917; LU 10389 (Library of Congress
Registration Number).
Two reels.

Lonesome Luke on Tin Can Alley.
Rel. Apr. 15; © Mar. 16, 1917; LU 10390.
Two reels.

* *Lonesome Luke's Honeymoon.*
Rel. May 20; © Mar. 16, 1917; LU 10391.
Two reels.

 * *Lonesome Luke, Plumber.*
Rel. June 17; © June 7, 1917; LU 10905.
Two reels.

* *Stop! Luke! Listen!*
Rel. July 15; © June 7, 1917; LU 10904.
Two reels.

* *Lonesome Luke, Messenger.*
Rel. Aug. 5; © June 27, 1917; LU 10994.
Two reels.

* *Lonesome Luke, Mechanic.*
Rel. Aug. 19; © June 27, 1917; LU 10995.
Two reels.

* *Lonesome Luke's Wild Women.*
Rel. Sept. 2; © Aug. 8, 1917; LU 11216.
Two reels.

* *Lonesome Luke Loses Patients.*
Rel. Sept. 16; © Aug. 25, 1917; LU 11292.
Two reels.

* *Lonesome Luke in Birds of a Feather.*
Rel. Oct. 7; © Sept. 12, 1917; LU 11386.
Two reels.

* *Lonesome Luke from London to Laramie.*
Rel. Oct. 21; © Oct. 8, 1917; LU 11520.
Two reels.

* *Lonesome Luke in Love, Laughs and Lather.*
Rel. Nov. 4; © Oct. 19, 1917; LU 11588.
Two reels.

* *Lonesome Luke in Clubs Are Trumps.*
Rel. Nov. 18; © Oct. 20, 1917; LU 11593.
Two reels.

* *Lonesome Luke in We Never Sleep.*
Rel. Dec. 2; © Oct. 20, 1917; LU 11600.
Two reels.

THE GLASSES CHARACTER SHORTS (1917–21)

All films: One reel (unless otherwise noted).
Produced by Rolin Film Co. Released by Pathé Film Exchange.
Directors: Unknown for most films.
Writers: Unknown for most films.
Photography: Walter Lundin.
Titles: H. M. Walker.
Cast: Lloyd, Daniels, Pollard, and Hal Roach Stock Company.

* Indicates that the film is not known to exist.

1917
Over the Fence.
Rel. Sept. 9; © Aug. 25, 1917; LU 11293.
Directors: J. Farrell Macdonald and Harold Lloyd.

Pinched.
Rel. Sept. 23; © Aug. 25, 1917; LU 11297.

By the Sad Sea Waves.
Rel. Sept. 30; © Sept. 12, 1917; LU 11378.

Bliss.
Rel. Oct. 14; © Oct. 18, 1917; LU 11522.

Rainbow Island.
Rel. Oct. 28; © Oct. 8, 1917; LU 11521.

The Flirt.
Rel. Nov. 11; © Oct. 19, 1917; LU 11587.

All Aboard.
Rel. Nov. 25; © Oct. 20, 1917; LU 11599.

Move On.
Rel. Dec. 9; © Nov. 5, 1917; LU 11658.

Bashful.
Rel. Dec. 23; © Nov. 5, 1917; LU 11667.

Step Lively.
Rel. Dec. 30; © June 24, 1918; LU 12582.

1918
* *The Tip.*
Rel. Jan. 6; © Dec. 8, 1917; LU 11797.

The Big Idea.
Rel. Jan. 20; © June 1, 1918; LU 12470.
Director: Hal Mohr.

* *The Lamb.*
Rel. Feb. 3; no copyright.

* *Hit Him Again.*
Rel. Feb. 17; no copyright.

* *Beat It.*
Rel. Feb. 24; no copyright.

* *A Gasoline Wedding.*
Rel. Mar. 3; no copyright.

Look Pleasant Please.
Rel. Mar. 10; © June 4, 1918; LU 12415.

Here Come the Girls.
Rel. Mar. 17; © Dec. 4, 1918; LU 12414.

* *Let's Go.*
Rel. Mar. 24; no copyright.

On the Jump.
Rel. Mar. 31; © Mar. 22, 1918; LU 12416.

* *Follow the Crowd.*
Rel. Apr. 7; © June 14, 1918; LU 12585.

Pipe the Whiskers.
Rel. Apr. 14; © June 24, 1918; LU 12581.

It's a Wild Life.
Rel. Apr. 21; © June 8, 1918; LU 12505.
Director: G. W. Pratt.

Hey There.
Rel. Apr. 28; © June 1, 1918; LU 12476.

* *Kicked Out.*
Rel. May 5; © June 1, 1918; LU 12475.

The Non-Stop Kid.
Rel. May 12; © June 1, 1918; LU 12474.

Two-Gun Gussie.
Rel. May 19; © June 1, 1918; LU 12473.

Fireman, Save My Child.
Rel. May 26; © June 1, 1918; LU 12472.

The City Slicker.
Rel. June 2; © June 1, 1918; LU 12471.

* *Sic 'Em Towser.*
Rel. June 8; © June 8, 1918; LU 12507.

Somewhere in Turkey.
Rel. June. 16; © June 24, 1918; LU 12583.

Are Crooks Dishonest?
Rel. June 23; © June 8, 1918; LU 12504.

* *An Ozark Romance.*
Rel. July 7; © June 8, 1918; LU 12506.

* *Kicking the Germ Out of Germany.*
Rel. July 21; © July 15, 1918; LU 12649.

* *That's Him.*
Rel. Aug. 4; © July 23, 1918; LU 12670.

* *Bride and Gloom.*
Rel. Aug. 18; © June 24, 1918; LU 12580.

* *Two Scrambled.*
Rel. Sept. 1; © July 15, 1918; LU 12651.

* *Bees in His Bonnet.*
Rel. Sept. 15; © July 23, 1918; LU 12669.

* *Swing Your Partners.*
Rel. Sept. 29; © July 23, 1918; LU 12668.

Why Pick On Me?
Rel. Oct. 13; © Aug. 10, 1918; LU 12757.

* *Nothing But Trouble.*
Rel. Oct. 27; © Sept. 27, 1918; LU 12904.

* *Hear 'Em Rave.*
Rel. Dec. 1; © Aug. 10, 1918; LU 12738.

Take a Chance.
Rel. Dec. 15; © Nov. 21, 1918; LU 13054.

* *She Loves Me Not.*
Rel. Dec. 29; © Nov. 21, 1918; LU 13055.

1919

Wanted—$5000.
Rel. Jan. 12; © Nov. 21, 1918; LU 13056.

Going! Going! Gone!
Rel. Jan. 26; © Dec. 4, 1918; LU 13094.

Ask Father.
Rel. Feb. 9; © Dec. 17, 1918; LU 13149.

On the Fire.
Rel. Feb. 23; © Dec. 4, 1918; LU 13095.

I'm On My Way.
Rel. Mar. 9; © Jan. 23, 1919; LU 13296.

* *Look Out Below.*
Rel. Mar. 16; © Dec. 1, 1918; LU 13096.

The Dutiful Dub.
Rel. Mar. 23; © Jan. 23, 1919; LU 13295.

Next Aisle Over.
Rel. Mar. 30; © Dec. 17, 1918; LU 13150.

A Sammy in Siberia.
Rel. Apr. 6; © Feb. 27, 1919; LU 13443.

* *Just Dropped In.*
Rel. Apr. 13; © Jan. 31, 1919; LU 13336.

* *Crack Your Heels.*
Rel. Apr. 20; © Jan. 31, 1919; LU 13335.

Ring Up the Curtain.
Rel. Apr. 27; © Nov. 21, 1918; LU 13052.

Young Mr. Jazz.
Rel. May 4; © Feb. 27, 1919; LU 13442.

* *Si, Senor.*
Rel. May 11; © Feb. 27, 1919; LU 13441.

* *Before Breakfast.*
Rel. May 18; © Mar. 13, 1919; LU 13488.

The Marathon.
Rel. May 25; © Mar. 13, 1919; LU 13485.

* *Back to the Woods.*
Rel. June 1; © Mar. 13, 1919; LU 13486.

* *Pistols for Breakfast.*
Rel. June 8; © Apr. 12, 1919; LU 13589.

* *Swat the Crook.*
Rel. June 15; © Apr. 24, 1919; LU 13637.

Off the Trolley.
Rel. June 22; © Apr. 12, 1919; LU 13588.

Spring Fever.
Rel. June 29; © May 10, 1919; LU 13690.

Billy Blazes, Esq.
Rel. July 6; © June 19, 1919; LU 13852.

Just Neighbors.
Rel. July 13; © May 24, 1919; LU 13752.

At the Old Stage Door.
Rel. July 20; © May 6, 1919; LU 13674.

* *Never Touched Me.*
Rel. July 27; © Aug. 4, 1919; LU 14026.

A Jazzed Honeymoon.
Rel. Aug. 3; © May 6, 1919; LU 13675.

Count Your Change.
Rel. Aug. 10; © July 15, 1919; LU 13950.

Chop Suey and Co.
Rel. Aug. 17; © June 24, 1919; LU 13882.

Heap Big Chief.
Rel. Aug. 24; © July 22, 1919; LU 13982.

Don't Shove.
Rel. Aug. 31; © Aug. 4, 1919; LU 14025.

* *Be My Wife.*
Rel. Sept. 7; © Aug. 4, 1919; LU 14024.

* *The Rajah.*
Rel. Sept. 14; © July 22, 1919; LU 13983.

* *He Leads, Others Follow.*
Rel. Sept. 21; © July 22, 1919; LU 13981.
Director: Hal Roach.

* *Soft Money.*
Rel. Sept. 28; © Aug. 23, 1919; LU 14106.

* *Count the Votes.*
Rel. Oct. 5; © Aug. 23, 1919; LU 14104.

Pay Your Dues.
Rel. Oct. 12; © Aug. 23, 1919; LU 14107.

* *His Only Father.*
Rel. Oct. 19; © Aug. 23, 1919; LU 14105.

Bumping into Broadway.
Rel. Nov. 2; © Mar. 18, 1920; LU 14893.
Cast: Harold Lloyd (The Boy), Bebe Daniels (The Girl), Harry Pol-
   lard (Director of Musical Comedy), Helen Gilmore ("Bearcat"
   The Landlady), Noah Young, Freddie Newmeyer, Charles Ste-
   venson, Sammy Brooks, and Gus Leonard (Voices Off Stage).
Two reels.

Captain Kidd's Kids.
Rel. Nov. 30; © Mar. 18, 1920; LU 14896.
Director: Hal Roach
Cast: Harold Lloyd (The Boy), Bebe Daniels (The Girl), Harry Pol-
   lard (The Valet), Freddie Newmeyer (The Nix, Chinese Cook),
   Helen Gilmore (The Girl's Mother).
Two reels.

From Hand to Mouth.
Rel. Dec. 28; © Mar. 18, 1920; LU 14895.
Director: Alf Goulding.
Cast: Harold Lloyd (The Boy), Mildred Davis (The Girl), Harry Pol-
   lard (The Kidnapper), Peggy Courtwright (The Waif).
Two reels.

1920
His Royal Slyness.
Rel. Feb 8; © Nov. 22, 1919; LU 14459.
Director: Hal Roach.
Cast: Harold Lloyd (The American Boy), Mildred Davis (Princess
   Florelle), Harry Pollard (Prince of Roquefort), Gus Leonard
   (King Louis XIVIIX), Noah Young (Count Nichole Throwe),
   Gaylord Lloyd (The Prince, Harold's Double).
Two reels.

Haunted Spooks.

Rel. Mar. 31; © Mar. 8, 1920; LU 14825.

Directors: Hal Roach and Alf Goulding.

Cast: Harold Lloyd (The Boy), Mildred Davis (The Girl), Wallace
Howe (The Uncle), Sunshine Sammy Morrison (a little boy).

Two reels.

An Eastern Westerner.

Rel. May 2; © Apr. 13, 1920; LU 15000.

Director: Hal Roach. Story: Frank Terry.

Cast: Harold Lloyd (The Boy), Mildred Davis (The Girl), Noah
Young (The Bully).

Two reels.

High and Dizzy.

Rel. July 11; © June 23, 1920; LU 15284.

Director: Hal Roach. Story: Frank Terry.

Cast: Harold Lloyd (The Boy), Roy Brooks (His Friend), Mildred
Davis (The Girl), Wallace Howe (Her Father).

Two reels.

Get Out and Get Under.

Rel. Sept. 12; © Aug. 28, 1920; LU 15463.

Director: Hal Roach.

Cast: Harold Lloyd (The Boy), Mildred Davis (The Girl), Fred
McPherson (The Rival), Sunshine Sammy Morrison (a little
boy).

Two reels.

Number Please.

Rel. Dec. 26; © Dec 2, 1920; LU 15860.

Director: Hal Roach. Co-Director: Fred Newmeyer.

Cast: Harold Lloyd (The Boy), Mildred Davis (The Girl), Roy Brooks
(The Rival), Charles Stevenson (a cop), Sunshine Sammy
Morrison (a little boy).

Two reels.

1921

Now or Never.

Rel. May 5; © Feb. 12, 1921; LU 16131.

Directors: Hal Roach and Fred Newmeyer. Scenario: Sam Taylor.

Film Editor: T. J. Crizer.

Cast: Harold Lloyd (The Boy), Mildred Davis (The Girl), Anna May
    Bilson (The Lonesome Little Girl).
Distributed by Associated Exhibitors, Inc.
Three reels.

Among Those Present.
Rel. July 3; © May 4, 1921; LU 16477.
Director: Fred Newmeyer. Story: Hal Roach and Sam Taylor.
Film Editor: T. J. Crizer.
Cast: Harold Lloyd (The Boy), Mildred Davis (The Girl), Aggie Her-
    ring (Her Mother), James Kelly (The Father), Vera White
    (The Society Pilot), William Gillespie (The "Hard-Boiled
    Party").
Distributed by Associated Exhibitors, Inc.
Three reels.

I Do.
Rel. Sept. 11; © July 2, 1921; LU 16723.
Director: uncredited. Story: Hal Roach and Sam Taylor.
Cast: Harold Lloyd (The Boy), Mildred Davis (The Girl), Noah
    Young (The Brother-In-Law, "The Agitation"), Jackie Morgan
    (The Older Child, "The Disturbance"), Jackie Edwards (The
    Baby, "The Annoyance").
Distributed by Associated Exhibitors, Inc.
Two reels.

Never Weaken.
Rel. Oct. 22(?); © Sept. 28, 1921; LU 17018.
Director: Fred Newmeyer. Story: Hal Roach and Sam Taylor.
Film Editor: T. J. Crizer.
Cast: Harold Lloyd (The Boy), Mildred Davis (The Girl), Roy Brooks
    (The Other Man), Mark Jones (The Acrobat), Charles Steven-
    son (The Police Force).
Distributed by Associated Exhibitors, Inc.
Three reels.

THE SILENT FEATURES

1921
A Sailor-Made Man. 4 reels. Associated Exhibitors. Distributed by
Pathé.
Presented by Hal Roach.

Rel. Dec. 25; © Dec. 6, 1921; LU 17298.

Director: Fred Newmeyer. Story: Hal Roach, Sam Taylor, and Jean Havez. Photog.: Walter Lundin. Titles: H. M. Walker.

Cast: Harold Lloyd (The Boy), Mildred Davis (The Girl), Noah Young (The Rowdy Element), Dick Sutherland (Maharajah of Khaipura-Bhandanna), Charles Stevenson, Gus Leonard, Fred Guiol, Leo Willis.

1922

Grandma's Boy. 5 reels. Associated Exhibitors. Distributed by Pathé. Presented by Hal Roach.

Rel. Sept. 3; © Apr. 27, 1922; LU 17796.

Director: Fred Newmeyer. Story: Hal Roach, Sam Taylor, and Jean Havez. Photog.: Walter Lundin. Titles: H. M. Walker. Editor: T. J. Crizer.

Cast: Harold Lloyd (Grandma's Boy/Granddaddy), Mildred Davis (His Girl), Anna Townsend (His Grandma), Charles Stevenson (His Rival), Dick Sutherland (Tramp), Noah Young (Sheriff of Dabney County), Sammy Brooks, Gus Leonard, Wallace Howe, William Gillespie.

Doctor Jack. 5 reels. Pathé Distributors.
Presented by Hal Roach.

Rel. Dec. 19; © Oct. 9, 1922; LU 18289.

Director: Fred Newmeyer. Assistant Director: Robert A. Golden. Story: Hal Roach, Sam Taylor, and Jean Havez. Photog.: Walter Lundin. Titles: H. M. Walker. Editor: T. J. Crizer.

Cast: Harold Lloyd (Dr. Jackson), Mildred Davis (The Sick-Little-Well-Girl), John T. Prince (Her Father), Erich Mayne (Dr. Ludwig Von Saulsbourg), C. Norman Hammond (The Lawyer), Charles Stevenson, Mickey Daniels, Jackie Condon, Anna Townsend.

1923

Safety Last. 7 reels. Pathé Distributors.
Presented by Hal Roach.

Rel. Apr. 1; © Jan. 25, 1923; LU 18608.

Director: Fred Newmeyer and Sam Taylor. Assistant Director: Robert A. Golden. Story: Hal Roach, Sam Taylor, and Tim Whelan. Photog.: Walter Lundin. Titles: H. M. Walker. Editor: T. J. Crizer. Technical Staff: Fred L. Guiol, C. E. Christensen, and J. L. Murphy.

Cast: Harold Lloyd (The Boy), Mildred Davis (The Girl), Bill Strothers (The Pal), Noah Young (The Law), Westcott B. Clarke

(The Floorwalker), Mickey Daniels, Anna Townsend, Charles Stevenson.

Why Worry? 6 reels. Pathé Exchange Inc.
Presented by Hal Roach.
Rel. Sept. 16; © Aug 11, 1923; LU 19294.
Directors: Fred Newmeyer and Sam Taylor. Assistant Director: Robert A. Golden. Story: Sam Taylor, Ted Wilde, and Tim Whelan. Photog.: Walter Lundin. Titles: H. M. Walker. Editor: T. J. Crizer.
Cast: Harold Lloyd (Harold Van Pelham), Jobyna Ralston (The Nurse), Johan Aasen (Colosso), Leo White (Herculeo the Mighty), Wallace Howe (The Valet), James Mason (Jim Blake), Mark Jones, Gaylord Lloyd, Charles Stevenson.

1924
Girl Shy. 8 reels. A Pathé Picture.
Rel. Apr. 20; © Mar. 12, 1924; LU 19987.
Directors: Fred Newmeyer and Sam Taylor. Assistant Director: Robert A. Golden. Story: Sam Taylor, Ted Wilde, and Tim Whelan. Titles: Thomas J. Grey. Photog.: Walter Lundin and Henry N. Kohler. Editor: Allen McNeil. Production Manager: John L. Murphy. Technical Director: William MacDonald. Art Director: Liell K. Vedder.
Produced by The Harold Lloyd Corp.
Cast: Harold Lloyd (Harold Meadows, "The Poor Boy"), Jobyna Ralston (Mary Buckingham, "The Rich Girl"), Richard Daniels (Jerry Meadows, "The Poor Man"), Carlton Griffin (Ronald DeVore, "The Rich Man"), Charles Stevenson (The Train Conductor), Joe Cobb, Mickey Daniels, Jackie Condon.

Hot Water. 5 reels. A Pathé Picture.
Rel. Nov. 2; © Sept. 24, 1924; LP 20638 and LP 20596.
Directors: Fred Newmeyer and Sam Taylor. Assistant Director: Robert A. Golden. Story: Sam Taylor, Thomas J. Grey, Tim Whelan, and John Grey. Titles: Thomas J. Grey. Photog.: Walter Lundin and Henry N. Kohler. Editor: Allen McNeil. Technical Director: William MacDonald. Production Assistant: King Vedder.
Produced by The Harold Lloyd Corp.
Cast: Harold Lloyd (Hubby), Jobyna Ralston (Wifey), Josephine Crowell (Her Mother), Charles Stevenson (Charley, Her Older Brother), Mickey McBan (Bobby, Her Little Brother).

1925

The Freshman. 7 reels. A Pathé Picture.

Rel. Sept. 20; © July 27, 1925; LP 21675.

Directors: Sam Taylor and Fred Newmeyer. Assistant Director: Robert A. Golden. Story: Sam Taylor, John Grey, Ted Wilde, Tim Whelan, Clyde Bruckman, Lex Neal, Jean Havez, and Brooks B. Harding. Titles: Thomas J. Grey. Photog.: Walter Lundin and Henry N. Kohler. Editor: Allen McNeil. Production Manager: John L. Murphy. Technical Director: William MacDonald. Art Direction: Liell K. Vedder.

Produced by The Harold Lloyd Corp.

Cast: Harold Lloyd (Harold "Speedy" Lamb), Jobyna Ralston (Peggy), Brooks Benedict (The College Cad), James Anderson (Chester A. "Chet" Trask), Hazel Keener (The College Belle), Joseph Harrington (The College Tailor), Pat Harmon (The College Coach).

1926

For Heaven's Sake. 6 reels. Paramount.

Rel. Apr. 5; © Apr. 6, 1926; LP 22577.

Director: Sam Taylor. Assistant Director: Robert A. Golden. Story: John Grey, Ted Wilde, and Clyde Bruckman. Titles: Ralph Spence. Photog.: Walter Lundin and Henry N. Kohler. Editor: Allen McNeil. Production Manager: John L. Murphy. Technical Director: William MacDonald. Art Direction: Liell K. Vedder.

Produced by The Harold Lloyd Corp.

Cast: Harold Lloyd (J. Harold Manners, "The Uptown Boy"), Jobyna Ralston (Hope, "The Downtown Girl"), Noah Young (The Roughneck), James Mason (The Gangster), Paul Weigel (Brother Paul, "The Optimist").

1927

The Kid Brother. 8 reels. Paramount.

Rel. Jan 22; © Jan. 18, 1927; LP 23563.

Directors: Ted Wilde, J. A. Howe, and Lewis Milestone. Assistant Director: Gaylord Lloyd. Story: John Grey, Ted Wilde, and Tom Crizer. Scenario: John Grey, Lex Neal, and Howard Green. Photog.: Walter Lundin and Henry N. Kohler. Production Manager: John L. Murphy. Editor: Allen McNeil. Art Director: Liell K. Vedder. Technical Director: William MacDonald.

Produced by The Harold Lloyd Corp.

Cast: Harold Lloyd (Harold Hickory), Jobyna Ralston (Mary Powers),

Walter James (Jim Hickory), Leo Willis (Leo Hickory), Olin Francis (Olin Hickory), Constantine Romanoff (Sandoni), Eddie Boland ("Flash" Farrell), Frank Lanning (Sam Hooper), Ralph Yearsley (Hank Hooper).

1928
Speedy. 8 reels. Paramount.
Rel. Apr. 7; © Apr. 7, 1928; LP 25135.
Director: Ted Wilde. Story and Scenario: John Grey, Lex Neal, Howard Rogers, and Jay Howe. Titles: Albert DeMond. Photog.: Walter Lundin. Production Manager: John L. Murphy. Dog Trainer: Ebenezer Henry.
Produced by The Harold Lloyd Corp.
Cast: Harold Lloyd (Harold "Speedy" Swift), Ann Christy (Jane Dillon), Bert Woodruff (Pop Dillon, Her Grand-Daddy), Brooks Benedict (Steve Carter), George Herman "Babe" Ruth (Himself), King Tut (Himself, a dog), Dan Wolheim, Hank Knight.

THE SOUND FEATURES

1929
Welcome Danger. 115 minutes (12 reels). Paramount.
Rel. Oct. 12; © Oct. 20, 1929; LP 13476 and LP 777.
Directors: Clyde Bruckman and Mal St. Clair.* Assistant Director: Gaylord Lloyd. Story: Felix Adler, Lex Neal, and Clyde Bruckman. Dialogue: Paul Gerard Smith. Photog.: Walter Lundin and Henry N. Kohler. Film Editors: Bernard Burton and Carl Himm. Production Manager: John L. Murphy. Musical Arrangement: Bakaleinikoff. Technical Director: William MacDonald. Art Director: Liell K. Vedder. Sound Technicians: Cecil Bardwell and Lodge Cunningham.
Recorded by Western Electric System.
Produced by The Harold Lloyd Corp.
Cast: Harold Lloyd (Harold Bledsoe), Barbara Kent (Billie Lee), Noah Young (Patrick Clancy), Charles Middleton (John Thorne), William Walling (Capt. Walton), James Wang (Doctor Chang Gow), Douglas Haig (Buddy Lee).

---

* St. Clair worked 18 weeks on this picture.

1930

Feet First. 90 minutes (10 reels). Paramount.

Rel. Nov. 8; © Nov. 11, 1930; LP 1738.

Director: Clyde Bruckman. Assistant Directors: Gaylord Lloyd and Mal De Lay. Story: John Grey, Al Cohn, and Clyde Bruckman. Scenario: Felix Adler and Lex Neal. Dialogue: Paul Gerard Smith. Photog.: Walter Lundin and Henry Kohler. Film Editor: Bernard Burton. Production Manager: John L. Murphy. Sound Technicians: Cecil Bardwell and William R. Fox. Art Director: Liell K. Vedder. Technical Director: William MacDonald.

Recorded by Western Electric Sound System.

Produced by The Harold Lloyd Corp.

Cast: Harold Lloyd (Harold Horne), Barbara Kent (Barbara), Robert McWade (John Quincy Tanner), Lillianne Leighton (Mrs. Tanner), Henry Hall (Endicott), Alec B. Francis (Old Timer, Mr. Carson), Noah Young (Ship's Officer), Arthur Housman (Drunken Clubman), Willie Best, "Sleep 'n' Eat" (Charcoal, a janitor).

1932

Movie Crazy. 96 minutes (later cut to 84 minutes). Paramount.

Rel. Sept. 23; © Sept 15, 1932; LP 3246.

Director: Clyde Bruckman. Assistant Director: Gaylord Lloyd. Story: Agnes Christine Johnston, John Grey, and Felix Adler. Continuity: Clyde Bruckman, Frank Terry, and Lex Neal. Screenplay and Dialogue: Vincent Lawrence. Photog.: Walter Lundin. Film Editor: Bernard Burton. Art Direction: Harry Oliver and William MacDonald. Production Manager: John L. Murphy.

Produced by The Harold Lloyd Corp.

Cast: Harold Lloyd (Harold Hall), Constance Cummings (The Girl, Mary Sears), Kenneth Thomson (The Gentleman, Vance), Sidney Jarvis (The Director), Eddie Featherstone (an assistant director), Robert McWade (The Producer, Wesley Kitterman), Louise Closser Hale (The Producer's Wife), Harold Goodwin (Miller, a director), DeWitt Jennings (Mr. Hall), Lucy Beaumont (Mrs. Hall), Arthur Housman (a drunk), Noah Young (traffic cop), Constantine Romanoff (sailor in movie).

1934

The Cat's Paw. 102 minutes. Fox.

Rel. Aug. 7; © Aug 17, 1934; LP 4895.

Screenplay and Direction: Sam Taylor and Clyde Bruckman.* Based on the story by Clarence Buddington Kelland. Photog.: Walter Lundin. Film Editor: Bernard Burton: Musical Direction: Alfred Newman. Art Director: Harry Oliver. Songs: Harry Akst and Roy Turk. Dances staged by Larry Ceballos. Production Manager: John L. Murphy. Produced by The Harold Lloyd Corp.

Cast: Harold Lloyd (Ezekiel Cobb), Una Merkel (Petunia Pratt), George Barbier (Jake Mayo), Nat Pendleton (Strozzi), Alan Dinehart (Mayor Morgan), Grace Bradley (Dolores Dace), Grant Mitchell (Silk Hat McGee), Warren Hymer (Spike Slattery), James Donlan (Red), Frank Sheridan (Commissioner Moriarity), Vincent Barnett (Vince), Fred Warren (Tien Wang), J. Farrell MacDonald (Chief Shigley), Edwin Maxwell (District Attorney), Fuzzy Knight (Fuzz), David Jack Holt (Ezekiel as a boy).

1936
The Milky Way. 88 minutes. Paramount.
Rel. Feb. 7; © Feb. 11, 1936; LP 6128.
Director: Leo McCarey. Assistant Director: Harry Scott. Producer: E. Lloyd Sheldon. Screenplay: Grover Jones, Frank Butler, and Richard Connell. Based on the play by Lynn Root and Harry Clork. Photog.: Alfred Gilks. Art Direction: Hans Dreier and Bernard Herzbrun. Film Editor: LeRoy Stone. Sound Recording: Earl Hayman and Louis Mesenkop. Interior Decorations: A. E. Freudman.
Presented by Adolph Zukor.
Cast: Harold Lloyd (Burleigh Sullivan), Adolphe Menjou (Gabby Sloan), Verree Teasdale (Ann Westley), Helen Mack (Mae Sullivan), William Gargan (Speed McFarland), George Barbier (Wilbur Austin), Dorothy Wilson (Polly Pringle), Lionel Stander (Spider Schultz), Marjorie Gateson (Mrs. E. Winthrope Lemoyne), Charles Lane (Willard).

1938
Professor Beware. 95 minutes. Paramount.
Rel. July 29; © July 29, 1938; LP 8174.
Directors: Elliott Nugent and Clyde Bruckman.† Assistant Director: George Hippard. Screenplay: Delmer Daves. Adaptation: Jack Cun-

---

* Bruckman worked 19 weeks on this picture.
† Bruckman was paid for 12 weeks as codirector and 23 weeks as writer.

ningham and Clyde Bruckman. Based on a story by Crampton Harris, Francis M. and Marian B. Cockrell. Photog.: Archie Stout. Film Editor: Duncan Mansfield. Art Director: Al D'Agostino. Sound: Earl Sitar. Producer: Harold Lloyd. Business Manager: Gaylord Lloyd.
Presented by Adolph Zukor.
Cast: Harold Lloyd (Professor Dean Lambert), Phyllis Welch (Jane Van Buren), Raymond Walburn (Judge James G. Parkhouse Marshall), Lionel Stander (Jerry), William Frawley ("Snoop" Donlan), Thurston Hall (J. J. Van Buren), Cora Witherspoon (Mrs. Pitts), Sterling Holloway (Bridegroom), Mary Lou Lender (Bride), Montague Love (Dr. Schmutz), Etienne Girardot (Judge), Christian Rub (Museum Attendant), Spencer Charters (Sheriff), Guinn Williams and Ward Bond (Motorcycle Policemen).

1947
The Sin of Harold Diddlebock. 89 minutes (later cut to 77 minutes as *Mad Wednesday*).
United Artists (Reissue: RKO-Radio).
Rel. Apr. 4, 1947 (Reissued Oct. 28, 1950); © Dec. 31, 1946; LP 591.
Produced by California Pictures Corp.
Screenplay and Direction: Preston Sturges. Photog.: Robert Pittack. Special Effects: John Fulton. Technical Director: Curtis Courant. Art Director: Robert Usher. Set Director: Victor A. Ganglin. Film Editor: Thomas Neff. Sound: Fred Lau. Music: Werner Richard Heymann. Production Manager: Cliff Broughton.
Cast: Harold Lloyd (Harold Diddlebock), Frances Ramsden (Miss Otis), Jimmy Conlin (Wormy), Raymond Walburn (E. J. Waggleberry), Arline Judge (Manicurist), Edgar Kennedy (Bartender "Jake"), Franklin Pangborn (Form-Fit Franklin), Lionel Stander (Max), Margaret Hamilton (Flora), Rudy Vallee (a banker).

MISCELLANEOUS

I. Cameo Appearances

1923
Dogs of War. One reel. Pathé.
Rel. July 1, 1923; © July 19, 1923; LU 19216.
Cast: Our Gang, Harold Lloyd, Jobyna Ralston.
(No print is known to exist).

II. Harold Lloyd Productions

1941

A Girl, a Guy and a Gob. 91 minutes. RKO-Radio Pictures.
Rel. Mar. 14; © Mar. 14, 1941; LP 10335.
Director: Richard Wallace. Screenplay: Frank Ryan and Bert Granet.
Based on a story by Grover Jones. Photog.: Russell Metty. Special Effects: Vernon L. Walker. Art Director: Van Nest Polglase. Musical
Score: Roy Webb. Film Editor: George Crane.
Cast: George Murphy, Lucille Ball, Edmond O'Brien, Henry Travers,
Franklin Pangborn, George Cleveland.

1942

My Favorite Spy. 86 minutes. RKO-Radio Pictures.
Rel. June 12; © Apr. 29, 1942; LP 11414.
Director: Tay Garnett. Screenplay: William Bowers and Sig Herzig.
Based on a story by M. Coates Webster. Photog.: Robert de Grasse.
Musical Score: Roy Webb. Musical Direction: C. Bakaleinikoff. Songs
by Johnny Burke and James Van Heusen.
Cast: Kay Kyser, Ellen Drew, Jane Wyman, Robert Armstrong, Helen
Westley, William Demarest, Una O'Connor.

III. Compilation Pictures

1948

Down Memory Lane. About 60 minutes.
Rel. None; no copyright. A compilation film made in 1948 for the
Shriners.
Producer: Harold Lloyd.
This includes excerpts from *Haunted Spooks* and virtually every feature from *Grandma's Boy* to *Professor Beware.*
Cast: Harold Lloyd, Mildred Davis, Jobyna Ralston, Noah Young.

1951

Harold Lloyd's Laugh Parade. About 60 minutes.
Rel. None; no copyright.
A compilation film made for the Shriners.
Producer and Narrator: Harold Lloyd, Editorial Supervision: Harvey
C. Johnston.

This includes excerpts from nearly all of Lloyd's features.
Cast: Harold Lloyd, Mildred Davis, Jobyna Ralston, Noah Young.

1962
Harold Lloyd's World of Comedy. 94 minutes.
Rel. June 4; © Mar. 5, 1962; LP 21938.
Producer: Harold Lloyd. Associate Producer: Jack Murphy. Narration
Writer: Arthur Ross. Music: Walter Scharf. Orchestrations: Lew
Schuken and Jack Hayes. Production Editor: Duncan Mansfield.
Music Editor: Sid Sidney. Sound Effects: Del Harris. Music Record-
ings: Vinton Vernon. Story Consultant: Harold Lloyd, Jr.
Contains excerpts from: *Safety Last, The Freshman, Hot Water, Why
Worry?, Girl Shy, Professor Beware, Movie Crazy,* and *Feet First.*
Cast: Harold Lloyd, Jobyna Ralston, Josephine Crowell, Charles Ste-
venson, Johan Aasen, Raymond Walburn, Lionel Stander, Louise
Closser Hale, and Willie Best.

1966
Harold Lloyd's Funny Side of Life. 99 minutes.
Rel. Nov. 9, 1966; © Aug. 1, 1963; LP 25723.
Producer: Harold Lloyd. Associate Producer: Jack Murphy. Narration
Writer: Arthur Ross. Music: Walter Scharf. Song "There Was a Boy,
There Was A Girl": Music, Walter Scharf; Lyrics, Ned Washington.
Production Editor: Duncan Mansfield. Music Editor: Sid Sidney.
Sound Effects: Del Harris. Music Recordings: Vinton Vernon. Story
Consultant: Harold Lloyd, Jr.
Contains excerpts from *Speedy, For Heaven's Sake,* and *The Kid
Brother* and the complete feature, *The Freshman.*
Cast: Harold Lloyd, Ann Christy, Noah Young, Constantine Romanoff,
Jobyna Ralston.

IV. Television Appearances

1954
This Is Your Life.
Televised: NBC, Wed., Sept. 29, 9:30 p.m.
Ralph Edwards hosts a testimonial to Bebe Daniels and Ben Lyon in
which Harold Lloyd is one of the guests.

1955
This Is Your Life.
Televised: NBC, Wed., Dec. 14, 9:30 p.m.
Ralph Edwards hosts a testimonial to Harold Lloyd.

1960s
Harold Lloyd appeared on many talk programs to promote his compilation features from the early to the mid 1960s.

BIBLIOGRAPHY

Agee, James. *A Death in the Family.* New York: McDowell, Obolensky, 1957.

———. *Agee on Film: Reviews and Comments.* New York: McDowell, Obolensky, 1958.

Balio, Tino. *United Artists: The Company Built by the Stars.* Madison (Wis.): The University of Wisconsin Press, 1975.

Brownlow, Kevin. *The Parade's Gone By.* New York: Alfred A. Knopf; London: Secker & Warburg, 1969.

———. *Hollywood: The Pioneers.* New York: Alfred A. Knopf; London: Secker & Warburg, 1979.

Cahn, William. *Harold Lloyd's World of Comedy.* New York: Duell, Sloan and Pearce, 1964.

Chaplin, Charles. *My Autobiography.* London: The Bodley Head; New York: Simon & Schuster, 1964.

Cohen, Hubert I. "The Serious Business of Being Funny" in Lloyd, H. L. and Stout, W. W. *An American Comedy.* New York: Dover Publications, 1971.

Dardis, Tom. *Keaton: The Man Who Wouldn't Lie Down.* New York: Charles Scribner's Sons, 1979; Penguin Books, 1980; London: André Deutsch, 1979; Penguin Books, 1981.

Deutelbaum, Marshal, ed. *"Image"—The Art and Evolution of the Film.* New York: Dover Publications, 1979.

Elkin, Stanley. *Criers and Kibitzers, Kibitzers and Criers.* New York: Random House, 1966.

Everson, William K. *American Silent Film.* New York: Oxford University Press, 1978.

———. *The Films of Laurel and Hardy.* New York: The Citadel Press, 1967.

Farber, Manny. *Negative Space—Manny Farber on the Movies.* New York and Washington: Praeger Publishers, 1971.

Ferguson, Otis. *The Film Criticism of Otis Ferguson.* Edited by Robert Wilson. Philadelphia: Temple University Press, 1971.

Fowler, Gene. *Father Goose.* New York: Covici-Friede, 1934.

Gebhart, Myrtle. "Mildred's Ambitions." *Picture Play* 90 (October 1922):96–97.

Geduld, Harry M. *The Birth of the Talkies, From Edison to Jolson.* Bloomington and London: Indiana University Press, 1975.

Gleason, Bill. "Harold Lloyd—Automaniac." *Film* (BFFS) series 2, no. 15 (June 1974):17–18.

Kaminsky, Stuart. "Harold Lloyd: A Reassessment of His Film Comedy." *Silent Picture* no. 16 (Autumn 1972):21–29.

Kerr, Walter. *The Silent Clowns.* New York: Alfred A. Knopf, 1975.

Leyda, Jay, ed. *Voices of Film Experience.* New York: The Macmillan Company, 1977.

Lloyd, Harold, and Stout, W. W. *An American Comedy.* New York: Longmans, Green & Co., 1928. Expanded edition, New York: Dover Publications, 1971.

———. "The Autobiography of Harold Lloyd." *Photoplay* vol. 25, no. 6, 7, 8 (May, June, and July 1924).

———. "The Funny Side of Life." *Films and Filming* vol. 10, no. 4 (January 1964):19–21.

McCabe, John. *Charlie Chaplin.* New York: Doubleday & Company, 1978.

McCaffrey, Donald. *Four Great Comedians: Chaplin, Lloyd, Keaton, Langdon.* London: A. Zwemmer; New York: A. S. Barnes, 1968.

———. *Three Classic Silent Screen Comedies Starring Harold Lloyd.* Rutherford (N.J.): Fairleigh Dickinson University Press, 1975.

Pratt, George C. *Spellbound in Darkness—A History of the Silent Film.* Greenwich, Conn.: New York Graphic Society, 1973.

Reilly, Adam. *Harold Lloyd—"The King of Daredevil Comedy."* New York: Collier Books; London: André Deutsch, 1977.

Rosenberg, Bernard, and Silverstein, Harry. *The Real Tinsel.* New York: The Macmillan Company, 1970.

St. Johns, Adela Rogers. "How Lloyd Made 'Safety Last.' " *Photoplay* vol. 24, no. 2 (July 1923):33.

Schickel, Richard. *The Shape of Laughter.* Boston: New York Graphic Society, 1974.

Seldes, Gilbert. *The Seven Lively Arts.* New York: Harper & Brothers, 1924.

Sennett, Mack. *King of Comedy.* New York: Doubleday, 1954.

Slide, Anthony. "Harold Lloyd." *The Silent Picture* 11/12 (Summer/ Autumn 1971):5–8.

Walker, Alexander. *The Shattered Silence—How the Talkies Came to Stay*. London: Elm Tree Books, 1978; New York: William Morrow and Company, 1979.

Unpublished Material

Transcripts of the Joan and Bob Franklin interviews with Lloyd, A. Edward Sutherland, Elliott Nugent, Reginald Denny, and Gloria Swanson are on deposit in the Oral History Project at Columbia University, New York City, as is a transcript of Arthur Friedman's interview with Mary Pickford.

A transcript of the interview with Lloyd at the American Film Institute Seminar in 1969 is available at the Charles K. Feldman Library of the American Film Institute in Los Angeles.

The Rolin-Roach correspondence is available at the Special Collections Library of the University of Southern California Library in Los Angeles. The Preston Sturges material is available at the Library of the University of California in Los Angeles.

NOTES AND SOURCES

Chapter I

Page
1 "in the state." Harold Lloyd, "The Autobiography of Harold Lloyd," *Photoplay*, May 1924, p. 32.

1 "realizing it" Joan and Bob Franklin, Transcript of interview with Harold Lloyd, New York, January 1959, p. 1.

1 "different places." Lloyd, "Autobiography," p. 32.
2 "his mother." Ibid.
2 "pretty busy." Ibid.
3 "Beatrice there." Lloyd-Franklin interview, p. 1.
4 "American kid." Lloyd, "Autobiography" (May), p. 32.
5 "could sit down." Ibid., pp. 33–34.
6 "I did." Ibid., p. 116.
7 "ended the job." Harold Lloyd, *An American Comedy*, p. 14. (Page numbers refer to the Dover edition.)

7 "is America." Stanley Elkin, *Criers and Kibitzers, Kibitzers and Criers*, p. 41.

7 "like that." Lloyd, "Autobiography" (May), p. 116.

8 "behind me." Lloyd, *An American Comedy*, p. 8.
8 "my character." Lloyd, "Autobiography" (May), p. 116.

9 "for amusement." Ibid.
9 "Shakespeare's own." Lloyd, *An American Comedy*, p. 4.
9 "murder them." Lloyd-Franklin interview, p. 2.

Page

9	"finish it out."	Ibid.
10	"Saturn's rings?"	Lloyd, "Autobiography" (May), p. 117.
10	"ever seen."	Ibid., p. 118.
11	"his bidding."	Ibid.
11	"beyond me."	Lloyd, *An American Comedy*, p. 27.
13	"histrionic art,"	Scrapbook.
15	*"lots of love,"*	Harold Lloyd to J. Darsie Lloyd, October 17, 1909.
15	*"kisses from,"*	Harold Lloyd to J. Darsie Lloyd, November 27, 1909.
16	"the Coast."	Lloyd-Franklin interview, p. 3.
16	"into the world."	Lloyd, "Autobiography" (May), p. 118.
17	"if I came."	Lloyd-Franklin interview, p. 3.
17	"wreath side up."	Lloyd, *An American Comedy*, p. 33.
17	"stock company."	Lloyd-Franklin interview, p. 4.
19	"I loved it."	Harold Lloyd, "The Autobiography of Harold Lloyd," *Photoplay*, June 1924, p. 42.
19	"remember where."	Ibid.
20	"as puppets."	Lloyd, *An American Comedy*, p. 21.
20	"put it on."	Anthony Slide, "Harold Lloyd," *The Silent Picture*, p. 5.
21	"else offered."	Lloyd, *An American Comedy*, p. 43.

Chapter II

23	"these movies?"	Lloyd, "Autobiography," *Photoplay*, June 1924, p. 107.
23	"on the weather."	Joan and Bob Franklin, Transcript of interview with Harold Lloyd, p. 6.
24	"for the day."	Ibid.
26	"the idea."	Ibid.
26	"try it."	Ibid.
26	"be in it."	Lloyd, "Autobiography" (June), pp. 108–109.
27	"post office."	Bernard Rosenberg and Harry Silverstein, *The Real Tinsel*, p. 15.
27	"to do it."	Ibid., p. 16.
27	"was 1913."	Ibid.
31	"called Edendale."	Kevin Brownlow, *The Parade's Gone By*, p. 308.

Page

31 "of events."   Mack Sennett, *King of Comedy*, p. 65.
31 "the Pathés"   Ibid.
32 "express train."   James Agee, *Agee on Film*, p. 6.
33 "BUILDING BROADWAY."   Charles Chaplin, *My Autobiography*,
                            p. 145.
33 "WITH MOVIES."   Gene Fowler, *Father Goose*, p. 229.
34 "made good."   Chaplin, *Autobiography*, p. 155.
34 "could stand up."   Joan and Bob Franklin, Transcript of
                            interview with Gloria Swanson, New
                            York, 1958, p. 38.
34 "in the park."   Joan and Bob Franklin, Transcript of
                            interview with Eddie Sutherland,
                            New York, February 1959, p. 17.
35 "exclusively exteriors." Lloyd, "Autobiography" (June), p.
                            109.
35 "we will be set."   Lloyd, *An American Comedy*, p. 49.
36 "watching you."   Lloyd-Franklin interview, p. 16.
37 "aspire to that."   Ibid., p. 13.
38 "go with Roach!"   Ibid., p. 17.
38 "little pond."   Ibid.
42 "young actress."   *Moving Picture World*, June 1, 1920,
                            p. 27.
43 "two cents."   Swanson-Franklin interview, p. 15.
43 "with lights."   Rosenberg and Silverstein, *The Real
                            Tinsel*, p. 17.
44 "own was."   Dolly Twist to Dwight Whiting, Au-
                            gust 4, 1915.
44 "to explain."   Ibid.
44 "slapstick ideas."   Dolly Twist to Dwight Whiting, Octo-
                            ber 27, 1915.
44 "funny stuff?"   Ibid., October 31, 1915.
46 "DO IT OVER."   Dwight Whiting to Hal Roach, March
                            25, 1915.
48 "is marvelous."   Lloyd, *An American Comedy*, p. 57.
48 "that category."   Lloyd-Franklin interview, p. 19.
48 "like Chaplin."   Ibid.
49 "over Toto."   Ibid., p. 23.

Chapter III

50 "or anyone."   Joan and Bob Franklin, Transcript of
                            interview with Harold Lloyd, p. 25.
50 "the opposite."   Ibid., p. 26.

Page

53 "the other two." Ibid., p. 23.
53 "and the same." Scrapbook.
56 "train to catch." Lloyd, *An American Comedy*, pp. 58–59.
56 "wind it up." Kevin Brownlow, *The Parade's Gone By*, p. 468.
56 glasses character. Interview with Hal Roach, January 1980.
62 "THE BACON." Hal Roach to Dwight Whiting, 1917.
63 "very lovely." Joan and Bob Franklin, Transcript of interview with Reginald Denny, New York, 1958, p. 20.
63 "I'd say." Joan and Bob Franklin, Transcript of interview with Eddie Sutherland, p. 28.
64 "stick for nothing." Dwight Whiting to Hal Roach, March 4, 1916.
66 "now receiving." Dwight Whiting to Frank A. Garbutt, May 4, 1917.
66 "under contract." Frank A. Garbutt to Dwight Whiting, May 5, 1917.
67 "what they thought." Kevin Brownlow, *Hollywood: The Pioneers*, p. 92.
68 "for a gag." Marshal Deutelbaum, ed., *"Image,"* p. 218.
70 *"small pictures of me—"* Elizabeth Lloyd to Harold Lloyd, January 1, 1919.
70 "can pay more." Paul Brunet to Hal Roach, March 11, 1919.
71 "IN THE PROFITS." Hal Roach to Paul Brunet, March 17, 1919.
74 "big French doll." Lloyd, "Autobiography," *Photoplay*, July 1924, p. 56.
74 "REGARDING THIS GIRL." Hal Roach to Paul Brunet, May 21, 1919.
74 "YOU GET HER." Paul Brunet to Hal Roach, May 22, 1919.

Chapter IV

75 "lowered your hand?" Lloyd, *An American Comedy*, p. 76.
76 "thing exploded." Ibid., p. 75.
77 "began to heal." Ibid., p. 76.

Page

77	"all & self."	Scrapbook.
79	"CAN DO IT AGAIN."	Scrapbook.
81	"for laughs."	Jay Leyda, ed., *Voices of Film Experience*, p. 395.
86	"that rainbow."	Lloyd, *An American Comedy*, p. 80.
87	"OVER THREE HOURS."	*Moving Picture World*, December 27, 1919, p. 77.
90	"and drove away."	Lloyd, *An American Comedy*, p. 81.
92	"to say 'we.' "	New York *Herald Tribune*, 1929.
92	"it helped them."	Transcript of American Film Institute Seminar with Harold Lloyd, September 23, 1969, p. 35.
93	"and not length?"	*Moving Picture World*, April 21, 1921, p. 21.
93	"back again."	Ibid., January 27, 1920, p. 334.
93	"New York City."	Ibid., August 17, 1921, p. 676.
97n	"nasty little walk!"	James Agee, *A Death in the Family*, p. 11.

Chapter V

100	"little canary."	Myrtle Gebhart, "Mildred's Ambitions," p. 90.
102	"the wallpaper."	Interview with Harvey Parry, June 1980.
103	"happy with it."	Anthony Slide, *The Silent Picture*, pp. 5–6.
105	"so long."	Walter Kerr, *The Silent Clowns*, p. 98.
105	"act fast."	Tom Dardis, *Keaton*, p. viii.
106	"the gods."	Walter Kerr, *The Silent Clowns*, p. 98.
108	"first feature."	Joan and Bob Franklin, Transcript of interview with Harold Lloyd, p. 27.
109	"we ever had."	Ibid.
109	"feature picture."	Ibid., p. 28.
109	"lied to him."	Ibid., p. 27.
110	"that had won."	Ibid., p. 28.
110	"ever since."	Transcript of American Film Institute Seminar with Harold Lloyd, p. 10.
112	"tremendously likable."	James Agee, *Agee on Film*, p. 10.

Page

112	"to go ahead."	Charles Chaplin to Robert Wagner, May 23, 1922. Scrapbook.
114	"indefatigable energy"	Gilbert Seldes, *The Seven Lively Arts*, p. 15.
117	"hear himself play."	*Moving Picture World*, June 2, 1923, p. 109.
117	"from your body."	Kevin Brownlow, *The Parade's Gone By*, p. 471.
117	"believe me."	Hubert I. Cohen, "The Serious Business of Being Funny," in Lloyd, *An American Comedy*, p. 123.
118	" 'been done before.' "	Lloyd-Franklin interview, pp. 29–30.
119	"all cameramen worked"	Hal Roach's work diary. Collection of the University of Southern California.
120	"looked straight down."	Adela Rogers St. Johns, "How Lloyd Made 'Safety Last,' " p. 117.
120	"crazy to do it."	Brownlow, *Parade*, p. 470.
120	"would be the end."	Lloyd-Franklin interview, p. 33.
121	"It was better."	Ibid.
121	"they didn't see."	Ibid., p. 34.
123	"the second story."	Lloyd, *An American Comedy*, p. 86.
125	"to the next."	Agee, *Agee on Film*, pp. 11–12.
128	"with the stunt."	AFI Seminar with Harold Lloyd, pp. 11–13.
129	"the last word."	Harold Lloyd Corporation versus Witwer, Circuit Court of Appeals, Ninth Circuit, April 10, 1933, in *The Federal Reporter*, volume 65, 2nd series, p. 7.
129	"the next one."	Ibid.
129	"with those boys."	Ibid., p. 8.
130	" 'from the cuff.' "	Ibid., p. 7.
130	"THAT I KNOW OF."	To Hal Roach, December 6, 1922.

Chapter VI

137	"Amen."	Lloyd, *An American Comedy*, p. 96.
137	" 'our own way.' "	Transcript of American Film Institute Seminar with Harold Lloyd, p. 16.
137	"of teamwork."	Lloyd, *An American Comedy*, p. 89.

Page

142 *Why Worry?* All figures on this page drawn from Price, Waterhouse report on Harold Lloyd films made for Roach, September 21, 1923. Courtesy of the Harold Lloyd Estate.

145 "eat that?" Arthur Friedman interview with Mary Pickford, 1958, p. 49.

148 "time and space." *The Listener*, 23/30, p. 833.

148 "treatment and appeal." *Moving Picture World*, July 28, 1923, p. 320.

148 "real perfectionist." Joan and Bob Franklin, Transcript of interview with Eddie Sutherland, p. 46.

156 "styles in clothes." *The New York Times*, April 2, 1973.

157 "football film!" Harold Lloyd Corporation versus Witwer, Circuit Court of Appeals, Ninth Circuit, April 10, 1933, in *The Federal Reporter*, volume 65, 2nd series, p. 8.

157 " 'win this game.' " Joan and Bob Franklin, Transcript of interview with Harold Lloyd, p. 61.

158 "gave them nothing." *Federal Reporter*, p. 6.

159 "to his story." Ibid., p. 11.

159 "to use them." Ibid.

160 "in the gag room." Kevin Brownlow, *The Parade's Gone By*, p. 465.

163 "it went fine." AFI Seminar with Harold Lloyd, p. 28.

165 "pure guts." Ibid., p. 22.

166 "EVER PRODUCED!" *Moving Picture World*, August 1, 1925, p. 79.

Chapter VII

169 "generally the best." Transcript of American Film Institute Seminar with Harold Lloyd, p. 31.

171 "can do that?" Scrapbook.

171 "directing comedy." Charles Chaplin, *My Autobiography*, p. 222.

172 "Sequences are funny." Interview with Hal Roach, January 1980.

Page

| 178 | not to release it. | *News*, Glen Cove, N.Y., April 28, 1926. |

179   "got it!"   Interview with Richard Correll, July 1981.

189   "was the best."   Joan and Bob Franklin, Transcript of Interview with Harold Lloyd, pp. 64–65.

189   only four days.   "We started a picture with Lewis Milestone in *Kid Brother*. The only thing is that he hadn't been on it less than about four days. He had a contract with Warner Brothers he wasn't too happy with, and he found out if he wasn't working on another picture he could get out of the contract. He came to me and said, "This is the most unprofessional thing I've ever wanted to do, Harold . . . I'm so unhappy with this contract." I said, "I'm not going to hold you here. We'd hate to lose you. Nevertheless, if you can get out of it, you're through right now." AFI Seminar with Harold Lloyd, p. 35.

Chapter VIII

192   "counts in comedy."   Interview, *Commercial News*, February 12, 1928.

193   Mrs. Parrish   Interview, Robert Parrish, London, January 1980.

200   Chart   Chaplin figures from University of Wisconsin Theater Collection, courtesy of Tino Balio; Keaton figures courtesy of MGM.

201   "something's wrong."   Interview with Richard Correll, July 1981.

201   "before it thought."   Alexander Walker, *The Shattered Silence*, p. 1.

201   "in this business."   *Moving Picture World*, January 6, 1925, p. 7.

202   "medium of dialogue."   *Film Spectator*, July 19, 1930, p. 3.

203   "arrest its development."   Ibid., December 22, 1928, p. 2.

Page

203	"flesh and blood humans."	Ibid., January 12, 1929, p. 3.
204	"pictures in general."	Ibid., December 22, 1928, p. 3.
204	"TO HEAR VOICES"	Ibid., January 12, 1929, p. 1.
205	"*a . . . ride. . . .* "	Walker, *Shattered Silence*, p. 71.
206	"of any language."	New York *Post*, March 23, 1929, p. 39.
206	"a sound picture."	Joan and Bob Franklin, Transcript of interview with Harold Lloyd, pp. 38–39.
208	" (music) and dialogue."	New York *American*, December 10, 1928, p. 52.
208	"don't know why."	Lloyd-Franklin interview, p. 50.
209	"almost obsolete."	Creed Neeper to William Fraser, April 20, 1929.
209	"roaring at these things."	Transcript of American Film Institute Seminar with Harold Lloyd, p. 23.
210	"or Griffith work."	William K.Everson, *The Films of Laurel and Hardy*, p. 54.
210	"to carry on."	Hubert I. Cohen, "The Serious Business of Being Funny," in Lloyd, *An American Comedy*, p. 131.
211	"one was coughing."	Lloyd-Franklin interview, p. 39.
211	"marks on it"	AFI Seminar with Harold Lloyd, p. 24.
211	"going to talk."	Lloyd-Franklin interview, p. 39.
214	"*keep the pace.*"	New York *Telegram*, October 19, 1929, p. 27.
214	"Buster Keaton."	*Brooklyn Daily Eagle*, October 21, 1929, p. 39.
215	"further cutting."	Memo, L. D. Netter to Sam Dembow, Jr., August 26, 1929.
215	"dialogue version."	Memo, Milton H. Feld to Sam Dembow, Jr., August 26, 1929.
215	"old silent pictures."	Memo, A. M. Botsford to Sam Dembow, Jr., August 26, 1929.

Chapter IX

217	"wasn't slumming."	*Show Business Illustrated*, April 1962, p. 42.
217	"sound of water."	Ibid., p. 44.

Page

218 –19	"true distinction,"	Richard Schickel, *The Shape of Laughter*, p. 109.
219	"didn't work out."	Ibid., p. 111.
224	"sea of dialogue."	*The Film Spectator*, February 1, 1936, p. 14.
224	"there is no movie."	*The New York Times Magazine*, March 1, 1980, p. 27.
224	"things he did."	*The Film Spectator*, May 24, 1930, p. 8.
229	"Harold passed on."	Kevin Brownlow, *Hollywood: The Pioneers*, p. 134.
230	"any more of it."	Pratt, "Mind over Matter: Harold Lloyd Reminisces," in Marshal Deutelbaum, ed., *"Image,"* p. 208.
232n	"no escaping them."	*The Film Spectator*, February 15, 1930, p. 3.
233	"silent films could be."	Yasujiro Ozu, quoted in the Oct. 13–15, 1982, program of the Japan Film Center, Japan Society, New York, N.Y.
233	"to do is look."	*The New Yorker*, May 21, 1962, p. 30.
239	"stop that trend."	George Schaefer to William Fraser, December 20, 1932.
240	"many years to come."	Ibid.
242	"play them better."	*The Film Spectator*, February 1, 1936, p. 14.

Chapter X

243	"luncheon the next day."	Gladys Hill, *Photoplay*, September 1932, p. 59.
244	"than we used last."	Ibid.
245	"abided by that."	Joan and Bob Franklin, Transcript of interview with Harold Lloyd, p. 59.
250	"wherever it belonged."	Ibid., pp. 58–59.
251	"it was better."	Ibid., p. 59.
252	*"deserve Rogers terms."*	Frank Harris to William Fraser, December 31, 1934.
253	"into middle age."	Jay Leyda, ed., *Voices of Film Experience*, p. 395.
258	" 'Oh boy!' "	Marshal Deutelbaum, ed., *"Image,"* p. 209.

Page

259	"family it honored."	Otis Ferguson, *The Film Criticism of Otis Ferguson*, p. 24.
260	"with dialogue."	Joan and Bob Franklin, Transcript of interview with Elliott Nugent, p. 62.
260	Maurice Chevalier.	Interview with Kitty Lippiatt, January 1981.
261	he was thirteen.	Interview with Peggy Lloyd, July 1981.

Chapter XI

263	"all Lloyd's money."	Joan and Bob Franklin, Transcript of interview with Elliott Nugent, p. 65.
265	"*did* improve it."	Ibid.
269	"what they can for you."	Joan and Bob Franklin, Transcript of interview with Harold Lloyd, p. 73.
272	"in the *Bois*."	*The New Yorker*, May 26, 1962, p. 19.
273	"ring very often."	Interview with Kitty Lippiatt, January 1981.
274	as they chose.	Interviews with Gloria and Peggy Lloyd, July 1981.
274	"from a plumber."	Ibid.
275	lucrative form.	Interview with Thomas Sheppard, January 1981.
276	"a talking picture."	Manny Farber, *Negative Space*, p. 94.
276	"firecracker tempo."	Ibid., p. 96.
277	"of other films."	Ibid., p. 95.
279	*The Sin of Madelon Claudet*	Sturges Collection, Library of the University of Southern California in Los Angeles.
281	"complete harmony."	Lloyd-Franklin interview, p. 69.
281	"week or less."	Ibid.
281	"entertainment, laughs."	Ibid., p. 71.
282	"to help you."	Ibid., p. 72.
282	"two scenes, each way."	Ibid. p. 70.
283	"reach a climax."	Ibid., p. 72.

Chapter XII

285	"saw them."	Transcript of American Film Institute Seminar with Harold Lloyd, pp. 41–42.

Page

285	"about it."	London *Times*, September 23, 1970.
286	Harry S. Truman.	*Time*, "The World of Hiram Abif," July 25, 1949, p. 14.
286	celebrity again.	Interview with Colleen Moore, June 1982.
286	"the Shrine."	Lloyd-Franklin interview, p. 75.
289	"come to see it."	AFI Seminar with Harold Lloyd, p. 14.
289	"That's it."	Ibid., p. 16.
295	"human being."	Interview with John Meredith, July 1981.
295	"alive again!"	Interview with Richard Correll, July 1981.
297	"astonishing violence."	*American Film*, May 1978, p. 75.

INDEX

Greenacres (Lloyd's estate),
217–23, *218, 219, 221, 222,*
244, 254, *299*
construction of, 169, 206–207
cost of, 145–46
cost of upkeep of, 270, 303
increasing dilapidation of, 278–79,
302
increasing loneliness of, 260,
272–73, 298
Lloyd's death at, 304
Lloyd's superstition at, 91
1943 film vault explosion at, 48,
300
sale of main house of, 305
wrecking of, xiii–xiv
Grey, John, 156, 184, 265, 322–25
Grey, Thomas J., 322, 323
Griffin, Carlton, 322
Griffith, D. W., 42, 79, 171, 173, 181
Griffith, Raymond, 173, 174
Guasti, Suzanne, *see* Lloyd, Suzanne
Guasti, William, 291
Guiol, Fred L., 321

Haig, Douglas, 324
Hal Roach Productions, *see* Rolin
Company
Hal Roach Stock Company, 307, 313
Hale, Louise Closser, 325, 329
Hall, Henry, 325
Hall, Thurston, 327
Hamilton, Lloyd, 96
Hamilton, Margaret, 327
Hammond, C. Norman, 321
Harding, Brooks B., 156*n*, 323
Harding, Warren G., 128
Harmon, Pat, 323
Harold Lloyd Corporation (HL Cor-
poration)
end of, 270
founding of, 140
marketing by, 174–75, 238–39
productions of, 148–66, 175–201,
206–38, 322–26
profits of, 146, 166–67, 179, 190,
199, 200, 215–16, 230–31,
238, 246, 252
salary cuts at, 243–44, 269, 270
studios of, 140, 141

Harold Lloyd Foundation, 305
Harold Lloyd Productions, 270, 328
Harrington, Josephine, 323
Harris, Crampton, 327
Harris, Del, 329
Harrison, Estelle, *40,* 308
Havez, Jean, 92, *106, 107,* 154,
156*n,* 321, 323
Hayes, Jack, 329
Hayman, Earl, 326
Henie, Sonja, *240,* 241
Henry, Ebenezer, 324
Herring, Aggie, 320
Herzbrun, Bernard, 326
Herzig, Sig, 328
Heymann, Werner Richard, 327
Himm, Carl, 324
Hippard, George, 326
Holloway, Sterling, 262, 264, 327
Hollywood Producers' Association,
raiding forbidden by, 66
Holt, David Jack, 326
Hope, Bob, 259, 264
Hoppé, Linda, 300
Hornbeck, William, 31
Housman, Arthur, 325
Howe, J. A., 323
Howe, Jay, 324
Howe, Wallace, 140, 319, 321, 322
Howell, Alice, 96
Hughes, Howard, 279, 283
Hymer, Warren, 326

Income
Arbuckle's, 71, 78–79
Chaplin's, 33, 34, 200–201, 232
Daniels's, 63, 71, 73
of extras, 26–28
Keaton's, 71, 173, 234, 239
of leading actor (1913), 26
Lloyd's
guaranteed by Pathé, 62
in own firm, 155, 166, 179, 199,
200, 215–16, 230–31, 238,
246, 252, 263–64, 267–68
profit sharing at Rolin, 81,
88–89, 113, 116, 128, 136,
138
as salaried player for California,
279, 283–84

DATE DUE

MAR 1 1 1985			